FOR THE RECORD
Women in Sports

FOR THE RECORD
Women in Sports
by

Robert Markel

Nancy Brooks

Susan Markel

World Almanac Publications
New York, New York

Dates and places of birth have been supplied where available and confirmed.

Newspaper Enterprise Association ISBN 0-911818-75-8
Ballantine Books ISBN 0-345-32192-8
Printed in the United States of America
World Almanac Publications
Newspaper Enterprise Association, Inc.
A Scripps Howard Company
200 Park Avenue
New York, New York 10166

CONTENTS

Swimming (*continued*)

INTRODUCTION

Women athletes have participated in a multitude of sports and competitive events since the Games of Hera. Over the centuries since then, barriers to women's involvement in organized sport have been raised and then stormed; many, but not all, have fallen. Women have challenged records in popular and less well known sports and have performed feats of physical prowess. But until now it has been possible to find out about their accomplishments only by tedious and frustrating search that as often as not yielded incomplete or inaccurate information. The records established by women in sports have not been publicized in any organized or systematic format, and the stories behind the statistics—of such inspiration to young athletes and interest to fans—have not been widely known. I have, it is true, received recognition for my accomplishments, but probably more readily because I was the youngest ever on the team than because of my specific achievements. In the past, when women athletes have been noticed, it has generally been for some secondary or even frivolous distinction.

This is a time for change. Women athletes are entitled to have their feats recorded and recognized, and they deserve to be seen as part of a tradition. Fans, who in ever-growing numbers are watching women in sports, are entitled to have access to the best information about women athletes past and present to enhance their understanding and enjoyment. And perhaps most important are the young, who will carry on our standards and traditions. Joe Di Maggio and Willie Mays are, rightly, heroes to boys who play baseball; girls playing softball should have a similar opportunity to admire and emulate Bertha Tickey and Joan Joyce. This book is the place to begin.

Donna de Varona
President, Women's Sports Foundation
Gold Medalist, 1964 Olympics

FOREWORD

What's new in sports? Women. The dramatic rise in female participation in sports has not gone unrecognized by the sports experts or the public. When Bonne Bell racers increase from 20,000 to 60,000 in five short years, when schools struggle to provide facilities and coaching for the population explosion of girls and women in sports programs, when women's professional tennis draws as many fans as the men's game, and when women's swimming records are better than the best men's records of only a few years ago, there is reason to take notice. Nonetheless, sports pages, sports news, and televised coverage still focus primarily on men, and this focus will continue until women athletes are accepted in the mainstream of sport and are respected for their accomplishments. Women in sport are not an aberration; they have a proud history, but their records and victories have not been well publicized, and as a result the new records being set today lack context and significance.

In hopes of changing this situation the Women's Sports Foundation was established by America's finest female athletes, among them founder Billie Jean King, Wyomia Tyus, Donna de Varona, Micki King Hogue, and Carol Mann. They knew that by banding together, women athletes—all women athletes—could attract more attention. And with attention comes encouragement and support, providing a climate for participation and excellence.

Encouragement—at various times from parents, peers, teachers, and the public—is essential to the making of an athlete. Encouragement is essential in early childhood when both sexes develop their motor skills; it is essential through the school years, when skills in specific sports are acquired; it is essential during the amateur and professional years of peak performance.

For girls and women to become the best they can be in sport they must also be given the continuing societal support afforded boys and men throughout their careers. This means recognition of their accomplishments in sports history books, on the sports pages, in sports halls of fame, by endorsements and earnings and by all the ways in which our society makes a hero of a male sports star. To supplement their inner motivation, young girls who are aspiring athletes need role models and heroines to provide them with incentives and goals; fulfillment of this need is one of the reasons the Foundation established the Women's Sports Hall of Fame.

This women's sports record book will help to give young girls a sense of their sports heritage and give sports fans a basis of comparison when they read about Martina Navratilova's win record or Mary Decker's times. We commend the publishers of this book for recognizing that the place of women in sports history is a sufficiently marketable subject to warrant a volume of its own.

Eva Auchincloss
Executive Director
Women's Sports Foundation

BADMINTON

The origins of the game (but not the name) of badminton are confused—is it an ancient game of Eastern, possibly Chinese, roots? Or was it developed by some fun-loving nineteenth-century British officers in India who stuck some feathers in a cork and batted it around? What we do know is that the game was being played by the British at Poona in the 1870's, and that officers home on leave demonstrated it for the Duke of Beaufort in 1873 at his estate—Badminton, in Gloucestershire. The game was quickly popular in England, and within 20 years local clubs had joined together to form, in 1893, the Badminton Association of England, the first national organization, which held the first All-England championships in 1899. In 1925 and 1930, an English team toured Canada; Canadians took to the sport and taught it to their American neighbors. In the late 20's British players toured Denmark, and within ten years the Danes were playing a world-class game. More recently, Asian, particularly Japanese and Indonesian, players have come to the fore. In the U.S., the American Badminton Association (later the U.S. Badminton Association) was founded in 1936, and the first national championships were held the following year. The Thomas Cup (for men in international competition) was established in 1948; the corresponding Uber Cup for women was first played in England in 1957, with the U.S. team defeating Denmark for the championship. Badminton was a demonstration sport at the 1972 Olympics. Deceptively simple, badminton at its highest level is a fast, hard, demanding game, requiring tremendous coordination, accuracy, and strategy successfully to return and place a missile that can be fired off the racket at 110 miles an hour.

The Uber Cup was donated by **Betty Uber** of Great Britain, who won eight All-England titles (singles in 1935; doubles in 1931 with **Marianne Horsley**, 1937 and 1938 with Diana Doveton, and 1949 with Queenie Allen; mixed doubles in 1935 and 1936 with Donald Hume, in 1938 with R. M. White). Uber, a fine doubles player, played for England in international competition for 25 years. Danish players dominated in most of the post-war years: **Tonni Olsen Ahm** and **Kirsten Thorndahl** took the doubles title in 1947, 1948, 1950, and 1951; Ahm had also won in 1939, playing with Ruth Dalsgard, and in 1952, with **Aase Schiött Jacobsen**.

1

Thorndahl was singles champion in 1948, Ahm in 1950 and 1952, Jacobsen in 1949 and 1951. The early record for All-England titles—17—was held by the English player **Mary Lucas**, who was singles champion 1902, 1905, 1907-10; doubles champion with a Ms Graeme in 1899 and 1900, with Ethel Thomson 1902 and 1904-06, with G. L. Murray 1907-09, and with Mary Bateman in 1910; playing with Norman Wood, she was mixed doubles champion in 1908. Her record for total number of titles is matched— and for singles titles surpassed—by that of **Judith Devlin Hashman** of the U.S., considered the greatest woman player ever. She won a record ten All-England singles titles (1954, 1957, 1958, 1960-64, 1966, 1967); playing with her sister, **Susan Devlin Peard**, she won doubles in 1954, 1956, 1960, 1961, 1963, and 1966, and, with Mrs. T. Holst-Christensen, in 1962. (The sisters were daughters of the Irish player, J. F. Devlin, regarded as the best badminton player of all time: he held six All-England singles titles, six doubles, and five mixed doubles.) At home, Devlin Hashman was U.S. singles champion in 1954, 1956-63, 1965, and 1967, and held twelve doubles titles, ten of them played with her sister (1953-55, 1957-60, 1961, 1963, 1966); in 1962 she won with Pat Stephens and in 1967 with Rosine Jones. Devlin Hashman also held mixed doubles titles for seven consecutive years, in 1956-58 and 1960 playing with the great Danish player, Finn Kobberö, in 1959 with Michael Roch and in 1961 and 1962 with Wynn Rogers. In the 15 years of her reign, Devlin Hashman demonstrated extraordinary talent, both in physical coordination and in strategy; she also possessed what has been described as a "sense of perfection," practicing smash after smash, clear after clear, for hours on end. Her dedication and knowledge of badminton were apparent in her work as a teacher and a writer. She was elected to the Badminton Hall of Fame in 1963 (her sister was elected in 1976); she received the U.S. Badminton Association's Kenneth Davidson Award in 1966.

The Devlin Cup is played every three years between the U.S. and Canada. In 1983, the U.S. was the defending champion, but nonetheless lost the tournament 5-0, a dramatic testament to the rapidly rising levels of play in Canada. **Cheryl Carton** of San Diego was U.S. singles champion in 1983 (as she had been in 1978); in the Devlin Cup tournament in November 1983 she was defeated by Canadian player Denise Julien.

BASKETBALL

An ensemble consisted of a daring, mid-calf-length dress with long sleeves, black stockings, and leather shoes does not sound much like a basketball uniform—but in the 1890's that's exactly what it was. Basketball was developed in 1891 by James Naismith at a Springfield, Massachusetts, YMCA. It came to the attention of Senda Berenson, physical education director at Smith College, who in 1893 organized a freshman-sophomore game. Across the continent, the first intercollegiate women's game was held in 1896, between Stanford and Berkeley (Stanford won, 2-1!). Not quite 75 years later, in 1966, the first intercollegiate women's tournament was held in Pennsylvania. International competition for women's teams began in 1953; women's basketball became an Olympic sport at the Montreal Games in 1976 (the Soviet team, undefeated in international competition since 1958, easily won the gold medal). In the U.S., the emphasis is on college basketball, and the Wade Trophy recognizes each year's outstanding college player. The professional Women's Basketball League was founded in 1977, but lasted only three seasons. Another effort was being made in 1984, by the Women's American Basketball Association. International competition has been led by the Soviet team for almost 30 years, but the U.S. team offered a strong challenge at the 1983 world championships, where the Soviet Union defeated the U.S. team in the championship game 84-82. Outstanding Soviet players are center **Iuliana Semenova** (6'10½") and forward **Olga Sukharnova** (6'8"); both played on the gold-medal-winning Olympic teams at Montreal in 1976 and Moscow in 1980. Semenova was high scorer in both tournaments; Sukharnova is fast and responsive, and some observers consider her the key Soviet player. The Soviets boycotted the 1984 Los Angeles Olympics; the U.S. team, which *might* have won the gold medal if the Soviets had come, *did* win it in their absence, defeating the South Korean team in the championship game 85-55. In 1983 South Korea placed fourth at the world championships and has developed a tight team which, while not the tallest, is among the fastest. The leading scorer in the Olympic game against the U.S. was **Aei Young Choi** with 20 points. China defeated Canada to take the bronze medal; **Song Xiaobo**, 6'0", who led her team to the bronze at the 1983 world championships as well, was high scorer with 16 points.

3

Carol Blazejowski

Carol Blazejowski
born Cranford, New Jersey

As Nancy Lieberman had her early basketball education on the streets of New York, so Blazejowski is the veteran of innumerable New Jersey playground games, in which she, like Lieberman, was the only girl. She watched pro games on television and imitated what she saw, but her style is her own, easy and natural. In her last year at Montclair State College, 1978, she was awarded the Wade Trophy; she had amassed 3,199 points in her college career and scored 40 points or more in each of her last three games. Outspoken and exuberant, she was perhaps too overwhelming for the team concept held by the selection committee for the 1976 Olympics, and she was not chosen for the team, even as an alternate. She was, however, on the U.S. team at the World University Games in Bulgaria in 1977, where the U.S. won the silver medal. In the U.S.-Soviet game, the Blaze made 38 points; she was U.S. top scorer in the tournament. Patricia Head, who played on the 1976 Olympic team (and coached the 1984 squad), said, "I don't see how she can miss in 1980." And indeed, Blazejowski stayed amateur for two years after college (the years of the Women's Basketball League) to preserve her Olympic eligibility. Her Olympic hopes thwarted by the U.S. boycott of the Moscow Games, she signed with the New Jersey Gems. In the second go-round for women's professional basketball, the Women's American Basketball Association, organized in 1984, Blazejowski crossed the Hudson to join the New York club.

Denise Curry
born Davis, California, August 22, 1959

In her years as a UCLA forward, Curry amassed 3,198 career points, the most points in a single game (47), and, in her last years, more points than any other player in UCLA history—man or woman. Even with this record, Curry feels that she's not naturally that quick, that strong, nor that good a jumper. What she is is an excellent team player, effective at any position. She made the 1980 Olympic team that never got to play; then, after college, she joined the U.S. national team and played its 1982 East European tour, when the U.S. upset the Soviet Union 85-83. In 1983 she played for a West German club. How does the opposition see her? After the Seventh Soviet Games in 1980, center Iuliana Semenova remarked, "I admired the new one, Curry, from the U.S.A. She is a universal player." Curry was a member of the gold-winning 1984 Olympic team.

Denise Curry   Anne Donovan

Anne Donovan
born Ridgewood, New Jersey, November 1, 1961

Center Donovan, at 6'8" the tallest U.S. player, was at school at Old Dominion, where she won the 1983 Naismith College Player of the Year award: she played all 136 games scheduled during her 4-year career, she totaled 2,719 points and averaged 14.5 rebounds per games. She was named to two Kodak All-American teams, and to the 1980 Olympic team, which did not play because of the boycott. In 1983, she played on the U.S. team at the world championship in Brazil, going against 6'10½" center Iuliana Semenova of the Soviet Union twice (the two had faced off twice before). Although the Soviet Union won on both occasions in Brazil, Donovan said, "I know I felt a lot more comfortable and not in quite as much awe as I was the first two times." In 1983 she won the first Champion Player of the Year award of the Women's Basketball Coaches Association. After college, Donovan went to Japan, where her team won the Japanese championship. In January 1984 she returned to the U.S. to coach at Old Dominion; she was a member of the first-place 1984 Olympic team.

Janice Lawrence
born Lucedale, Mississippi, June 7, 1962

A senior at Louisiana Tech in 1983-84, center-forward Lawrence won the 1984 Wade Trophy, averaging 20.7 points and 9.1 rebounds a game (she also led her team in steals). She was a member in 1983 of the first-place U.S. team at the Pan American Games, of the U.S. World University Games team, which took second, and of the Kodak All-American team. In her years as Louisiana Tech center, her team was consistently in the finals and won two national championships (in 1983 Lawrence was named Most Valuable Player of the tournament). A member of the gold-winning U.S. team at the Los Angeles Olympics in 1984, Lawrence compared her earlier career to an Olympic victory—"That was college—this is the world!" She was the first college senior picked by the professional Women's American Basketball Association in 1984, and signed with the New York franchise.

Janice Lawrence   Cheryl Miller

Nancy Lieberman
born Brooklyn, New York, July 1, 1958

New York has always been hospitable to basketball, in the sports arenas and in the streets. Lieberman's first courts were the New York City playgrounds, where she played with and against boys until high school. At sixteen she was the youngest member of the 1976 U.S. Olympic basketball team, which won the silver medal at the Montreal Games. She played forward and point guard at Old Dominion University, where she led her team to national collegiate championships in 1979 and 1980, and in both those years she was awarded the Wade Trophy. In 1979 she played on the U.S. team that won the silver medal at the Pan American Games. After college, she was the first draft choice of the Dallas Diamonds in the last season of the Women's Basketball League. For many years committed to the goal of a professional basketball league for women, Lieberman was again the first draft choice of Dallas in the newly organized Women's American Basketball Association in the summer of 1984.

Ann Meyers

The first woman to attend the University of California at Los Angeles on a full athletic scholarship was also the first woman to sign, in 1979, a National Basketball Association contract, with the Indiana Pacers. Though the one-year NBA contract might have meant no more than publicity, there is no doubt that Meyers's visibility had a significant impact on women's basketball; in her day, she has said, "Basketball hadn't yet become an 'acceptable' sport for women." By 1984, that was simply no longer true. Meyers had excelled in track in high school, and dreamed of going to the Olympics—as a high jumper. When she came to basketball, she was successful as both shooter and passer despite her size—5′ 9″, 140 pounds. She was a four-time All-American, and UCLA coach Billie Moore has said of her, "I've never seen anyone have more of an impact on a team than Annie did." At the 1976 Montreal Olympics the U.S. fielded a team, coached by Moore, that included, as well as Meyers, Nancy Lieberman and Patricia Head, who was later the coach of the gold-winning U.S. team in 1984. In 1976, the U.S. won the silver, defeating Czechoslovakia, Canada, and Bulgaria (which took the bronze) in the course of the tournament; the gold medal went to the Soviet Union, which, led by Iuliana Semenova, defeated the U.S. 112-77 (Meyers was U.S. high scorer with 17 points). Earlier in 1976 Meyers had been a member of the gold-winning U.S. team at the Pan American Games. After her brief association with the NBA in 1979, Meyers played for the New Jersey Gems in the Women's Basketball League. Before the 1984 Olympics at Los Angeles, Meyers thought that a gold medal for the U.S. team was "a real possibility"—she

Lynette Woodard   Pat Head Summitt, U.S. coach

was absolutely right. That summer, she was drafted by the New York franchise team of the newly formed women's professional league, the Women's American Basketball Association.

Cheryl Miller
born Riverside, California, January 3, 1964

When the University of Southern California defeated defending champion Louisiana Tech in 1983, it was terrific basketball, and forward Miller commented, "It was a shame someone had to lose." The final score was 69-67, and Miller was responsible for 27 of the winning points. Miller was named Most Valuable Player for the tournament that year, and again in 1984, when USC successfully defended against Tennessee. In Miller's high school career at Riverside Poly, the team's record was 132-4 and she set three California high school records: total points scored (3,405), season points (1,156), and game points (105). In 1983, Miller led USC in scoring, blocking, and steals; she was the first player, man or woman, to be selected four times to the Parade All-American team; and she was on the Kodak All-American team. She was top scorer on the U.S. team at the 1983 Pan American Games (winning the gold medal) and the World University Games (winning the silver), and was a member of the U.S. team at the world championships. Miller averages 20 points and 10 rebounds a game. Says co-coach Leon Barmore of Louisiana Tech, "She is one of the few women who can singlehandedly turn the tide of the game." She was top scorer in the Olympic competition at Los Angeles in 1984, leading her team to the gold.

LaTaunya Pollard
born East Chicago, Indiana, July 26, 1960

The 1983 Wade Trophy went to Pollard, guard on the Long Beach State team, recognizing her average of 29.3 points and 8.9 rebounds per game; she scored 2,913 total points at Long Beach. She was named to the 1980 Olympic team (which did not play) and to the 1981 World University Games team. After college, she played in Italy. She suffered an ankle injury at the 1983 world championships, which gave her trouble at the Pan American Games a few weeks later; she could not play her full schedule on either occasion. She was a member of the 1983 Kodak All-American team. During the 1984 Olympic trials in April, another injury caused cartilage damage in her right knee, which required surgery; she was named an alternate on the 1984 Olympic team.

Lynette Woodard
born Wichita, Kansas, August 12, 1959

Guard Woodard, chosen for the non-playing 1980 Olympic team, is possibly the finest one-on-one player in the U.S. Winner of the 1981 Wade Trophy, at the University of Kansas she set a record for career scoring (3,649 points); as a freshman she was number one in the country in rebounds with an average of 15 per game. A four-time member of the Kodak All-American team, Woodard played a season for an Italian club, and led her league in scoring. She was captain of the U.S. team that defeated the Soviet Union in 1982 and contributed to the U.S. gold medal won at the

Pan American Games in 1983. On the coaching staff at Kansas, she was a member of the gold-winning 1984 Olympic team, and was the first free agent picked in the professional Women's American Basketball Association, joining the Columbus club.

Pamela McGee, center, 1984 U.S. Olympic team

Kim Mulkey, guard, 1984 U.S. Olympic team

OLYMPIC CHAMPIONSHIPS

Year	Gold	Silver	Bronze
1976 Montreal	USSR	USA	Bulgaria
1980 Moscow	USSR	Bulgaria	Yugoslavia
1984 Los Angeles	USA	South Korea	China

U.S. COLLEGIATE CHAMPIONS

Year	School
1982	Louisiana Tech
1983	University of Southern California
1984	University of Southern California

BOWLING

Quick—what is America's most widely played sport? Right. In 1916, 40 bowlers formed the Women's International Bowling Congress, and today, with more than four million members, it is the largest women's sports organization in the world. The 1916 WIBC championship total purse was $222; in 1983, it was $1,617,878. On the college level, there are more than 500 teams across the country; 24 of them (12 men's, 12 women's) competed for the national collegiate bowling championship in San Jose, California, in 1984. A highly competitive series of events is administered by the Ladies Pro Bowlers Tour (LPBT), whose members must carry a league average of 175 or more for two years. Not only Americans bowl; the ancient Egyptians did, and so did Martin Luther. In modern times, international competition is supervised by the Fédération Internationale des Quilleurs, which sponsors world and American zone championships. Bowling will be a demonstration sport at the 1988 Olympics, and possibly a medal sport in 1992.

Donna Adamek
born Duarte, California, Februrary 1, 1957

A bowler since the age of ten, Adamek—known as "Mighty Mite"—has bowled in every pro tournament since 1976. She was BWAA Woman Bowler of the Year 1978-81, Queens tournament champion 1979 and 1980, and winner of the U.S. Women's Open in 1978 and 1981. With partner Dorothy Fothergill, she woh the Brunswick Great and Greatest in 1979. When she won the Northeast Fabrics Classic in May 1983, she captured her fifteenth LPBT title. Adamek is the first woman to have bowled six 300 games.

Dorothy Fothergill
born Lincoln, Rhode Island

In a 12-year career, Fothergill won 18 WIBC and pro titles, including the WIBC all-events and singles in 1970, doubles 1971-73, the Queens in 1972 and 1973, the all-star championship in 1968 and 1969, and had eight professional wins in the period 1967-72. BWAA Bowler of the Year in 1968 and 1969, Fothergill came out of retirement in 1979 to win the first Brunswick Great and Greatest Tournament with partner Donna Adamek. She was elected to the WIBC Hall of Fame in 1980.

Loa Boxberger won 1978 Queens   Dorothy Fothergill

Nikki Gianulias
born Vallejo, California, December 5, 1959

Six times collegiate champion, Gianulias was 1979 LPBT Rookie of the Year, four-time WIBC All-American (1980-83), and 1982 Woman Bowler of the Year. She was the winner of the 1982 California all-events and member of the 1983 California state team. Winner of the Clearwater Classic in 1982 and 1983, she was out most of the rest of the 1983 season with pneumonia, but made a terrific return at the Ormond Beach Classic in March 1984: her 276 winning score was the fourth highest in LPBT history. Gianulias is the first woman ever to bowl three 800 series.

Marion Ladewig
born Grand Rapids, Michigan

Ladewig was possibly the greatest woman bowler of all time. Winner of the 1950 and 1955 WIBC all-events, she was nine times BWAA Bowler of the Year (1950-54, 1957-59, 1963). She was all-star champion in 1949-54, 1957, 1959, 1963; in 1961 she won the PWBA national championship. Named Michigan Woman Athlete of All Time and a member of the Michigan Athletic Hall of Fame, she was elected to the WIBC Hall of Fame in 1964 and to the Women's Sports Hall of Fame in 1984.

Carol Norman
born Ardmore, Oklahoma, August 6, 1961

Winner of several regional and state titles, Norman joined the LPBT in 1982 and was Rookie of the Year: she was first in match play winning percentage (.6074), fifteenth in average (201), and twenty-second in com-

Nikki Gianulias   Marion Ladewig

petition points. In 1983 she was fourth (just behind Lisa Rathgeber) in the $25,000 Clearwater Classic, and fifth in the Inside Sports Open. Norman has power and endurance—and the discipline of practice, up to twenty games a day.

Lisa Rathgeber
born Hillsboro, Illinois, May 19, 1961

LPBT Rookie of the Year in 1980, Rathgeber did not really fulfill her promise until 1983. Before that year, she had often been a runner-up, never a winner. Her first LPBT title, Robby's Midwest Classic, came on her twenty-second birthday; she followed it up with another win the next week, taking the Greater Milwaukee Open (and incidentally becoming the first bowler in five years to win back-to-back titles). In August she won the Hush Puppies Classic. At the end of the 1983 season she led the tour in match play winning percentage (.6351), average (208.50), and competition points (9,070); she was named Woman Bowler of the Year by the Bowling Writers Association of America, and members of the LPBT voted her Lind Shoe Player of the Year. In 1984, Rathgeber easily won her first event of the season, the Roto Grip Classic.

Aleta Rzepecki Sill
born Detroit, Michigan, September 9, 1962

Rzepecki Sill started bowling at five and had her first professional title at nineteen. She won the 1982 WIBC all-events, but 1982 was not overall a good year for her. Then, "I made myself practice, which I didn't do in 1982." Practice paid off—literally. Her 1983 LPBT earnings topped the list. She won the 1983 WIBC single and the 1983 Queens (she was the second youngest champion) and the Dallas-Fort Worth Classic, in which she bowled her first 300 game. She was third in the Ormond Beach Classic in March 1984. In May, she lost her Queens title to Kazue Inahashi of Japan, who is number one in her country. Said second-place Sill, "The money is nice but the title is nicer."

WIBC SINGLES CHAMPIONS

Year	Bowler	Score
1916	Mrs. A. J. Koester	486
1917	not played	
1918	Frances Steib	537
1919	B. Husk	594
1920	Birdie Humphries	559
1921	Emma Jaeger	579
1922	Emma Jaeger	603
1923	Emma Jaeger	594
1924	Alice Feeney	593
1925	Eliza Reich	622
1926	Evelyn Weisman	579
1927	Florence Amrein	577
1928	Anita Rump	622
1929	Agnes Higgins	637
1930	Anita Rump	613
1931	Myrtle Schulte	650
1932	Audrey McVay	668
1933	Sally Twyford	628
1934	Marie Clemensen	712
1935	Marie Warmbier	652
1936	Ella Mankie	612
1937	Ann Gottstine	647
1938	Rose Warner	622
1939	Helen Hengstler	626
1940	Sally Twyford	626
1941	Nancy Huff	662
1942	Tillie Taylor	659
1943-45	not played	
1946	Val Mikiel	682
1947	Agnes Junker	650
1948	Shirlee Wernecke	696
1949	Clara Mataya	658
1950	Cleo McGovern	669
1951	Ida Simpson	639
1952	Lorene Craig	672
1953	Marge Baginski	637
1954	Helen Bassett	668
1955	Nellie Vella	695
1956	Lucille Noe	708
1957	Eleanor Towles	664
1958	Ruth Hertel	622
1959	Mae Bolt	664
1960	Marge McDaniels	649
1961	Dorothy Wilkinson	653
1962	Martha Hoffman	693
1963	Dorothy Wilkinson	653
1964	Jean Havlish	690

Year	Bowler	Score
1965	Doris Rudell	659
1966	Gloria Simon	675
1967	Gloria Griffith	652
1968	Norma Parks	691
1969	Joan Bender	690
1970	Dorothy Fothergill	695
1971	Mary Scruggs	698
1972	D. D. Jacobson	737
1973	Bobbie Soldan	706
1974	Shirley Garms	702
1975	Barbara Leicht	689
1976	Beverly Shonk	686
1977	Akiko Yagama	714
1978	Mae Bolt	709
1979	Betty Morris	674
1980	Betty Freeman	652
1981	Virginia Norton	672
1982	Gracie Freeman	652
1983	Aleta Rzepecki Sill	726

WIBC QUEENS TOURNAMENT CHAMPIONS

Year	Bowler	Average	Runner-up	Average
1961	Janet Harman	199	Eula Touchette	188
1962	Dorothy Wilkinson	195	Marion Ladewig	195
1963	Irene Monterosso	194	Georgette DeRosa	192
1964	D. D. Jacobson	199	Shirley Garms	198
1965	Betty Kuczynski	190	LaVerne Carter	196
1966	Judy Lee	188	Nancy Peterson	190
1967	Mildred Martorella	215	Phyllis Massey	208
1968	Phyllis Massey	200	Marian Senser	197
1969	Ann Feigel	213	Mildred Martorella	200
1970	Mildred Martorella	216	Joan Holm	201
1971	Mildred Martorella	202	Katherine Brown	191
1972	Dorothy Fothergill	210	Maureen Harris	215
1973	Dorothy Fothergill	211	Judy Soutar	203
1974	Judy Soutar	211	Betty Morris	201
1975	Cindy Powell	190	Pat Costello	185
1976	Pamela Buckner	200	Shirley Sjostrom	193
1977	Dana Stewart	197	Vesma Grinfelds	200
1978	Loa Boxberger	196	Cora Fiebig	198
1979	Donna Adamek	218	Shinobu Saitoh	205
1980	Donna Adamek	205	Sheryl Robinson	197
1981	Katusko Sugimoto	192	Virginia Norton	198
1982	Katsuko Sugimoto	189	Nikki Gianulias	192
1983	Aleta Rzepecki Sill	205	Dana Miller	211
1984	Kazue Inahashi	248	Aleta Rzepecki Sill	222

ALL-STAR U.S. OPEN CHAMPIONS

Year	Bowler	Runner-up	Champion's Average
1949	Marion Ladewig	Catherine Burling	200.53
1950	Marion Ladewig	Stephanie Balogh	199.87
1951	Marion Ladewig	Sylvia Martin	211.46
1952	Marion Ladewig	Shirley Garms	205.34
1953	Marion Ladewig		
1954	Marion Ladewig	Sylvia Martin	196.87
1955	Sylvia Martin	Sylvia Fanta	193.12
1956	Anita Cantaline	Doris Porter	190.02
1957	Marion Ladewig	Marge Merrick	194.11
1958	Merle Matthews	Marion Ladewig	191.91
1959	Marion Ladewig	Donna Zimmerman	201.03
1960	Sylvia Martin	Marion Ladewig	193.95
1961	Phyllis Notaro	Hope Ricilli	194.46
1962	Shirly Garms	Joy Able	199.02
1963	Marion Ladewig	Bobbie Kostelny	204.21
1964	Laverne Carter	Evelyn Teal	200.10
1965	Ann Slattery	Sandy Hooper	194.78
1966	Joy Abel	Bette Rockwell	198.95
1967	Gloria Simon	Shirley Garms	195.52
1968	Dorothy Fothergill	Doris Coburn	205.40
1969	Dorothy Fothergill	Kayoka Suda	203.67
1970	Mary Daker	Judy Soutar	208.33
1971	Paula Carter	June Lllewellyn	204.58
1972	Lorrie Nichols	Mary Baker	197.46
1973	Mildred Martorella	Patty Costello	212.83
1974	Pat Costello	Betty Morris	196.67
1975	Paula Carter	Lorrie Nichols	199.48
1976	Patty Costello	Betty Morris	226.27
1977	Betty Morris	Virginia Norton	218.98
1978	Donna Adamek	Vesma Grinfelds	212.78
1979	Diane Silva	Pat Costello	218.05
1980	Pat Costello	Shinobu Saitoh	206.00
1981	Donna Adamek	Nikki Gianulias	201.10
1982	Shinobu Saitoh	Robin Romeo	210.07
1983	Dana Miller	Aleta Rzepecki Sill	213.46

WOMAN BOWLER OF THE YEAR

Year	Bowler
1948	Val Mikiel
1949	Val Mikiel
1950	Marion Ladewig
1951	Marion Ladewig
1952	Marion Ladewig
1953	Marion Ladewig
1954	Marion Ladewig

Year	Bowler
1955	Sylvia Martin
1956	Anita Cantaline
1957	Marion Ladewig
1958	Marion Ladewig
1959	Marion Ladewig
1960	Sylvia Martin
1961	Shirley Garms
1962	Shirley Garms
1963	Marion Ladewig
1964	LaVerne Carter
1965	Betty Kuczynski
1966	Joy Abel
1967	Mildred Martorella
1968	Dorothy Fothergill
1969	Dorothy Fothergill
1970	Mary Baker
1971	Paula Carter
1972	Patty Costello
1973	Judy Soutar
1974	Betty Morris
1975	Judy Soutar
1976	Patty Costello
1977	Betty Morris
1978	Donna Adamek
1979	Donna Adamek
1980	Donna Adamek
1981	Donna Adamek
1982	Nikki Gianulias
1983	Lisa Rathgeber

CANOEING/KAYAKING

If riding a log propelled through the water is canoeing, then canoeing has been around for a very long time. Refinements—shaping the log, digging it out—appeared independently in many societies. The woodland Indians of northeast North America used a birchbark canoe; on it, Europeans based their larger explorer and voyager canoes, in which they took 1,000-mile trips as they pursued the fur trade. The design of the canoe is almost perfect: light, with a shallow draft, it is fast and maneuverable, even with a large load. Canoe competition includes flat-water classes, white-water events, and marathons—women compete in all. More than a thousand canoes enter the Mid-American Canoe Race on the Fox River, near Chicago; the longest race is the 419-mile Texas Water Safari. Like "drafting" in cycling, "riding the wash" in canoeing is a legitimate technique that, skillfully employed, can be the key to victory. As an Olympic sport, events are either in kayaking (both men and women compete, women at 500 meters, using a paddle with a blade at each end), or the men-only Canadian canoeing, which uses a single-bladed paddle.

The great women kayakers are the Europeans, and perhaps the greatest was **Ludmila Khvedosyuk-Pinayeva** of the Soviet Union, Olympic singles champion in 1964 and 1968 and, with **Ekaterina Kuryshko**, pairs champion in 1972. The West German team of **Roswitha Esser** and **Annemarie Zimmerman** were gold medalists in 1964 and 1968. More recently, **Birgit Fischer** of East Germany was gold medalist in singles at the 1980 Moscow Olympics, and since then world champion three times before the next Olympiad; she and her partner in pairs events, **Carsta Kuhn**, were 1983 world champions. **Eva Rakusz** of Hungary, silver medalist in the 1981 world championships, bronze medalist in 1982, and fourth place in 1983, upset Fischer at the Lake Casitas International Regatta in 1983. Neither woman competed in the 1984 Olympics because of the Soviet-led boycott of the Los Angeles Games. At that competition, as King Carl XVI Gustav and Queen Sylvia watched, **Agneta Andersson** and **Anna Olsson** of Sweden won the pairs event and Andersson won the gold medal in singles. Americans at the top of the sport are **Cathy Marino**, 1983 national singles champion, who placed sixth in the singles at the world championships in 1983 but who did not make the 1984 Olympic team because of injury and impaired training; **Leslie Klein**, a world champion whitewater canoeist who shared the 1983 national pairs title with Marino; 1976 and 1980 Olympic team vet **Ann Turner, Jojo Toeppner**, and **Sheila Conover**, who, like Klein, were members of the four-member team that was third at the 1983 Lake Casitas event, behind the East German boat; **Anne Kobylenski** and **Valerie Fons**, marathon canoeists who were the first women to complete the grueling 240-mile Au Sable race in Michigan, finishing in under 17 hours, tenth in a field of 15, in July 1984.

CYCLING

"Woman has taken her stand, and her seat in the saddle. . . . This is not a revolt, it is a revolution. I am tolerably certain that the net result will be that woman will take her true position as man's equal." Thus the English cycling magazine *Northern Wheeler* in 1893. Women had ridden earlier— Frenchwomen had raced at Bordeaux in 1868—but for the next thirty years the issue of a woman riding a bicycle was a highly charged as any contemporary discussion of gun control. The controversy reached its shrill peak in 1893, when sixteen-year-old **Tessie Reynolds** of Brighton rode to London and back, a distance of some 120 miles, in 8½ hours. Her feat outraged even some supporters of women's cycling, for Reynolds had worn the shocking "rational dress"—a long jacket over knickers-style trousers—and this flouting of convention, it was feared, would only set back the cause. But within two years, cycling for women was a craze, indulged in by titled ladies and even some royals. The bicycle is an extremely efficient machine, women have a high endurance potential, and strategy and tactics are essential to racing success. Thus cycling may be one of the few sports in which a woman could defeat a man in head-to-head competition. In the U.S., national championships have been held since 1937 (with women competing); women were admitted to the world championships in 1958. The most rigorous event in the U.S. is the Coors International Classic, a nine- or ten-day competition that includes criteriums (short flat races, usually 1-3K, with perhaps four 90-degree turns), time trials, and road races—including 40 miles through the Colorado mountains. The first women's Tour de France, 616 miles, was held in July 1984; in first place was **Marianne Martin** of the U.S. (elapsed time of 29:39:2), second was **Helene Hage** of The Netherlands (29:42:19) and **Deborah Schumway** of the U.S. was third. Men's cycling events have been part of the Olympics since 1896; the first Olympic competition for women— a 79K road race—was held at Los Angeles in 1984.

Marianne Berglund
born Sweden, July 26, 1963
   In the 1983 season Berglund moved rapidly to top rank. Swedish national road champion, she won the Ruffles Tour of Texas in March, defeating Sue Novara-Reber (second) and Rebecca Twigg (third) of the U.S. In the

19

Coors International Classic she placed sixth overall, winning the difficult 40-mile stage through the mountains of Colorado. At the world championships she won the road race, defeating Twigg (second) and Maria Canins of Italy (third). Like Novara-Reber, she rides for Raleigh. Also like Novara-Reber, she has a terrific finishing kick, but she had no chance to use it in the 1984 Olympic 79K road race: she finished twenty-fifth, in 2:20:16.

Beryl Burton, O.B.E.
born England, 1937

Arguably the world's greatest woman cyclist, Burton holds 80 English titles and seven world championships (five in pursuit, 1959, 1960, 1962, 1963, 1966, and two in road racing, 1960 and 1967). She won the Women's Best British All-Rounder (BBAR) in 1958 for the first time, and continued to win it every year through 1980. In 1967, her twelve-hour race distance of 277.37 beat the men's top distance (previously, Burton had done 237 and 251). In the 1980 BBAR she raced 25 miles in 54:54, 50 miles in 1:55:38, 100 miles in 4:10:42—and all three events were held in the heat of the last week of August.

Maria Canins
born Italy

Like other great cyclists, Canins has a second sport—unlike theirs it's nordic skiing, not speed skating. She was Italian national nordic champion before she began cycling in 1982. She was then thirty-three. That September she won the silver medal in the world championship road race; the following July (1983) she was second overall in the Coors International Classic. Returning to the world championships in September, she placed third in the road race. Going into the 1984 Olympics, she held five national championships. Her endurance and strength, hallmarks of a cross-country skier, make her formidable in competition. In the 79K Los Angeles road race, Canins, now thirty-five and the mother of two, stayed with the lead pack of six, and despite taking a bad fall, she finished fifth.

Connie Carpenter-Phinney
born Madison, Wisconsin, February 26, 1957

Carpenter-Phinney was primarily a road racer, and she was also probably the best all-around American cyclist. Like Beth Heiden and Sheila Young Ochowicz, she was a top speed skater; she placed seventh in the 1500-meter at the Sapporo Olympics in 1972, but injury kept her from the 1976 Olympic speed skating team and she turned to cycling. In her first year of competition (1976), she won the national championship in road race and pursuit; she won both titles again the following year (when she also won second place in the world championship road race) and again in 1978. She was winner of the Coors International Classic in 1977, 1981, and 1982. In 1981 she also picked up three national titles and won the bronze medal in the world championship road race; the next year she won the world championship silver medal in pursuit. A broken wrist forced her to withdraw from the 1983 Coors, but that year she successfully defended her national criterium title and, a month after Coors, won the world championship in pursuit (Rebecca Twigg, concentrating on road racing, did not defend), setting a world record of 3:49.53. Carpenter-Phinney, who rode on the Raleigh team, was named 1983 Colorado Sportswoman of the Year. Between 1976 and the 1984 Los Angeles Olympics, she had won twelve national championships, four world championship medals, and three Coors International Classics—more victories than any other American cyclist, man or woman, had ever achieved. At the Los Angeles Games, in her last race before retirement, she won the gold medal in the 79K road race in 2:11:14—the first Olympic cycling medal for the U.S. since 1912.

Beth Heiden
born Madison, Wisconsin, September 27, 1959

An Olympic medal in one sport, and a world gold in another, make for a pretty good year: that's what Heiden had in 1980, when she took the 3000-meter speed skating bronze medal at Lake Placid, and in cycling won the world championship road race (and the national road championship and the Coors International Classic as well). She left cycling competition in 1982; while at school at the University of Vermont, she began cross-country skiing and picked up the NCAA first division title in that sport. She returned to cycling in 1983, riding with the 7-Eleven team.

Sue Novara-Reber
born Flint, Michigan, November 22, 1955

In 1975, at nineteen, Novara-Reber was the youngest woman ever to win the world sprint championship, and she won it again in 1980. Because the 1984 Olympic cycling event was road only, the seven-time national track champion chose to make the transition from sprint to road racing in order to be competitive in Los Angeles. She made extensive changes in her training regimen, and slowly but steadily she was making it: in 1982 she took the national championship in the road race, two road-race stages of the Coors International Classic, and the Eastern Division of the *Self* Magazine Cycling Circuit. In 1983 she placed second to Sweden's Marianne Berglund (and ahead of Rebecca Twigg, third) in the Ruffles Tour of Texas, won two stages of the French Tour, and took the *Self* Cycling Circuit (East) for the second time. That year she placed second in the criterium nationals, in which she successfully blocked for Connie Carpenter's win. Later in the year, possibly because of overtraining, Novara-Reber was not so successful, and she did not make the 1983 world team. Her last year of racing was 1984; in May she won the 24-mile Central Park Grand Prix in New York, an important race on the *Self* circuit. Because of her sprint experience, her finishing kick was always a force to be reckoned with.

Ochowicz, Sheila Young. See Speed Skating.

Cindy Olavarri
born Pleasant Hill, California, March 23, 1955

In cycling, teamwork doesn't just mean working together; it can mean sacrificing your chances, manipulating the field so that another member of your team can win. That is what a *domestique* does, and Olavarri is one of the best: a key member of the 7-Eleven team, she prepared the way for Rebecca Twigg's victory in the national road championship in 1983. Olavarri is also a top road racer herself: she won the 1983 40K national time trial championship in 1:01.42, and in the track nationals (in which Twigg and Connie Carpenter did not compete), she won the kilometer in 1:16.80 and the 3000 meter individual pursuit.

Rebecca Twigg
born Seattle, Washington, March 26, 1963

It's simple enough to Twigg: "I like to go fast. I always have." At fourteen, in 1977, she entered the University of Washington and the national championships, coming in fifth in the intermediate track event and third in the road race. Two years later she held the national junior title in time trials. In 1981, still a junior, she won the senior pursuit race (as well as the junior time trials and road race), defeating three-time champion Connie Carpenter. The following year, Twigg won the pursuit again and the senior time trials, and won the gold medal in pursuit at the world championships, the first American ever to do so; she defeated Carpenter again in all these contests. Concentrating on training for the 1984 Olympic road race, Twigg did not defend her national title in the 40K time trial nor the pursuit; she did win the 1983 Coors International Classic, coming in 2 minutes 23 seconds ahead of Maria Canins of Italy (Carpenter had had to withdraw because of injury). She also won the national road race title, doing 57.6 miles in 2:54.10. In the world championship road race, Twigg made the mistake of turning her head just meters from the finish, and Marianne Berglund of Sweden got the gold medal while Twigg took the silver. In 1983, Twigg was named Rider of the Year by *Cycling USA* (for the second time) and Cyclist of the Year by *The Olympian*; she is a member of the 7-Eleven team. She finished the 1984 Olympic 79K road race a hair behind Carpenter-Phinney to win the silver medal.

U.S. NATIONAL ROAD CHAMPIONS

Year	Champion
1937	Doris Kopsky
1938	Dolores Amundson
1939	Gladys Owen
1940	Mildred Kugler
1941	Jean Michels
1942-44	not held
1945	Mildred Dietz
1946	Mildred Dietz
1947	Doris Travani
1948	Doris Travani
1949	Doris Travani
1950	Doris Travani
1951	Anna Piplak
1952	Jeanne Robinson

Year	Champion
1953	Nancy Nelman
1954	Nancy Nelman
1955	Jeanne Robinson
1956	Nancy Nelman
1957	Nancy Nelman
1958	Maxine Conover
1959	Joanne Specklin
1960	Edith Johnson
1961	Edith Johnson
1962	Nancy Burghart
1963	Edith Johnson
1964	Nancy Burghart
1965	Nancy Burghart
1966	Audrey McElmury
1967	Nancy Burghart
1968	Nancy Burghart
1969	Audrey McElmury
1970	Jeanne Kloska
1971	Sheila Young Ochowicz
1972	Sue Novara-Reber
1973	Sheila Young Ochowicz
1974	Sue Novara-Reber
1975	Sue Novara-Reber
1976	Sheila Young Ochowicz
1977	Sue Novara-Reber
1978	Sue Novara-Reber
1979	Sue Novara-Reber
1980	Sue Novara-Reber
1981	Sheila Young Ochowicz
1982	Connie Pareskevin
1983	Connie Pareskevin

EQUESTRIAN SPORTS

The Amazons rode astride; Persian women played polo; Charlemagne's six daughters, wearing divided skirts, rode out with him. Isabella of Spain refused to ride the mule protocol dictated; when not hunting, she devoted time to organizing stud farms (one of them today supplies the Lippizaners for the Spanish Riding School in Vienna). Equestrian exhibitions were popular in Rome and through the Middle Ages. On the battlefield, though, new weapons—crossbow and firearms—found the armored knight on a heavy horse too slow to maneuver. Sixteenth-century observers of the natural movements of the horse developed exercises that would train the horse to quick response and refine coordination between horse and rider. The French word for such training is *manéger*, the ring where it takes place is the *manège*; *dressage*, referring to the "dressed" or raised carriage of the neck and head, has come to mean the entire repertoire of exercises. Soon these movements became an art in themselves, taught at riding and cavalry schools throughout Europe. England, on the other hand, with the sea for defense, never depended on her cavalry as much as did the Continent, and the art of dressage was never as important there—in fact, there were those who regarded it as a bag of tricks. On seeing a precise *passage*, Colonel Blimp was heard to mutter, "If my horse did that I'd shoot it." From the British tradition of hunting and racing comes steeplechase (originally a race from visible landmark to visible landmark, often church to church) and show jumping, first seen at rural fairs: a "leaping" contest was part of a show at the Agricultural Hall in Islington in 1864, and the earliest modern show jumping was part of the 1907 International Horse Show at Olympia, London. Show jumping became an Olympic event in 1912. In the U.S. today, show-jumping events are organized by the American Grandprix Association (AGA); the national team for all events is the U.S. Equestrian Team. Women are seen hunting with men in the great medieval tapestries, but they are not seen competing with men in the Olympics until 1952, when four women entered the dressage class. One of them, Denmark's **Lis Hartel**, who had retrained herself to ride after being stricken with paralytic polio, took the silver medal; she repeated her performance at the Stockholm Games four years later. Another Dane, **Anne-Grethe Jensen**, was in her seventeenth year of dressage competition in 1984. She and Marzog were fifth at the 1982 world championships, and in 1983 they defeated world champion Reiner Klimke of West Germany and Ahlerich—twice (the second occasion made Jensen European champion). At Los Angeles, the five Olympic judges agreed on all three places: Klimke had the gold, Jensen the silver, and Otto Hofer of Switzerland the bronze. The Olympic three-day event (a combination class for individuals and teams of jumping, dressage, and speed and endurance tests in cross-country and steeplechase) was barred to women until 1964; in that year Helena Dupont of the U.S. was the only woman to compete. The picture has changed since then: in 1984, 18 of the 48 riders in the three-day event were women, and 2 of them were individual medalists. Overall, the world best is probably Britain's **Lucinda Green**. At the last world championship before the Los Angeles Games, held in 1982, Green won both the individual and team golds on Regal Realm. She has won the European championship twice, and the Badminton International six times—on six different horses. Her Olympic performances have never reflected her talents: she had to withdraw in the 1976 Montreal Games when her horse, Be Fair, injured a tendon, and in 1980, at the alternate competition at Fontainebleau, on Village Gossip, their dressage test was so bad that even clean cross-country and jumping brought the pair only to seventh. The Los Angeles Games were a slight improvement: riding Regal Realm, she finished sixth, and shared in Great Britain's team silver. Although women were barred from competition for so long, it is interesting that today in all equestrian classes, unlike many other sports, women compete head to head with men, not in separate divisions.

Leslie Burr
born Westport, Connecticut

In 1979, her first year on the AGA tour, Burr had two Grandprix wins, both on Chase the Clouds. In 1980 she was on two winning Nations Cup teams, and in 1981 she was fifth at the World Cup final. In 1982 Chase the Clouds died, and Burr had to take time to school suitable mounts. Now she has three, Albany, Boing, and Corsair. In August 1983, when the U.S. team took the gold medal in team jumping at the Pan American Games, Burr was riding Boing; at the American Gold Cup in September, she took first on Albany (32 fences, no faults, in 31.032) and third on Corsair (4 faults). At the National Horse Show in New York in November, Burr and Albany had a clean jump-off in 35.49 to win the Mercedes Grandprix; riding Corsair, Burr also took third place with 37.46. In 1983 Burr took three Grandprix events in a row, a record; she was named Mercedes Rider of the Year, Albany was Horse of the Year. Burr and Albany went to the 1984 Los Angeles Olympics, where they shared the first U.S. team jumping gold with Melanie Smith on Calypso, Joe Fargis on Touch of Class, and Conrad Homfeld on Abdullah.

Hilda Gurney
born Moorpark, California

When Gurney led the bronze-winning U.S. team in points in the team dressage event at the 1976 Montreal Games she was riding Keen, and on Keen she won the gold medal in dressage (individual and team) at the

1979 Pan American games. Then Keen suffered a series of injuries to back
and foreleg; though he had recovered after four years of rest, the retirement
of the seventeen-year-old chestnut was generally expected. Instead, Gurney
announced that she would be riding Keen in the trials for the 1984 Olympics—and she did. Her second mount is the gray stallion Chrysos, whom
she rode at the 1983 Pan American Games, when the U.S. team took first
in team dressage and Gurney and Chrysos took second in the individual
competition. Gurney's riding career began in eventing—she was 1967
national intermediate champion—but she recognized dressage is her forte.
At the Los Angeles Games the U.S. placed sixth—and Gurney was riding
Keen.

Edith Master
   The most experienced U.S. woman dressage rider, Master was on U.S.
teams competing in the Olympics in 1968, 1972, and 1976. In 1968, the
U.S. placed eighth, Master riding Helios. But at home she was the best
in the country and a national champion. To progress she had to go to
Europe, where dressage was performed at a much higher level: "When I
got there, it was like starting over." Although in 1972 the U.S. team came
in ninth out of ten, in 1976 it took the bronze medal, with Master on
Dahlwitz. In 1980, she did not make the team, which competed at the
alternate Goodwood Dressage Festival (the team came in seventh, after a
difficult year in which its coach, Bengt Ljundquist, died). At the trials for
the 1984 Olympic team, Master rode Azur, a twelve-year-old Hanoverian.
They didn't make it, but in dressage, age is not a factor for horse or rider,
and Master looks forward to 1988.

Melanie Smith

Melanie Smith
born Litchfield, Connecticut

In her first (and successful) years on the AGA tour, which she joined in 1976, Smith rode Val de Loire and Radnor II (she and Val de Loire were on the gold-winning U.S. team at the Pan American Games in 1979). Then she worked with Calypso, a Dutch bay gelding, and a stunning partnership began. Smith is the only rider to have jumped Calypso, and together they won the 1979 International Jumping Derby; in 1980 they were second at the World Cup final, won the Grand Prix of Paris, and took the individual bronze medal at the Rotterdam Show Jumping Festival (the alternate to the 1980 Moscow Olympics). By 1982 the pair was busy— too busy; in March they won the American Invitational, in April the World Cup final (which took place in Sweden), and back in the U.S., the American Gold Cup in September. The schedule and the transatlantic flights took their toll. Smith and Calypso, like the rest of the American team, did not fare well at the world championships in Dublin. But the pair is a strong combinations, contributing heavily to the U.S. team's 1983 Nations Cup victory, and at the 1983 World Cup final, Smith came in first of the women and third overall. They entered few events in spring 1984, to be fresh and ready for the Los Angeles Olympics. They were, and so were the rest of the team (Leslie Burr on Albany, Joe Fargis on Touch of Class, and Conrad Homfeld on Abdullah): the U.S. won its first-ever Olympic gold medal in team jumping.

Karen Stives
born Wellesley, Massachusetts

The last rider in the three-day event at the Los Angeles Olympics in 1984, Stives was the first woman individual medalist—ever. She won the silver on Ben Arthur, and another woman, Virginia Holgate of Great Britain, riding Priceless, won the bronze (the gold went to Mark Todd of New Zealand and Charisma). A rider since the age of seven, Stives competed successfully in dressage as well as eventing: in 1978 she decided to concentrate on eventing, because of the variety of challenges it presents, particularly in the cross-country, which she has described as a "real high." Four years later her career was almost over after a bad accident at the Kentucky Three-Day Event, when her horse, Silent Partner, fell on her; three months after that, she rode The Saint at the world championships in a slow but clean round, to finish twenty-fifth. After that competition she bought Ben Arthur, who had finished thirty-ninth; in June 1983 the pair was third at the Kentucky, and Stives calls him "the best horse I've ever ridden." At Los Angeles in 1984, Stives and Ben Arthur shared another medal: with their teammates, Torrance Fleishmann (who finished fourth in individual standings, riding Finivarra), J. Michael Plumb, and Bruce Davidson, they won the team gold.

FENCING

"Oh, come, everyone knows what touché means," says Georgie in Odets's *The Country Girl*. And parry, and riposte. And foible—the "weak" part of a blade, from middle to point. The language of fencing has entered common speech more than we may realize. A form of sword has been known since earliest recorded combat, but as armor grew thicker and weapons heavier, refined swordplay moved from the battlefield to the medieval guilds and the education of gentlemen. The weapons used, manipulated with finesse and nuance of movement, were the lightweight rapier in Italy and later, in France, the foil. Modern fencing as we know it stems from two developments of the seventeenth century: the button tip on the point and the convention of "right of way," which gave the sport its recognizable pattern of alternating attack and defense. For dueling, a heavier weapon was needed: this was the épée. Epée fencing remembers its origin, and in this event there is no right-of-way rule and the entire body (not just the torso) is the allowable target. (For these reasons the épée has been called the "realistic weapon.") In the nineteenth century the Hungarians began fencing with the sabre, a version of the scimitar. Unlike foil and épée, the sabre has a cutting edge. Schooled by the Italian master Italo Santelli in the 1930's, the Hungarians became the absolute masters of sabre fencing. In the Olympics, men have competed in foil and sabre events since 1896, in épée since 1900; women compete only in foil events, first seen at the Paris Olympics in 1924. In the 80's, the top American fencers are **Jana Angelakis** of Peabody, Massachusetts, **Vincent Bradford** of San Antonio, Texas, and **Debra Waples** of Portland, Oregon. Angelakis has won just about everything available in American fencing; six times junior champion, at seventeen she was the youngest to win the senior title, and she took it again in 1981 and 1982. Named to the non-competing 1980 Olympic team, Angelakis finished twelfth that year at the junior world championships, the best individual finish by an American woman in world championship competition. When she went for her third national championship in 1983 she lost to Waples, who won her first national title in that competition. Waples had come to fencing relatively late (in 1973, when she had turned twenty). She made the 1980 Olympic team as an alternate, and has since trained in Europe, a background she feels has been advantageous to her; she was third in American point standing in the summer of 1984. Proficient in both foil and épée, Bradford is tall, left-handed, and quick. Twice collegiate foil champion, she was national épée champion 1982-84, and runner-up to Angelakis in the 1982 national foil championship. She had an excellent season in 1983, finishing second in overall points. In 1984 she defeated defending champion Waples twice in early rounds and ended up with her first national foil title.

Maria Cerra Tishman
born New York, New York

A fencer at the age of nine at the Salle Vince in Brooklyn (where she was later on the salle's national championship team 1935-39), Cerra Tishman attended Hunter College, was twice national collegiate champion, and shared in Hunter's two team titles during her undergraduate years. National champion in 1945, she was also a member of national championship teams in 1943 (Salle Santelli) and 1945-47 (Fencers Club). Named to the U.S. Olympic team for the London Games in 1948, she finished fourth in individual foil, the highest placing an American woman had achieved. A member also of the U.S. world championship team that year, Cerra Tishman and her teammates achieved fifth place, again the best American showing. After retiring from competition, Cerra Tishman was actively involved in committee work for women's fencing; she was the first woman appointed to the U.S. Olympic Committee for fencing. She is a member of the Helms Hall of Fame.

Ilona Schacherer Elek
born Budapest, Hungary, May 17, 1907

The European champion, lefthanded Schacherer Elek was the oldest woman gold medalist at the 1936 Berlin Olympics: she was in her thirtieth year when she won the individual foil event, defeating Helene Mayer, who was competing for Germany. These two women were both brilliant fencers, the best ever; the next year Schacherer Elek was runner-up to Mayer at the world championships. The Olympics, suspended during World War II, were not held again until the London Games of 1948. There, twelve years later almost to the day since her first gold, Schacherer Elek again was the oldest woman gold medalist, coming from behind in the next to last bout to defeat Maria Cerra Tishman of the U.S. with four straight hits. (In that Olympiad, Ilona's sister Margit placed sixth in the same event.) In 1952, at the Helsinki Games, Schacherer Elek won her third Olympic medal, a silver; after winning her first 20 bouts, two losses forced her into a barrage, or fence-off, in which she was defeated for the gold by Irene Camber of Italy.

Marion Lloyd Vince
born Brooklyn, New York, April 16, 1906; died November 2, 1969

Two years after she began fencing in 1925, Lloyd Vince was nationally ranked; a year after that, she was a member of the U.S. Olympic team (in one of her bouts defeating eventual gold medalist Helene Mayer). Twice national champion (1928 and 1931), Lloyd Vince appeared again at the 1932 Olympics, and was the first American woman to attain the fencing finals (she finished ninth); she was named to the Olympic team again in 1936. At the Salle Vince, directed by her husband, Joseph, she was a key member of the Salle Vince team for nine of its ten consecutive national team championships. She and her husband were both named to fencing's Helms Hall of Fame; after her death, the Amateur Fencing League of America honored her memory by naming the national championship trophy for under-nineteens for her.

Helene Mayer
born Konigstein, Germany, 1910; died October 1953

National champion for the first time at the age of thirteen, Mayer won a gold medal in foil at the Amsterdam Olympics in 1928 before her eighteenth birthday, taking 18 of her 20 bouts. She was European champion in 1929 and 1931, and competed again in the Olympics at Los Angeles in 1932; because of illness she did not place. She chose to stay in the U.S., but competed again for Germany (possibly under pressure—Mayer was Jewish) at the 1936 Olympics in Berlin, where she placed second to Ilona Elek of Hungary. The following year she beat Elek in the world championships; she never again competed internationally. In her adopted country, Meyer took part in nine U.S. championships (1934, 1935, 1937-39, 1941, 1942, 1946, 1947); she was first in all but the last, when she lost in her last bout to Helena Mroczkowska Dow and came in second. Tall (5'10") and physically superb, a tremendous competitor, Mayer is regarded by many as the greatest woman fencer ever and a classic stylist.

Janice-Lee York Romary
born California, August 6, 1928

The Commissioner of Fencing for the Los Angeles Olympic Organizing Committee for 1984, York Romary had an impressive background for the job: she was a member of the six U.S. Olympic fencing teams from 1948 through 1968. In 1952 and 1956 she reached the finals in individual foil and finished fourth both times. She holds ten national championships (1950, 1951, 1956, 1957, 1960, 1961, 1964, 1965, 1966, 1968) and was a member of the national championship team seven times (1948, 1950, 1952, 1956, 1957, 1962, 1967). She was on the U.S. women's foil team that achieved fifth place in the 1948 world championships. The first woman to carry the U.S. flag at an Olympiad (Mexico City, 1968), York Romary is a member of the Helms Hall of Fame for fencing.

WORLD CHAMPIONS
Women's Foil Individual

Year	Champion	Country
* 1924	Ellen Osiier	Denmark
* 1928	Helene Mayer	Germany
1929	Helene Mayer	Germany

Year	Champion	Country
1930	Jenny Addams	Belgium
1931	Helene Mayer	Germany
* 1932	Ellen Preis	Austria
1933	Gwen Neligan	Great Britain
1934	Ilona Elek	Hungary
1935	Ilona Elek	Hungary
* 1936	Ilona Elek	Hungary
1937	Helene Mayer	Germany
1938	Maria Sediva	Czechoslovakia
1939-46	not held	
1947	Ellen Preis	Austria
* 1948	Ilona Elek	Hungary
1949	Ellen Preis	Austria
1950 (tie)	Renee Garilhe	France
	Ellen Preis	Austria
1951	Ilona Elek	Hungary
* 1952	Irene Camber	Italy
1953	Irene Camber	Italy
1954	Karen Lachmann	Denmark
1955	Lidia Domolky	Hungary
* 1956	Gillian Sheen	Great Britain
1957	Aleksandra Zabelina	USSR
1958	Valentina Kisseleva	USSR
1959	Emma Efimova	USSR
* 1960	Heidi Schmid	West Germany
1961	Heidi Schmid	West Germany
1962	Olga Orban Szabo	Romania
1963	Ildiko Ujlaki-Rejto	Hungary
* 1964	Ildiko Ujlaki-Rejto	Hungary
1965	Galina Gorokhova	USSR
1966	Tatanya Samusenko	USSR
1967	Aleksandra Zabelina	USSR
* 1968	Elena Novikova	USSR
1969	Elena Novikova	USSR
1970	Galina Gorokhova	USSR
1971	Marie Chantal Demaille	France
* 1972	Antonella Ragno-Lonzi	Italy
1973	Valentina Nikonova	USSR
1974	Ildiko Bobis	Hungary
1975	Ekaterina Stahl	Romania
* 1976	Ildiko Schwarczenberger	Hungary
1977	Valentina Sidorova	USSR
1978	Valentina Sidorova	USSR
1979	Cornelia Hanisch	West Germany
* 1980	Pascale Trinquet	France
1981	Cornelia Hanisch	West Germany
1982	Nailia Guiliazova	USSR
1983	Dorina Vaccaroni	Italy
* 1984	Luan Jujie	China

*In Olympic years, the Games are considered the world championship competition.

U.S. CHAMPIONS
Women's Foil Individual

Year	Champion
1912	Adelaide Baylis
1913	W. H. Dewar
1914	Margaret Stimson
1915	Jessie Pyle
1916	Alice Voorhees
1917	Florence Walton
1918-19	not held
1920	Adeline Gehrig
1921	Adeline Gehrig
1922	Adeline Gehrig
1923	Adeline Gehrig
1924	Irma Hopper
1925	Florence Schoonmaker
1926	Florence Schoonmaker
1927	Stephanie Stern
1928	Marion Lloyd
1929	Florence Schoonmaker
1930	Evelyn Van Buskirk
1931	Marion Lloyd Vince
1932	Dorothy Locke
1933	Dorothy Locke
1934	Helene Mayer
1935	Helene Mayer
1936	Joanna de Tuscan
1937	Helene Mayer
1938	Helene Mayer
1939	Helene Mayer
1940	Helena Mroczkowska
1941	Helene Mayer
1942	Helene Mayer
1943	Helena Mroczkowska
1944	Madeline Dalton
1945	Maria Cerra
1946	Helene Mayer
1947	Helena Mroczkowska Dow
1948	Helena Mroczkowska Dow
1949	Polly Craus
1950	Janice-Lee York
1951	Janice-Lee York
1952	Maxine Mitchell
1953	Paula Sweeney
1954	Maxine Mitchell
1955	Maxine Mitchell
1956	Janice-Lee York Romary
1957	Janice-Lee York Romary
1958	Maxine Mitchell
1959	Maria Pilar Roldan
1960	Janice-Lee York Romary
1961	Janice-Lee York Romary
1962	Yoshie Takeuchi

Year	Champion
1963	Harriet King
1964	Janice-Lee York Romary
1965	Janice-Lee York Romary
1966	Janice-Lee York Romary
1967	Harriet King
1968	Janice-Lee York Romary
1969	Ruth C. White
1970	Harriet King
1971	Harriet King
1972	Ruth C. White
1973	Tatanya Adamovich
1974	Gay Jacobson
1975	Nikki Tomlinson
1976	Ann O'Donnell
1977	Sheila Armstrong
1978	Gay Jacobson Dasaro
1979	Jana Angelakis
1980	Nikki Tomlinson Franke
1981	Jana Angelakis
1982	Jana Angelakis
1983	Debra Waples
1984	Vincent Bradford

OLYMPIC CHAMPIONSHIPS
Women's Individual Foil

Year	Gold	Silver	Bronze
1924 Paris	Ellen Osiier Denmark	Gladys Davis Great Britain	Grete Heckscher Denmark
1928 Amsterdam	Helene Mayer Germany	Muriel Freeman Great Britain	Olga Oelkers Germany
1932 Los Angeles	Ellen Preis Austria	J. Heather Guinness Great Britain	Erna Bogathy Bogan Hungary
1936 Berlin	Ilona Elek Hungary	Helene Mayer Germany	Ellen Preis Austria
1948 London	Ilona Elek Hungary	Karen Lachmann Denmark	Ellen Preis Austria
1952 Helsinki	Irene Camber Italy	Ilona Elek Hungary	Karen Lachmann Denmark
1956 Melbourne	Gillian Sheen Great Britain	Olga Orban Romania	Renee Garilhe France
1960 Rome	Heidi Schmid West Germany	Valentina Rastuorova USSR	Maria Vicol Romania
1964 Tokyo	Ildiko Ujlaki-Rejto Hungary	Helga Mees West Germany	Antonella Ragno Italy

Year	Gold	Silver	Bronze
1968 Mexico City	Elena Novikova USSR	Maria Del Pilar Roldan Mexico	Ildiko Ujlaki-Rejto Hungary
1972 Munich	Antonella Ragno-Lonzi Italy	Ildiko Bobis Hungary	Galin Gorokhova USSR
1976 Montreal	Ildiko Schwarczenberger Hungary	Maria Consdata Collino Italy	Elena Novikova USSR
1980 Moscow	Pascale Trinquet France	Magda Maros Hungary	Barbara Wysoczanska Poland
1984 Los Angeles	Luan Jujie China	Cornelia Hanisch West Germany	Dorina Vaccaroni Italy

FIELD HOCKEY

Look carefully at a Greek frieze—that game with sticks is an ancestor of field hockey. In modern times women began playing field hockey at the women's colleges of Oxford and Cambridge in the 1880's. Constance M.K. Appleby introduced the game from England to a group of Harvard Summer School faculty and students—men and women—in 1901. Vassar College heard of the exhibition and asked for a similar demonstration of the game. The sport soon spread to other Eastern women's colleges, and clubs were formed. Today women are active in more than 2,000 high school and 400 college field hockey programs in the U.S., and in more than 2,000 amateur clubs. The first American women's team to compete internationally—in any sport—was the All-Philadelphia field hockey team; their application to the 1920 Olympics in Antwerp refused, they were invited by the English team to play in a tournament, which the Americans lost, 2 and 8. The U.S. Field Hockey Association was formed in 1922, and in 1927 the Federation of Women's Field Hockey Associations was established to promote competition among teams from the U.S., England, Scotland, and Ireland. Women's field hockey was an Olympic event for the first time at the Moscow Games in 1980, which were boycotted by the U.S. The first U.S. Olympic team appeared at Los Angeles in 1984, and won the bronze medal; West Germany won the silver. The gold-winning team, from The Netherlands, also held the 1982 American Cup, the 1983 European Cup, and the 1983 World Cup. Going into the Los Angeles Games, **Sophie von Weiler** of the Dutch team, the great left wing, was the only woman to have scored more than 100 goals in international competition. Her teammate **Fieke Boekhorst** is unsurpassed at the penalty corner; Boekhorst retired from competition in 1983 but returned to play at Los Angeles.

35

Beth Anders

Gwen Cheeseman

Beth Anders
born Norristown, Pennsylvania, November 13, 1951

As field hockey coach at Old Dominion University, Anders piloted her team to two national collegiate championships, in 1982 and 1983; as captain of the U.S. field hockey team, playing sweeper/midfielder, she is one of the world's best penalty corner scorers and a fine defense player. She has been a member of the national team since 1969; at the time of the 1984 Olympics, she had been team high scorer every year since she joined the team, and had played on every World Cup team since 1971. *Olympian* magazine voted her Co-Athlete of the Year in 1982; the other was teammate Charlene Morett. In the 1983 World Cup competition Anders scored six penalty corner goals in seven matches. The following year, at the Four Nations tournament in March (at which the U.S. team won the gold medal, defeating New Zealand, Australia, and tieing, then defeating, Canada), Anders scored four goals on penalty corners. The most experienced of the U.S. team in international competition, in 1984 she played her hundredth international match. She was named to the 1980 Olympic team, which did not compete because of the boycott. Four years later Anders led her team to the bronze medal at the Los Angeles Games.

Gwen Cheeseman
born Harrisburg, Pennsylvania, August 13, 1951

A member of the U.S. team since 1972, goalkeeper Cheeseman played on the World Cup team in 1975 and 1980, and in National Sports Festival competition in 1978 and 1979. She was named to the U.S. Olympic team in 1980, but the U.S. boycotted the Moscow Games; Cheeseman retired from the game in 1981, but by late 1982 she was back, and on the national team. In 1983 she again played in World Cup competition and at the National Sports Festival. By the beginning of 1984 she had played in almost 70 international matches. Small (5′ 2″, 127 pounds) but successful, Cheeseman was in goal for all four matches of the Four Nations tournament in March 1984, in which the U.S. team defeated New Zealand and Australia and tied and then defeated Canada: Cheeseman allowed only one goal; the other three games were shutouts. She was a member of the bronze-medal-winning team at the Los Angeles Olympics in August 1984.

Charlene Morett
born Darby, Pennsylvania, December 5, 1957

Playing left wing forward on the U.S. team, Morett's passing, fakes, and daring are superb—she is simply one of the best in the world. A member of the national team since 1977, she played in World Cup competition in 1979 and 1983, and at the National Sports Festival in 1979, 1981, and 1983; she was named to the U.S. Olympic team in 1980 and 1984. She works a fine partnership with teammate Beth Anders, especially at the penalty corner. In 1982, *Olympian* magazine voted Morett Co-Athlete of the Year; the other was Anders.

Charlene Morett

Julie Staver, midfielder, 1980 and 1984 U.S. Olympic teams

OLYMPIC CHAMPIONSHIPS

Year	Gold	Silver	Bronze
1980 Moscow	Zimbabwe	Czechoslovakia	Poland
1984 Los Angeles	Netherlands	West Germany	USA

U.S. COLLEGIATE CHAMPIONS

Year	School
1981	University of Connecticut
1982	Old Dominion
1983	Old Dominion

WORLD CUP CHAMPIONS

Year	Country
1983	Netherlands
(first year held)	

GOLF

Mary, Queen of Scots was an enthusiastic golfer—and the only woman known to play the sport for about 300 years. Then, women's golf clubs began appearing in the British Isles (the first was at St. Andrew's, Scotland, founded in 1867, followed a year later by the Westward Ho! Ladies Club in England). But there was no serious competition for women until the establishment in 1893 of the Ladies Golf Union, which sponsored the first British Ladies' championship that same year, won by Lady Margaret Scott. Two years later, Mrs. Charles S. Brown took the first U.S. Women's Amateur championship, held at the Meadow Brook Club in Hempstead, New York. Until the 1940's few women played professionally, and there were no cash prizes; the income that made them pros came from promotions, teaching, and consulting. In 1944 the Women's Professional Golf Association was formed, and in 1946 the new organization sponsored the first U.S. Women's Open championship; Patty Berg won the top prize of $1,500. But the WPGA was short-lived, and in 1950 it was succeeded by the Ladies Professional Golf Association, supported by the redoubtable Babe Zaharias. Through the 50's LPGA purses were small and conditions of the tour were primitive. By 1963, however, a record purse of $9,000 was offered at the U.S. Open and the event was televised; that was the beginning. Commercial sponsorship and television made the difference, both in prize money and gate receipts, and in 1984 the total LPGA purse for its tour of 38 events was $8,000,000.

Amy Alcott
born Kansas City, Missouri, February 22, 1956

Winner of the U.S. Junior Girls title in 1973, Alcott was second in the Canadian Amateur the next year. She joined the LPGA tour in 1975 (and was Rookie of the Year); she won the Orange Blossom Classic her first year out, and at least one tournament every year since. When still a teenager, Alcott shot 70 at the difficult Pebble Beach course, breaking the course record for women that had been set by Babe Zaharias. She won her first major event in 1979, the Peter Jackson Classic (later known as the DuMaurier). Her best year to date was 1980: she won the U.S. Women's Open and three other tournaments, and her 71.51 average earned her a

Vare Trophy. In 1983, she won the Nabisco-Dinah Shore Invitational (designated by the LPGA that year as one of its four major events). Off-season, Alcott works as a short-order cook at the Butterfly Bakery in Los Angeles. Her $55,000 from the Dinah Shore? "Maybe I'll put a down payment on my own bakery!" More for the bakery came in 1984, when she won the $200,000 Lady Keystone Open with a tournament-record round of 65; she also placed second in the LPGA championship and third in the U.S. Women's Open. By September, when she won the San Jose Classic, she had 21 career victories.

Patty Berg
born Minneapolis, Minnesota, February 13, 1918
   Who made the only hole in one in the history of the U.S. Women's Open? Patty Berg, in 1959. Berg was U.S. Amateur champion in 1938 and a member of the Curtis Cup team in 1936 and 1938. She had 26 amateur titles before turning pro in 1940, then accumulated 83 more trophies (41 of them with the LPGA). She was the winner of the first U.S. Women's Open in 1946 and a founder and first president of the LPGA. Three-time AP Athlete of the Year, and three-time winner of the Vare Trophy (1953, 1955, 1956), she was one of the first four golfers elected to the LPGA Hall of Fame (1951) and was chosen for the World Golf Hall of Fame (honoring both men and women golfers) in 1974. Berg's sportsmanship and concern for others have been recognized by the 1963 Bob Jones Award and the 1976 Humanitarian Sports Award from the United Cerebral Palsy Foundation (of which she was the first woman recipient). In 1978 the LPGA established the Patty Berg Award for her outstanding contribution to women's golf. (To date, the award, not presented annually, had been won by Marilynn Smith in 1979 and Betsy Rawls in 1980.) She was named to the Women's Sports Hall of Fame in 1980.

Amy Alcott   Patty Berg

Jane Blalock
born Portsmouth, New Hampshire, September 19, 1945

New Hampshire Junior champion and New England Junior champion in 1963, Blalock went on to win the New Hampshire Amateur four years in a row (1965-68) and the New England Amateur in 1968. As a student at Rollins College, she also took the Florida Intercollegiate in 1965. She joined the LPGA tour in 1969 and was named Rookie of the Year; that year she began her record streak, which lasted to 1981, of 299 tournaments without missing a cut. In 1983 Blalock had three top-ten finishes. Wind does not daunt her; she knows just how to play it. Blalock is a tremendous competitor, and her game is at its best when the pressure is on.

Jane Blalock   Beth Daniel, 1979 Rookie of the Year

JoAnne Gunderson Carner
born Kirkland, Washington, April 4, 1939

Carner started playing as a ten-year-old, and seven years later (1956) won the U.S. Girls' Junior championship. She holds five U.S. Amateur championships (1957, 1960, 1962, 1966, 1968). As a professional, Carner won her first tournament—the Wendell West Open—in 1970, her first year on the LPGA circuit. She won the U.S. Women's Open in 1971 and 1976. Her fortieth career victory came in May 1984, when she won the Corning Classic. She holds five Vare Trophies (1974, 1975, 1981, 1982, 1983). Friendly and popular with the crowds, Carner plays an aggressive and confident game. She won the Bob Jones Award in 1981 and was elected to the LPGA Hall of Fame in 1982. She had top earnings ($291,404.25) on the LPGA circuit in 1983, and was number one in career money— $1,644,348.63.

JoAnne Carner   Donna Caponi won U.S. Women's
                                 Open twice in a row, 1969 and 1970

Marlene Hagge
born Eureka, South Dakota, February 16, 1934

At sixteen Hagge was the youngest player to join the LPGA tour; in 1984, she was the senior active member, playing her thirty-fifth season. Her amateur career began with a victory in the Long Beach Boys Junior in 1944; she went on to win the Western and National Junior championships, the Los Angeles Junior, the Palm Springs Junior, and the Northern California Junior. In 1949, she was named AP Athlete of the Year, Golfer of the Year—and Teenager of the Year. As a pro, Hagge won the second LPGA championship (1956), beating Patty Berg in a sudden-death playoff; she also took seven other LPGA titles, leading the tour. That year Hagge was the top LPGA money winner, and has finished among the top ten in earnings in eight seasons. She was the first to establish the low nine-hole score of 29 (1971). A small woman (5'2"), Hagge has a compact and remarkably powerful swing.

Betty Jameson
born Norman, Oklahoma, May 19, 1919

Her high school had only a "boys' golf team"—and Jameson was on it. In those years she began her impressive amateur career: 1934 Southern Amateur champion, four-time Texas state champion, twice each the Trans-Mississippi, Texas Open, U.S. Amateur, and Western Amateur winner. She was the first player to win both the Western Open and the Western Amateur in the same year (1942). Two years after joining the LPGA tour, Jameson won the 1947 U.S. Women's Open with a 295 total; this was the first time a woman had scored below 300 in a 72-hole event. Her best year was 1955, when she won four events, including the Babe Zaharias

Sandra Haynie, elected to LPGA Hall   Nancy Lopez
of Fame in 1977

Open. A founder and charter member of the LPGA, in 1952 Jameson
donated the Vare Troy, named for Glenna Collett Vare and awarded annually to the player with the lowest scoring average in a minimum of 70
official rounds of tournament play.

Catherine Lacoste
born Paris, France, June 27, 1945
   A champion and the daughter of champions: her mother, golfer Simone
Thion de la Chaume, was the first foreigner to win the British Amateur;
René Lacoste, her father, held Wimbledon and U.S. tennis titles. Catherine
Lacoste's career was short and remarkable: twice winner of the French
Closed championship, three-time winner of the French Open, she also took
the British Amateur, the U.S. Amateur, and the U.S. Women's Open, all
between 1966 and 1970. At nineteen, she was already responsible for
France's victory in the first Women's World Amateur Team championships; two years later, in 1966, she was French national champion for the
first time. In 1967 she took the U.S. Women's Open; as of 1984 she is
one of only two foreigners to have won this event, the only amateur, and,
at twenty-two, the youngest. In 1979, Lacoste made the grand slam of
French, British, and U.S. amateur titles in one year.

Nancy Lopez
born Torrance, California, January 6, 1957
   Lopez grew up in Roswell, New Mexico, and—at twelve—won the
New Mexico Women's Amateur. She went on to take both the U.S. Junior
Girls' and Western Junior titles three years running (1972-74) and won

the Mexican Amateur in 1975. In 1976, she won the national collegiate championship and made the Curtis Cup and World Amateur teams. That year, still an amateur, she tied for second in the U.S. Women's Open. In her first full season of professional play (1978), Lopez won nine tournaments and was named Rookie of the Year *and* Player of the Year. Twice a Vare Trophy winner, her scoring average in 1978 was 71.76, an all-time LPGA record—until 1979, when Lopez broke it herself with a 71.20. She won the 1981 Dinah Shore championship, in which she played a career-low 64. Lopez joined the million-dollar club in 1983, a year in which she played only 12 events because of pregnancy. After the birth of her daughter in November, Lopez rejoined the tour, winning the $300,000 Uniden Invitational in March 1984. Of her style, Carol Mann has said, "She plays by feel. All her senses come into play. That's when golf is an art."

Carol Mann
born Buffalo, New York, February 3, 1941

Winner of the Western Junior and Chicago Junior titles in 1958, in 1960 she was medalist in the Trans-Mississippi and winner of the Chicago Women's Amateur. Mann turned pro that year, and in her twenty active years on the LPGA circuit she took multiple titles in eight seasons. She was winner of the U.S. Women's Open in 1965. Her best year, 1968: Mann took ten titles and the Vare Trophy with an average score of 72.04, a record that stood for ten years. She was elected to LPGA Hall of Fame in 1977 and the Women's Sports Hall of Fame in 1982. Sure in putting, controlled in driving, Mann's game reflects a secure knowledge and use of her strengths. She did not play in 1982 or 1983, but continues active in the game: she is a commentator for NBC-TV coverage of both men's and women's tours, and a member of the Women's Sports Foundation board of trustees.

Judy Rankin
born St. Louis, Missouri, February 18, 1945

Taught by her father, Rankin started playing golf at six; at eight she won her first title (her first of four St. Louis Pee Wees). At fourteen, she was the youngest player to win the Missouri Amateur, which she won again two years later, in 1961. In 1960, Rankin was the low amateur in the U.S. Women's Open. She turned pro at seventeen and won three tournaments in her third year on tour. She holds 26 LPGA victories (the last in 1979), won the Vare Trophy in 1973, 1976, and 1977, and was Player of the Year in 1976 and 1977. Rankin knows her own game well and is a patient and consistent player, but her career has been curtailed by a back injury in recent seasons.

Betsy Rawls
born Spartanburg, South Carolina, May 4, 1928

Rawls did not begin playing golf until she was seventeen, then made up for lost time. She won the Texas Amateur championship (Rawls grew up in Texas) in 1949 and 1950; in 1951 she won the first of her four U.S.

Judy Rankin   Betsy Rawls

Women's Opens (the others in 1953, 1957, and 1960). She was twice
LPGA champion (1959 and 1969). Holds 55 tournament titles (only Kathy
Whitworth and Mickey Wright have won more). Her best season was
1959, when she won ten titles and the Vare Trophy. She was elected to
LPGA Hall of Fame in 1960. A Phi Beta Kappa from the University of
Texas with a degree in math and physics, Rawls early acquired a com-
prehensive knowledge of the rules of golf, and on tour was known as the
"circuit judge." She was the first woman to serve on the Rules Committee
for the U.S. Men's Open. Rawls was the second recipient of the Patty
Berg Award.

Patty Sheehan
born Middlebury, Vermont, October 27, 1956

At thirteen, Sheehan was rated the best of her age in the country in her
sport—skiing! (Her father was Middlebury College ski coach and coached
the U.S. Olympic team in 1956; as a junior Sheehan competed with Tamara
McKinney.) Golf became her game after her family's move to Nevada;
she won the Nevada State Amateur 1975-78, the California Amateur in
1978 and 1979, and was national collegiate champion in 1980. Playing
on the 1980 Curtis Cup team, she won all four of her matches. As a pro,
Sheehan was named LPGA Rookie of the Year in 1981, and in 1982 she
had eighteen top-ten finishes, including three wins. At the start of 1983,
her play seemed to lack spark: it turned out she had pneumonia. Necessary
rest and ultra-sound treatments for arthritis in both hands periodically also
cut into her schedule, but she was still Player of the Year in 1983, winning
the Corning Classic, the Henredon Classic, the Inamori Classic (the second
year in a row), as well as the LPGA championship. Her 1984 season began
with a victory in the Elizabeth Arden Classic in February. In June, when

she won both the LPGA championship and the McDonald's Kids' Classic, she earned a bonus of $500,000 for winning two of the three last LPGA events (JoAnne Carner won the third, the Corning Classic), which together with her first-prize money made the largest award ever made to a professional golfer. The summer continued good: in August Sheehan won her second Henredon Classic. In lighter moments on tour she sings with the Unplayable Lies; off the course she is actively involved with Tigh Sheehan, a home for troubled girls she sponsors in California.

Jan Stephenson
born Sydney, New South Wales, Australia, December 22, 1951

New South Wales Schoolgirl champion 1964-69, Junior champion 1969-72, Stephenson won the Australian Junior championship three times, the New South Wales Amateur twice. As a professional, Stephenson took four titles on the Australian circuit, including the national championship. In the U.S., she was the LPGA's Rookie of the Year in 1974. Being a stunning blonde is not always smooth sailing in the world of women's professional golf, and some of Stephenson's publicity activities occasioned comment; but despite controversy (and injuries), she has proved herself a great golfer. In 1976 she had two tournament victories, another in 1978, another in 1980; since then, the sky has been the limit. She set the all-time LPGA low score of 198 for 54 holes (1981). In 1982, although she missed the first seven events of the season because of a foot injury, she still had three victories including the LPGA championship. Her best season to date was 1983: she had three wins, including the U.S. Women's Open, and finished in the top five in almost every category in which records are kept. A small woman (5' 5", 115 pounds), Stephenson has a swing that is not powerful, but is technically superb, thanks to natural talent—and hours of practice.

Jan Stephenson

Hollis Stacy, U.S. Women's Open Champion, 1977, 1978, 1984

Louise Suggs
born Atlanta, Georgia, September 7, 1923

Suggs owns a brilliant amateur record, followed by a professional history no less brilliant. Her amateur titles include the Southern, Western, Georgia (twice) and the North and South (three times). She followed Babe Zaharias as U.S. Amateur champion (1947) and as British Amateur champion the following year, and was a member of the 1948 Curtis Cup team. A founder and charter member of the LPGA, she won three events in her first year as a pro (1949)—the U.S. Women's Open, the Western Open, and the All-American Open. She won the U.S. Open again in 1952. Her scoring average of 74.64 earned her the Vare Trophy in 1957, the same year she was LPGA champion. Her three Titleholders victories came in 1954, 1956, and 1959. The first member of the LPGA Hall of Fame (1951), she is also honored in the Georgia Hall of Fame (the first woman elected, in 1966) and the World Golf Hall of Fame. Direct and businesslike in play, Suggs has often been compared with Ben Hogan.

Glenna Collett Vare
born Providence, Rhode Island, June 20, 1903

The Vare Trophy for lowest scoring average is named for a "tomboy" who at ten was playing baseball and driving a car; at eighteen she defeated the great British woman golfer, Cecil Leitch, for the Berthellyn Cup in Philadelphia in 1921. For the next ten years, Glenna Collett was the one to beat. In 1922, after winning the North and South and then the Eastern, (in which she averaged 82 for three rounds), she took the U.S. Women's Open championship, 5 and 4. The following year, she won the Canadian championship, and in 1924 won 59 of her 60 events, including her second Canadian title. Collett Vare won five more U.S. Women's Open championships (1925, 1928-30, 1935); in her sixth and last, she defeated the then unknown Patty Berg. She received the Bob Jones Award in 1965. With her fluid swing and long, powerful drives, she led the exciting trend of the 20's, when women were lowering their scores to the high and mid 70's—and she herself played a good 10 strokes lower than women had scored before the war. In 1981—still playing golf, with an 11 handicap— she was named to the Women's Sports Hall of Fame.

Joyce Wethered
born Maldon, Surrey, England, November 17, 1901

Said by many to be perhaps the finest woman golfer ever, Wethered entered only five English championships—in consecutive years, and won in all of them. She was also four-time winner of the British Amateur championship (1922, 1924, 1925, 1929). In the 1929 event, an opponent was Glenna Collett, who played the first nine holes in an amazing 34. Wethered took only 73 strokes to play the next eighteen—winning an average of every other hole— and took the title. She toured the U.S. in the 1930's but did not compete. Her balance was perfect, her swing not long but rhythmic and powerful. As Bobby Jones observed, "It was impossible to expect that Miss Wethered would miss a shot—and she never did."

Kathy Whitworth
born Monahans, Texas, September 27, 1939

Whitworth tried golf as a teenager: "Most sports had come naturally to me, but this one—gosh, it just bugged me. At first I just didn't catch on to it at all." Then it didn't take long: Whitworth took the New Mexico Amateur two years in a row (1957 and 1958). As a pro, she won the Vare Trophy seven times (1965-67, 1969-72), and was seven times LPGA Player of the Year (1966-69, 1971-73); in 1965 and 1967 she was AP Athlete of the Year. She was three times LPGA champion (1967, 1971,1975). With 86 career victories (the most recent in the Safeco Classic in September 1984, in her twenty-fifth year on tour), Whitworth is the all-time LPGA titleholder—yet she never took the U.S. Open. She was inducted into the LPGA Hall of Fame in 1975; in 1982, she made the Texas Golf Hall of Fame, the World Golf Hall of Fame, and Texas sportswriters elected her to the Texas Sports Hall of Fame. She was named to the Women's Sports Hall of Fame in 1984. An intense and dedicated golfer, Whitworth is amazingly flexible in adapting to various conditions of play.

Kathy Whitworth   Mickey Wright

Mickey Wright
born San Diego, California, February 14, 1935

The American golfer of the 60's, Wright was possibly the greatest in LPGA history. She started on the tour in 1955; beginning the following year, she won between one and thirteen titles each year for the next fourteen years. (Her thirteen wins in 1963 is a record that will probably stand forever.) She was four-time LPGA champion (1958, 1960, 1961, and 1963) and four-time U.S. Women's Open champion (1958, 1959, 1961, 1964). She won the Vare Trophy for five consecutive years (1960-1964) and was named AP Athlete of the Year in 1963 and 1964. She was elected to the

LPGA Hall of Fame in 1964, to the World Golf Hall of Fame in 1976, and to the Women's Sports Hall of Fame in 1981. Her record of 82 career victories (the last won in 1973) stood for ten years, until Kathy Whitworth achieved 84 in 1983. Tall and powerful, with a lovely swing and unrattled in competition, Wright was in many ways a champion of women's golf. Said Judy Rankin, "Mickey got the outside world to take a second hard look at women golfers, and when they looked they saw the rest of us."

Mildred "Babe" Didrikson Zaharias
born Port Arthur, Texas, June 26, 1914; died September 27, 1956

A "profile" of Zaharias? Impossible—there were too many sides to her. Zaharias came to golf already an All-American basketball player and an Olympic track and field gold medalist and world record-setter; she was also an expert swimmer, tennis player, bowler. In her two amateur years as a golfer (1946 and 1947) she won 17 tournaments in a row, which included the 1946 U.S. Amateur and the 1947 British Amateur. A founding member of the LPGA, Zaharias won three U.S. Women's Open championships (1948, 1950, 1954) and the 1954 Vare Trophy. In her eight-year career, Zaharias had 31 LPGA victories; she was elected to the LPGA Hall of Fame in 1951. In 1957, the year after her death, she was the first woman honored by the Bob Jones Award. Flamboyant, brash, and not everyone's cup of tea, yet she advanced the cause of women's professional golf immeasurably. **See also Track and Field.**

Mildred "Babe" Didrikson Zaharias

LPGA CHAMPIONSHIP

Year	Player	Score	Course
1955	Beverly Hanson	220-4&3*	Orchard Ridge C.C., Fort Wayne, IN
1956	Marlene Hagge	291†	Forest Lake C.C., Detroit, MI
1957	Louise Suggs	285	Churchill Valley C.C., Pittsburgh, PA
1958	Mickey Wright	288	Churchill Valley C.C., Pittsburgh, PA
1959	Betsy Rawls	288	Sheraton Hotel C.C., French Lick, IN
1960	Mickey Wright	292	Sheraton Hotel C.C., French Lick, IN
1961	Mickey Wright	287	Stardust C.C., Las Vegas, NV
1962	Judy Kimball	282	Stardust C.C., Las Vegas, NV
1963	Mickey Wright	294 (+10)	Stardust C.C., Las Vegas, NV
1964	Mary Mills	278 (−6)	Stardust C.C., Las Vegas, NV
1965	Sandra Haynie	279 (−5)	Stardust C.C., Las Vegas, NV
1966	Gloria Ehret	282 (−2)	Stardust C.C., Las Vegas, NV
1967	Kathy Whitworth	284 (−8)	Pleasant Valley C.C., Sutton, MA
1968	Sandra Post	294 (+2)−68‡	Pleasant Valley C.C., Sutton, MA
1969	Betsy Rawls	293 (+1)	Concord G.C., Kiamesha Lake, NY
1970	Shirley Englehorn	285 (−7)†	Pleasant Valley C.C., Sutton, MA
1971	Kathy Whitworth	288 (−4)	Pleasant Valley C.C., Sutton MA
1972	Kathy Ahern	293 (+1)	Pleasant Valley C.C., Sutton MA
1973	Mary Mills	288 (−4)	Pleasant Valley C.C., Sutton MA
1974	Sandra Haynie	288 (−4)	Pleasant Valley C.C., Sutton MA
1975	Kathy Whitworth	288 (−4)	Pine Ridge C.C., Baltimore, MD
1976	Betty Burfeindt	287 (−5)	Pine Ridge C.C., Baltimore, MD
1977	Chako Higuchi	279 (−9)	Bay Tree Plantation, N. Myrtle Beach, SC
1978	Nancy Lopez	275 (−13)	Jack Nicklaus G.C., Kings Island, OH
1979	Donna Caponi	279 (−9)	Jack Nicklaus G.C., Kings Island, OH

Year	Player	Score	Course
1980	Sally Little	285 (−3)	Jack Nicklaus G.C., Kings Island, OH
1981	Donna Caponi	280 (−8)	Jack Nicklaus G.C., Kings Island, OH
1982	Jan Stephenson	279 (−9)	Jack Nicklaus G.C., Kings Island, OH
1983	Patty Sheehan	279 (−9)	Jack Nicklaus G.C., Kings Island, OH
1984	Patty Sheehan	272 (−16)	Jack Nicklaus G.C., Kings Island, OH

*Won match-play final.
†Won sudden-death playoff.
‡Won 18-hole playoff.

U.S. WOMEN'S OPEN CHAMPIONSHIP

Year	Player	Score	Course
1946	Patty Berg	5 and 4	Spokane C.C., Spokane, WA
1947	Betty Jameson	295	Starmount Forest C.C., Greensboro, NC
1948	Mildred "Babe" Zaharias	300	Atlantic City C.C., Northfield, NJ
1949	Louise Suggs	291	Prince Georges G.&C.C., Landover, MD
1950	Mildred "Babe" Zaharias	291	Rolling Hills C.C., Wichita, KS
1951	Betsy Rawls	293	Druid Hills G.C., Atlanta, GA
1952	Louise Suggs	284	Bala G.C., Philadelphia, PA
1953	Betsy Rawls	302-70+	C.C. of Rochester, Rochester, NY
1954	Mildred "Babe" Zaharias	291	Salem C.C., Peabody, MA
1955	Fay Crocker	299	Wichita C.C., Wichita, KS
1956	Kathy Cornelius	302-72+	Northland C.C., Duluth, MN
1957	Betsy Rawls	299	Winged Foot G.C., Mamaroneck, NY
1958	Mickey Wright	290	Forest Lake C.C., Bloomfield Hill, MN
1959	Mickey Wright	287	Churchill Valley C.C., Pittsburgh, PA

Year	Player	Score	Course
1960	Betsy Rawls	292	Worcester C.C., Worcester, MA
1961	Mickey Wright	293	Baltusrol G.C., Springfield, NJ
1962	Murle Breer	301	Dunes G.&Beach C., Myrtle Beach, SC
1963	Mary Mills	289 (−3)	Kenwood C.C., Cincinnati, OH
1964	Mickey Wright	290 (−2)−70*	San Diego C.C., Chula Vista, CA
1965	Carol Mann	290 (+2)	Atlantic City C.C., Northfield, NJ
1966	Sandra Spuzich	297 (+9)	Hazeltine National G.C., Minneapolis, MN
1967	Catherine Lacoste	294 (+10)	Virginia Hot Springs G.&Tennis Club, Hot Springs, VA
1968	Susie M. Berning	289 (+5)	Moselem Springs G.C., Fleetwood, PA
1969	Donna Caponi	294 (−2)	Scenic Hills C.C., Pensacola, FL
1970	Donna Caponi	287 (−1)	Muskogee C.C., Muskogee, OK
1971	JoAnne G. Carner	288	Kahkwa Club, Erie, PA
1972	Susie M. Berning	299 (+11)	Winged Foot G.C., Mamaroneck, NY
1973	Susie M. Berning	290 (+2)	C.C. of Rochester, Rochester, NY
1974	Sandra Haynie	295 (+7)	La Grange C.C., La Grange, IL
1975	Sandra Palmer	295 (+7)	Atlantic City C.C., Northfield, NJ
1976	JoAnne G. Carner	292 (+8)	Rolling Green G.C., Springfield, PA
1977	Hollis Stacy	292 (+4)	Hazeltine National G.C., Chaska, MN
1978	Hollis Stacy	289 (+5)	C.C. of Indianapolis, Indianapolis, IN
1979	Jerilyn Britz	284	Brooklawn C.C., Fairfield, CT
1980	Amy Alcott	280 (−4)	Richland C.C., Nashville, TN
1981	Pat Bradley	279 (−9)	La Grange C.C., La Grange, IL
1982	Janet Anderson	283 (−5)	Del Pasco C.C., Sacramento, CA
1983	Jan Stephenson	290 (+6)	Cedar Ridge C.C., Tulsa, OK
1984	Hollis Stacy	290 (+2)	Salem C.C., Peabody, MS

*Won 18-hole playoff.

DU MAURIER CLASSIC

Year	Player	Score	Course
1973	Jocelyne Bourassa	214 (−5)	Montreal G.C., Montreal, QUE
1974	Carole Jo Callison	208 (−11)	Candiac G.C., Montreal, QUE
1975	JoAnne G. Carner	214 (−5)*	St. George's C.C., Toronto, ONT
1976	Donna Caponi	282 (−4)*	Cedar Brae C.C., Toronto, ONT
1977	Judy Rankin	214 (−4)	Lachute G&C.C., Montreal QUE
1978	JoAnne G. Carner	278 (−14)	St. George's C.C., Toronto, ONT
1979	Amy Alcott	285 (−7)	Richelieu Valley G.C., Montreal, QUE
1980	Pat Bradley	277 (−11)	St. George's C.C., Toronto, ONT
1981	Jan Stephenson	278 (−10)	Summerlea C.C., Dorion, QUE
1982	Sandra Haynie	280 (−8)	St. George's C.C., Toronto, ONT
1983	Hollis Stacy	277 (−11)	Beaconsfield G.C., Montreal, QUE
1984	Juli Inkster	279 (−9)	St. George's C.C., Toronto, ONT

*Won sudden-death playoff.

NABISCO DINAH SHORE INVITATIONAL

Year	Player	Score	Course
1972	Jane Blalock	213 (−3)	Mission Hills C.C., Rancho Mirage, CA
1973	Mickey Wright	284 (−4)	Mission Hills, C.C., Rancho Mirage, CA
1974	JoAnn Prentice	289 (+1)*	Mission Hills, C.C., Rancho Mirage, CA
1975	Sandra Palmer	283 (−5)	Mission Hills, C.C., Rancho Mirage, CA
1976	Judy Rankin	285 (−3)	Mission Hills, C.C., Rancho Mirage, CA
1977	Kathy Whitworth	289 (+1)	Mission Hills, C.C., Rancho Mirage, CA
1978	Sandra Post	283 (−5)*	Mission Hills, C.C., Rancho Mirage, CA
1979	Sandra Post	276 (−12)	Mission Hills, C.C., Rancho Mirage, CA
1980	Donna Caponi	275 (−13)	Mission Hills, C.C., Rancho Mirage, CA

Year	Player	Score	Course
1981	Nancy Lopez	277 (-11)	Mission Hills, C.C., Rancho Mirage, CA
1982	Sally Little	278 (-10)	Mission Hills, C.C., Rancho Mirage, CA
1983	Amy Alcott	282 (-6)	Mission Hills, C.C., Rancho Mirage, CA
1984	Juli Inkster	280 (-8)*	Mission Hills C.C., Rancho Mirage, CA

*Won sudden-death playoff.

LPGA PLAYER-OF-THE-YEAR AWARD

Year	Player
1966	Kathy Whitworth
1967	Kathy Whitworth
1968	Kathy Whitworth
1969	Kathy Whitworth
1970	Sandra Haynie
1971	Kathy Whitworth
1972	Kathy Whitworth
1973	Kathy Whitworth
1974	JoAnne G. Carner
1975	Sandra Palmer
1976	Judy Rankin
1977	Judy Rankin
1978	Nancy Lopez
1979	Nancy Lopez
1980	Beth Daniel
1981	JoAnne G. Carner
1982	JoAnne G. Carner
1983	Patty Sheehan

PGA HALL OF FAME
Of the 48 members of the PGA Hall of Fame only 2 are women: Patty Berg and Mildred "Babe" Zaharias.

LPGA LEADING MONEY WINNERS

Year	Player	Amount
1954	Patty Berg	$16,011
1955	Patty Berg	16,492
1956	Marlene Hagge	20,235
1957	Patty Berg	16,272

Year	Player	Amount
1958	Beverly Hanson	$12,629
1959	Betsy Rawls	25,774
1960	Louise Suggs	16,892
1961	Mickey Wright	22,236
1962	Mickey Wright	21,641
1963	Mickey Wright	31,269
1964	Mickey Wright	29,800
1965	Kathy Whitworth	28,658
1966	Kathy Whitworth	33,517
1967	Kathy Whitworth	32,937
1968	Kathy Whitworth	48,379
1969	Carol Mann	49,152
1970	Kathy Whitworth	30,235
1971	Kathy Whitworth	41,181
1972	Kathy Whitworth	65,063
1973	Kathy Whitworth	82,854
1974	JoAnne G. Carner	87,094
1975	Sandra Palmer	94,805
1976	Judy Rankin	150,734
1977	Judy Rankin	122,890
1978	Nancy Lopez	189,813
1979	Nancy Lopez	215,987
1980	Beth Daniel	231,000
1981	Beth Daniel	206,977
1982	JoAnne G. Carner	310,399
1983	JoAnne G. Carner	291,404

The first man to exceed $100,000 in a year was Arnold Palmer in 1963. He won $128,230. In 1980, Tom Watson was the top men's PGA money winner with $530,808.

GYMNASTICS

To the ancient Greeks, it was all one; their athletes routinely exercised with hoops and balls. But in modern times, "artistic" and "rhythmic" gymnastics have been separated into two distinct sports. "Artistic," or "Olympic," gymnastics includes floorwork, vaults, and work on the beam and uneven bars. "Rhythmic" gymnastics, based on dance movements, is floorwork with the rope, ball, hoop, clubs, and ribbon (in the 1984 Olympics the rope was not used). Women have competed in artistic gymnastics in the Olympics since 1928, and in the world championships since their establishment in 1934. Rhythmic gymnastics has had a more ragged history, largely because of its on-again, off-again relationship with the Olympics. It was first seen in the London Games in 1948, when the competitors had to perform both artistic and rhythmic programs. At the next Games, in Helsinki in 1952, the two forms were separate; and in 1956 rhythmic gymnastics was dropped from the Olympic schedule. It continued to be a popular sport in the Soviet Union and in Eastern Europe, but was not officially recognized by the International Federation of Gymnastics until 1962. The first world championships were held in Bulgaria in 1963 and have been held every two years since; only ten years later was rhythmic gymnastics recognized by the U.S. Gymnastics Federation, and its popularity in America has been slow to develop. The reappearance of rhythmic gymnastics as a distinct Olympic event at the Games hosted by Los Angeles in 1984 may well change that. The top American rhythmic gymnasts are **Valerie Zimring** of Los Angeles, who has placed as high as seventeenth against top international competition, including the Bulgarians, and **Michelle Berube** of Rochester, Michigan, 1983 national champion; both were members of the U.S. Olympic team in 1984 and made the finals at the Los Angeles Games, placing eleventh and fourteenth. The Soviet bloc boycotted the 1984 Olympics; the gold medal in rhythmic gymnastics was won by **Lori Fung** of Canada, the silver by Romanian **Doina Staiculescu,** and the bronze by **Regina Weber** of West Germany. **Anelia Ralenkova** of Bulgaria was all-around 1981 world champion, and tied for second at the next world championship in 1983 (she shared the silver with compatriot **Lilia Ignatova** and with **Galina Beloglazova** of the Soviet Union). Ignatova won the all-around gold medal at the first rhythmic gymnastics World Cup, held in 1982. The 1983 European all-around title was shared by Ralenkova and **Dalia Kutkaite** of the Soviet Union.

Lavinia Agache
born Deva, Romania

Consistent, controlled, possessed of smoothness and stylishness, Agache is 1983 Romanian national champion. She is a year older than teammate and friend Ekaterina Szabo; the two are from the same small Transylvania town. They go to school together, train together, and their careers touch at many points. At the Balkan championships in November 1982, Szabo fell from the uneven bars, Agache from the balance beam: they finished with Agache taking the silver medal in all-around, Szabo the bronze. The next year, at the 1983 European championships, Agache was second overall, first on balance beam, second on uneven bars, third in vault; Szabo finished third overall. Agache and Szabo both gave lovely performances, tieing for second in vault and uneven bars; Agache was third in balance beam, fourth in floor exercises, and sixth in the all-around. At the Los Angeles Olympics in 1984, Agache shared in the team gold and won the bronze medal in vault, but most of the golds went to Szabo—Agache's runner-up for the national title.

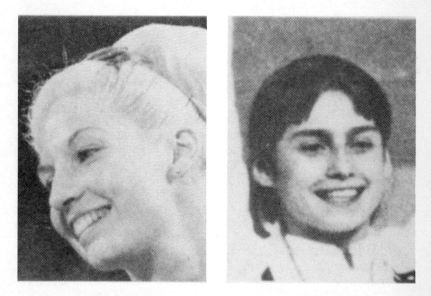

Vera Čáslavská   Nadia Comaneci

Vera Čáslavská
born Prague, Czechoslovakia, May 3, 1942

Trained as an ice skater, Čáslavská first competed internationally as a gymnast at the world championships in 1958; she won the silver medal.

For the next six years, she and Larissa Latynina of the Soviet Union were the top women gymnasts in the world. At the 1964 world championships Čáslavská finally defeated Latynina in the all-around event, and a new reign had begun. Her first Olympic appearance had been at Rome in 1960, where she was eighth in all-around, sixth in balance beam, and shared in the team silver; at the next Games, Tokyo in 1964, she won gold medals in all-around, vault, and balance beam, a team silver, and was fifth in uneven bars and sixth in floor exercises. In the 1968 Mexico City Games she won silver medals in balance beam and the team event, and four more golds (all-around, vault, uneven bars, and floor exercises), but she gave them away: Czechoslovakia had been invaded by the Soviet Union two months before the Games, and she presented her gold medals to nationalist Czech leaders Alexander Dubcek, Ludvik Svoboda, and Oldrich Cernik. In the floor exercises Čáslavská had performed a crowd-pleasing routine to the popular "Mexican Hat Dance," and tied for first place with Larissa Petrik of the Soviet Union; during the awards ceremony Čáslavská was seen to bow her head as her occupied country's anthem was played. But there was joy, too: during the Games she married countryman and fellow Olympian Josef Odložil, a national track champion who had won the silver medal in the 1500-meter run in 1964. In the period 1959-68, Čáslavská had 15 world and European titles in addition to her 7 Olympic championships. She was sparkling as a performer, gifted with star quality as well as ability.

Nadia Comaneci
born Gheorghe Gheorghiu-Dej, Romania, November 12, 1961
   "I was gifted, that's all." Not quite. Comaneci also worked very hard indeed, first under Gherche Munteamu, then under the demanding Bela Karolyi, who later coached Mary Lou Retton of the U.S. At age six she was "playing gymnast" in a school playground. Her first major competition was the 1975 Champions All tournament in London, where she won the gold medal; a month later she won the first of three consecutive European championships, defeating five-time champion Ludmila Tourischeva of the Soviet Union. In 1976 she won the first American Cup, with a score of 10 in the vault. Later that year, at the Montreal Olympics, she won gold medals in all-around, uneven bars, and balance beam; she was third in the floor exercises and fourth in vault. In the course of her performance she racked up an astounding seven perfect scores. After her self-contained and nearly flawless performances, the 4' 11", 86-pound fourteen-year-old was named a Hero of Socialist Labor by her country. In 1977 she won her second European championship, in 1979 her third. In 1980, at the Moscow Olympics, she narrowly missed the gold medal in the all-around, which went to Elena Davidova of the Soviet Union, and had to share the silver with Maxi Gnauck of East Germany; Comaneci won gold medals in the balance beam and floor exercises, was fifth in vault, and shared in the team silver. Her last major tournament was the World University Games in Bucharest in 1981, where she won gold medals in all-around, uneven bars, and floor exercises; after that competition she occasionally appeared in exhibitions with Romania's national team. In May 1984 she formally

retired from competition. She is a qualified judge, and later in 1984 she was preparing for the exacting national examinations that will qualify her as a coach. That summer she was an honored guest at the Los Angeles Olympics.

Dianne Durham
born Gary, Indiana, June 1968

An expert jazz dancer, Durham has said of gymnastics, "When I'm out there performing it feels like I'm dancing, and I love to dance." Her parents introduced their active four-year-old daughter to a gymnastics class at the local Y, and Durham was junior elite champion in 1981 and 1982. In her first senior national championship (1983), she won the gold medal in the all-around, balance beam, vault, and floor exercises, and tied for the silver in the uneven bars. The first black national champion, Durham confirmed her supremacy later in the year when she won the all-around gold medal and the silver in uneven bars in the McDonald's International Championships; she injured her knee, however, and had to withdraw from the other individual events. Surgery kept her out of the world championships in the fall, but by December she was third in all-around in the Chunichi Cup competition in Japan. Knee strain returned at the American Cup meet in March 1984, and Durham did not make the finals; in May at the nationals she finished ninth. Early in 1984 she had left coach Bela Karolyi, returning to work with him after the nationals. "I've accomplished a lot in the two weeks I've been back with him," she said at the Olympic trials in June, and she was a strong contender for the U.S. team; unhappily, she was injured in competition and had to withdraw.

Olga Korbut
born Grodno, Byelorussia, Soviet Union, May 16, 1955

Five years after starting in gymnastics in a school program, fifteen-year-old Korbut was a member of the Soviet national team and two years after that the sensation of the 1972 Munich Olympics. In the all-around she was doing well when she managed only a 7.5 on the uneven bars segment. She finished seventh and cried her disappointment. When she came back the next night to win the silver medal in uneven bars, and the gold in balance beam and floor exercises, she won the hearts of the spectators in the stadium and the millions watching on television all over the world. (She also shared in the team gold.) At home, the "cult of personality" surrounding her proved divisive for the Soviet effort. At the next Olympiad, Montreal in 1976, despite excellent performances she won no gold medals and was second to rising star Nadia Comaneci of Romania in the balance beam, Korbut's best event, and was fifth in uneven bars and all-around; again, she shared in the gold won by the Soviet team. She realized a new generation had come: "It is out of my character to be a fifth- or sixth-ranking member of a team." Retiring from competition, she went to work for the Byelorussian State Sport Committee as a coach. In 1982 she was named to the Women's Sports Hall of Fame.

Larissa Latynina
born Kherson, Ukraine, Soviet Union, December 27, 1934

The intricate and technically superb look of modern women's gymnastics owes much to Latynina, who raised the standards of the sport and revolutionized its performance. In a 12-year career (1954-66)—during which she had two children—she won 18 Olympic medals (in three consecutive Games) and in world competition had 10 individual and 5 team titles. In 1956 at the Melbourne Games she won gold medals in all-around, vault, floor exercises (in a tie with Ágnes Keleti of Hungary), and team, the silver medal in uneven bars, and tied for the bronze in balance beam. At the Rome Games in 1960 she won three more golds, in all-around, floor exercises, and team, silver medals in uneven bars and balance beam, and a bronze in vault. At her last Olympics, tied for Tokyo in 1964, she won the gold medal in floor exercises and team, the silver in all-around and vault, and the bronze in uneven bars and balance beam. In the three Soviet team victories, Latynina was high scorer. Her best event was the floor exercises, in which her grace and proficiency in transitions into and out of complex movements were clearly seen. After she retired from competition in 1966, she coached the Soviet team.

Julianne McNamara
born Flushing, New York, October 6, 1966

A perfectionist in life as well as in her sport, McNamara has said, "I'm striving for a ten every time out." She is also determined: she achieved her last-place berth on the 1980 Olympic team—only five years after she began gymnastics—despite a strained ankle ligament. The U.S. didn't go to the Moscow Games, but the next year McNamara placed seventh in the all-around—then the highest-ever American woman's finish—in the 1981 world championships. Also in 1981 she won the first of two consecutive American Cup titles (she was runner-up to Mary Lou Retton in 1983 and placed third in 1984). She was bronze medalist in vault at the 1982 World Cup, and in 1983 won the silver medal in the national championship, surpassing Retton (who tied for third with Pamela Bileck). Slimmer than Retton, McNamara appears more delicate than her solidly built teammate. But she has strength aplenty, and in her work on the uneven bars, her best event, she performs moves from the men's repertoire not often attempted by women gymnasts. At the Los Angeles Olympics in 1984, she shared the gold medal for uneven bars with Ma Yanhonjg of China and barely missed a medal in the all-around, placing .275 of a point behind bronze medalist Simona Pauca of Romania.

Mary Lou Retton
born Fairmont, West Virginia, January 24, 1968

Despite their strength and control, women gymnasts, though small, have traditionally appeared thin, almost frail—think of Korbut and Comaneci at their peak. With Retton a new and successful image exploded on the scene, compact, solid, muscular. At fourteen she was winning in international competition (in November 1982 she won the all-around in the

Sanlam Cup in South Africa, and three weeks later took the all-around, vault, balance beam, and floor exercises in the Sanlam International). In 1983 she won the American Cup and the Emerald Empire Cup, defeating Tracee Talavera, holder of three Empire titles. A wrist injury kept Retton out of the world championships in the fall, but she returned to competition in December to become the first American woman to win the Chunichi Cup. In 1984 she won the Caesar's Palace Invitational for the second year in a row, this time sweeping all four individual events as well as taking the all-around, and had a second American Cup victory. Her vaults are superb, often earning 10's. At the 1984 Olympics in Los Angeles—two months after arthroscopic surgery on her right knee—she won the all-around gold medal with a perfect vault, which she repeated for another 10 (two attempts are permitted, the higher score to count) to the delight of the crowd. She also took the silver in the individual vault event, and bronze medals in the uneven bars and the floor exercises; she was the only woman to qualify for the finals in all four events. Her daring, power, and exuberance endeared her to the Olympic audience. She has said that her heroine in gymnastics is Olga Korbut—"She was always smiling and real peppy." Retton has a smile that lights up the sky. The Women's Sports Foundation chose her and Olympic marathoner Joan Benoit to share honors as 1984 Sportswoman of the Year.

Cathy Rigby McCoy
born Los Alamitos, California, December 12, 1952

Before Rigby, women's gymnastics belonged to the Soviet Union and East Europe, and American audiences regarded the sport pretty much as a sideshow. Rigby's performances had two lasting results: they showed that the U.S. could be a contender in international competition, and they made American audiences sit up and take notice. Rigby was fifteen at her first Olympics, the Mexico City Games in 1968, where she placed sixteenth in the all-around and was high scorer on the sixth-place U.S. team. Two years later she won the silver medal in the balance beam event at the world championships. At the Munich Olympics in 1972, she was again team high scorer and led the U.S. to fourth place, then its best-ever finish; in the all-around, she placed tenth. Since she retired from competition at twenty-one, she has remained active in the sport, directing gymnastics schools and working as a television commentator for gymnastics events, including the competition at the 1984 Olympics at Los Angeles.

Ekaterina Szabo
born Deva, Romania

The heritage of Nadia Comaneci, her elegance and style, has come to another Romanian, whom her friends call Cati. Szabo's superb performance at the 1984 Olympics was perhaps overshadowed, for Americans at least, by the dynamism of Mary Lou Retton. Szabo, whose grace and fluidity are probably unmatched in the world, won gold medals in balance beam (tied with her teammate Simona Pauca), floor exercises, and vault, and the silver medal in the all-around, .05 of a point behind Retton; she also shared in the team gold. Possibly her excellent showing on balance beam was a particular pleasure for her: she had been ahead in the 1983 European championships when she fell from that apparatus, but nonetheless she tied for the all-around bronze medal with Albina Shishova of the Soviet Union. In individual apparatus events she was first in uneven bars and tied for first with Olga Bicherova of the Soviet Union in floor exercises. Six months later, at the world championships in Budapest, balance beam again was her nemesis, but the rest of her performances for the all-around, scored with 10's (vault and floor exercises) and a 9.95 (uneven bars), enabled her to finish third. (In individual events, she was tied for second with her teammate Lavinia Agache in vault and uneven bars, and was first in floor exercises.) But after her showing at the Los Angeles Games, in which her balance beam segment of the all-around earned her a 10, and her balance beam individual event gave her a gold, it's clear that Szabo now can do it all.

Julianne McNamara   Ludmila Tourischeva

Ludmila Tourischeva
born Soviet Union, October 7, 1952

The head judge in balance beam at the 1984 Los Angeles Olympics holds nine Olympic gymnastics medals herself—but at the very summit of her performing career, when she won the gold medal in all-around at the Munich Games in 1972, the world's attention was on a competitor whom she defeated, her compatriot Olga Korbut. Tourischeva's first Olympic appearance was at Mexico City in 1968, when she shared in the gold won by the Soviet team (the first of three consecutive such Soviet victories Tourischeva participated in). By the time of the next Olympics she was world champion, and in 1972 at Munich she won the gold medal in all-around, the silver in floor exercises, and the bronze in vault. Five times European champion, Tourischeva was defeated for her sixth title by Nadia Comaneci of Romania, who stole the show at the Montreal Olympics in 1976. Though the world watched Comaneci, as it had Korbut, Tourischeva gave brilliant performances, sharing in the team gold and winning the silver medal in floor exercises (incidentally, defeating Comaneci, who was third), tieing Carola Dombeck of East Germany for the silver medal in vault (again, surpassing Comaneci), and taking the bronze in the all-around. After the Montreal Games she married a fellow Olympian from the Soviet Union, runner Valery Borzov, who had won gold medals in 100- and 200-meter dash in 1972 and the bronze in 100 meters in 1976.

OLYMPIC ALL-AROUND CHAMPIONSHIPS

Year	Gold	Silver	Bronze
1952 Helsinki	Maria Gorokhovskaya USSR	Nina Bocharova USSR	Margit Korondi Hungary
1956 Melbourne	Larissa Latynina USSR	Ágnes Keleti Hungary	Sofia Muratova USSR
1960 Rome	Larissa Latynina USSR	Sofia Muratova USSR	Polina Astakhova USSR
1964 Tokyo	Vera Čáslavská Czechoslovakia	Larissa Latynina USSR	Polina Astakhova USSR
1968 Mexico City	Vera Čáslavská Czechoslovakia	Zinaida Voronina USSR	Natalia Kuchinskaya USSR
1972 Munich	Ludmila Tourischeva USSR	Karin Janz East Germany	Tamara Lazakovitch USSR
1976 Montreal	Nadia Comaneci Romania	Nelli Kim USSR	Ludmila Tourischeva USSR
1980 Moscow	Elena Davidova USSR	Nadia Comaneci/Maxi Gnauck Romania/East Germany	
1984 Los Angeles	Mary Lou Retton USA	Ekaterina Szabo Romania	Simona Pauca Romania

OLYMPIC VAULT CHAMPIONSHIPS

Year	Gold	Silver	Bronze
1952 Helsinki	Ekaterina Kalinchuk USSR	Maria Gorokhovskaya USSR	Galina Minalcheva USSR
1956 Melbourne	Larissa Latynina USSR	Tamara Manina USSR	Ann-Sofi Pettersson Sweden
1960 Rome	Margarita Nikolayeva USSR	Sofia Muratova USSR	Larissa Latynina USSR
1964 Tokyo	Vera Čáslavská Czechoslovakia	Larissa Latynina/Birgit Radochla USSR/East Germany	
1968 Mexico City	Vera Čáslavská Czechoslovakia	Erika Zuchold East Germany	Zinaida Voronina USSR
1972 Munich	Karin Janz East Germany	Erika Zuchold East Germany	Ludmila Tourischeva USSR
1976 Montreal	Nelli Kim USSR	Carola Dombeck/Ludmila Tourischeva East Germany/USSR	
1980 Moscow	N. Shaposhnikova USSR	Steffi Kraker East Germany	Melita Ruhn Romania
1984 Los Angeles	Ekaterina Szabo Romania	Mary Lou Retton USA	Lavinia Agache Romania

OLYMPIC UNEVEN BARS CHAMPIONSHIPS

Year	Gold	Silver	Bronze
1952 Helsinki	Margit Korondi Hungary	Maria Gorokhovskaya USSR	Ágnes Keleti Hungary
1956 Melbourne	Ágnes Keleti Hungary	Larissa Latynina USSR	Sofia Muratova USSR
1960 Rome	Polina Astakhova USSR	Larissa Latynina USSR	Tamara Lyukhina USSR
1964 Tokyo	Polina Astakhova USSR	Katalin Makray Hungary	Larissa Latynina USSR
1968 Mexico City	Vera Čáslavská Czechoslovakia	Karin Janz East Germany	Zinaida Voronina USSR
1972 Munich	Karin Janz East Germany	Olga Korbut/Erika Zuchold USSR/East Germany	
1976 Montreal	Nadia Comaneci Romania	Teodora Ungureanu Romania	Marta Egervari Hungary
1980 Moscow	Maxi Gnauck East Germany	Emilia Eberle Romania	Maria Filatova USSR
1984 Los Angeles	Ma Yanhonjg/Julianne McNamara China/USA		Mary Lou Retton USA

OLYMPIC BALANCE BEAM CHAMPIONSHIPS

Year	Gold	Silver	Bronze
1952 Helsinki	Nina Bocharova USSR	Maria Gorkhovskaya USSR	Margit Korondi Hungary
1956 Melbourne	Ágnes Keleti Hungary	Eva Bosakova/Tamara Manina Czechoslovakia/USSR	*
1960 Rome	Eva Bosakova Czechoslovakia	Larissa Latynina USSR	Sofia Muratova USSR
1964 Tokyo	Vera Čáslavská Czechoslovakia	Tamara Manina USSR	Larissa Latynina USSR
1968 Mexico City	Natalyia Kuchinskaya USSR	Vera Čáslavská Czechoslovakia	Larissa Petrik USSR
1972 Munich	Olga Korbut USSR	Tamara Lazakovitch USSR	Karin Janz East Germany
1976 Montreal	Nadia Comaneci Romania	Olga Korbut USSR	Teodora Ungureanu Romania
1980 Moscow	Nadia Comaneci Romania	Elena Davidova USSR	Natalia Shaposhnikova USSR
1984 Los Angeles	Simona Pauca/Ekaterina Szabo Romania/Romania		Kathy Johnson USA

*In 1956, Larissa Latynina (USSR) and Anna Marejkova (Czechoslovakia) tied for the bronze medal.

OLYMPIC FLOOR EXERCISES CHAMPIONSHIPS

Year	Gold	Silver	Bronze
1952 Helsinki	Ágnes Keleti Hungary	Maria Gorokhovskaya USSR	Margit Korondi Hungary
1956 Melbourne	Ágnes Keleti/Larissa Latynina Hungary/USSR		Elena Leusteanu Romania
1960 Rome	Larissa Latynina USSR	Polina Astakhova USSR	Tamara Lyukhina USSR
1964 Tokyo	Larissa Latynina USSR	Polina Astakhova USSR	Aniko Janosi-Ducza Hungary
1968 Mexico City	Vera Čáslavská/Larissa Petrik Czechoslovakia/USSR		Natalia Kuchinskaya USSR
1972 Munich	Olga Korbut USSR	Ludmila Tourischeva USSR	Tamara Lazakovitch USSR
1976 Montreal	Nelli Kim USSR	Ludmila Tourischeva USSR	Nadia Comaneci Romania
1980 Moscow	Nadia Comaneci Romania	Nelli Kim USSR	Maxi Gnauck East Germany
1984 Los Angeles	Ekaterina Szabo Romania	Julianne McNamara USA	Mary Lou Retton USA

WORLD ALL-AROUND CHAMPIONS

Year		Champion	Country
1950		Helena Rakoczy	Poland
1952		Maria Gorokhovskaya	USSR
1954		Galina Roudiko	USSR
1956		Larissa Latynina	USSR
1958		Larissa Latynina	USSR
1960		Larissa Latynina	USSR
1962		Larissa Latynina	USSR
1964		Vera Čáslavská	Czechoslovakia
1966		Vera Čáslavská	Czechoslovakia
1968		Vera Čáslavská	Czechoslovakia
1970		Ludmila Tourischeva	USSR
1972		Ludmila Tourischeva	USSR
1974		Ludmila Tourischeva	USSR
1976		Nadia Comaneci	Romania
1978		Elena Mukhina	USSR
1980		Elena Davidova	USSR
1982	(tie)	Olga Bicherova	USSR
		Natalia Yurchenko	USSR
1984		Mary Lou Retton	USA

WORLD VAULT CHAMPIONS

Year		Champion	Country
1950		Helena Rakoczy	Poland
1952		Ekaterina Kalinchuk	USSR
1954	(tie)	Ann-Sofi Pettersson	Sweden
		Tamara Manina	USSR
1956		Larissa Latynina	USSR
1958		Larissa Latynina	USSR
1960		Margarita Nikoayeva	USSR
1962		Vera Čáslavská	Czechoslovakia
1964		Vera Čáslavská	Czechoslovakia
1966		Vera Čáslavská	Czechoslovakia
1968		Vera Čáslavská	Czechoslovakia
1970		Erika Zuchold	East Germany
1972		Karin Janz	East Germany
1974		Olga Korbut	USSR
1976		Nelli Kim	USSR
1978		Nelli Kim	USSR
1980		Natalia Shaposhnikova	USSR
1982		Natalia Yurchenko	USSR
1984		Ekaterina Szabo	Romania

WORLD UNEVEN BARS CHAMPIONS

Year		Champion	Country
1950	(tie)	Trude Kolar	Austria
		Ann-Sofi Pettersson	Sweden
1952		Margit Korondi	Hungary
1954		Ágnes Keleti	Hungary
1956		Ágnes Keleti	Hungary
1958		Larissa Latynina	Hungary
1960		Polina Astakhova	USSR
1962		Irina Pervushina	USSR
1964		Polina Astakhova	USSR
1966		Natalia Kuchinskaya	USSR
1968		Vera Čáslavská	Czechoslovakia
1970		Karin Janz	East Germany
1972		Karin Janz	East Germany
1974		Annelore Zinke	East Germany
1976		Nadia Comaneci	Romania
1978		Marcia Frederick	USA
1980		Maxi Gnauck	East Germany
1982		Maxi Gnauck	East Germany
1984		Ma Yanhonjg	China

WORLD BALANCE BEAM CHAMPIONS

Year	Champion	Country
1950	Helena Rakoczy	Poland
1952	Nina Bocharova	USSR
1954	Keiko Tanaka	Japan
1956	Ágnes Keleti	Hungary
1958	Larissa Latynina	USSR
1960	Eva Bosakova	Czechoslovakia
1962	Eva Bosakova	Czechoslovakia
1964	Vera Čáslavská	Czechoslovakia
1966	Natalia Kuchinskaya	USSR
1968	Natalia Kuchinskaya	USSR
1970	Erika Zuchold	East Germany
1972	Olga Korbut	USSR
1974	Ludmila Tourischeva	USSR
1976	Nadia Comaneci	Romania
1978	Nadia Comaneci	Romania
1980	Nadia Comaneci	Romania
1982	Natalia Yurchenko	USSR
1984	Simona Pauca	Romania

WORLD FLOOR EXERCISES CHAMPIONS

Year		Champion	Country
1950		Helena Rakoczy	Poland
1952		Ágnes Keleti	Hungary
1954		Tamara Manina	USSR
1956	(tie)	Ágnes Keleti	Hungary
		Larissa Latynina	USSR
1958		Eva Bosakova	Czechoslovakia
1960		Larissa Latynina	USSR
1962		Larissa Latynina	USSR
1964		Larissa Latynina	USSR
1966		Natalia Kuchinskaya	USSR
1968		Larissa Petrik	USSR
1970		Ludmila Tourischeva	USSR
1972		Olga Korbut	USSR
1974		Ludmila Tourischeva	USSR
1976		Nelli Kim	USSR
1978		Nelli Kim	USSR
1980		Nadia Comaneci	Romania
1982		Olga Bicherova	USSR
1984		Ekaterina Szabo	Romania

U.S. ALL-AROUND CHAMPIONS

Year	Champion
1931	Roberta C. Ranck
1932	not held
1933	Consetta Caruccio
1934	Consetta Caruccio
1935	Thera Steppich
1936	Jennie Caputo
1937	Pearl Perkins
1938	Helm McKee
1939	Margaret Weissmann
1940	not held
1941	Pearl Perkins Nightingale
1942	not held
1943	Pearl Perkins Nightingale
1944	Helm McKee
1945	Clara M. Schroth
1946	Clara M. Schroth
1947	Helen Schifano
1948	Helen Schifano
1949	Clara M. Schroth
1950	Clara M. Schroth
1951	Clara M. Schroth
1952	Clara Schroth Lomady
1953	Ruth Grulkowski

Year	Champion
1954	Ruth Grulkowski
1955	Ernestine Russell
1956	Sandra Ruddick
1957	Muriel Davis
1958	Ernestine Russell
1959	Ernestine Russell
1960	Gail Sontgerath
1961	Kazuki Kadaowaki
1962	Dale McClemens
1963	Muriel Grossfeld
1964	Marie Walther
1965	Doris Ruchs Brause
1966	Linda Metheny
1967	Carolyn Hacker
1968	Linda Metheny
1969	Joyce Tanac
1970	Linda Metheny
1971	Linda Metheny
1972	Linda Metheny
1973	Joan Moore Rice
1974	Joan Moore Rice
1975	Ann Carr
1976	Roxanne Pierce
1977	Stephanie Willim
1978	Kathy Johnson
1979	Leslie Pyfer
1980	Julianne McNamara
1981	Tracee Talavera
1982	Tracee Talavera
1983	Dianne Durham
1984	Mary Lou Retton

ICE SKATING

Shank bones of horses and deer worked, but the Iron Age brought a big improvement to ice skating in Scandinavia, since metal gives better traction on the ice than bone does. In the Low Countries of the Middle Ages, the combination of cold winters, relatively little snow, and a good canal system made skating a basic means of transportation. Thus the Dutch were the first speed skaters, and the first race for women was held in Leeuwarden in 1805. The first women's world championship was held in Sweden in 1936, and women's speed skating has been a regular Olympic event since 1960. When English royalists were in exile in Holland during the Protectorate, they learned to skate from the Dutch—the Princess of Orange taught the Duke of Monmouth, son of Charles II. At the Restoration the Stuarts returned to England, bringing their skates with them. The English developed a shorter blade, making it possible to cut designs—"figures"—in the ice, which they did with precision. Meanwhile, on the Continent, figure skating was more influenced by dance. So the English gave the world compulsory school figures, and the waltzing Viennese developed what we know as "free skating"—the modern figure skater of course must be accomplished in both. The toe pick makes it possible to maintain longer and better balance in jumps and spins. Although in the 1920 Olympics the American Theresa Weld was cautioned by the judges on her jumps, which were deemed unsuitable for a lady, only four years later Sonja Henie streaked across the Olympic ice in shorter costumes permitting athletic leaps and sit spins that changed the look of figure skating from thenceforth. Still, the argument about "suitable style" goes on today (note the controversy generated by Elaine Zayak) and has affected men as well—the remarkable skater John Curry had to adjust his "too feminine" style for success in the 1976 Olympics.

Figure Skating

Tenley Albright
born Newton Center, Massachusetts, July 18, 1935
　　The first American woman figure skater to win the world championship

70

(in 1953) and the Olympic gold medal (at the Cortina Games in 1956), Albright was U.S. novice champion in 1949, junior champion in 1950; she was five times national champion, 1952-56. Albright had started skating at nine, then was felled by non-paralytic polio. She resumed skating to strengthen her weakened back muscles, and won her first competition (the Eastern Juvenile Girls Championship) in 1947. At her first Olympics, Oslo in 1952, she won the silver medal; in 1953 and 1955, Albright was national champion, North American champion, and world champion. Her Olympic gold medal at Cortina was won on a badly injured ankle; nonetheless she won the first-place votes of ten of the eleven judges, defeating sixteen-year-old Carol Heiss. The ankle was not healed by the time of the world championships two weeks later, and in a close contest, Heiss won. Albright's last competition was her sixth U.S. championship, in 1956, when she successfully defended her title and defeated Heiss. Her style combined athleticism and grace, and her exhibitions were distinctive, integrated, and quite beautiful. In 1979 Albright, a surgeon and sports medicine authority, became the first woman officer of the U.S. Olympic Committee; she was named to the Women's Sports Hall of Fame in 1983.

Theresa Weld Blanchard

Many "firsts" in figure skating belong to Blanchard: she was the first U.S. national champion (in 1914 and again, after World War I, 1920-24); she was the first North American champion (1923); she won the first Olympic figure skating medal for the U.S. (the bronze at the 1920 Antwerp Games). In pairs she worked throughout her career with Nathaniel W. Niles, and the partners were U.S. pairs champions nine times (1918, 1920-27) and North American pairs champions in 1925. (The two were partners off the ice as well—in 1923 they founded *Skating* magazine, which became the official publication of the U.S. Figure Skating Association.) Blanchard was a member of the U.S. Olympic team again in 1924 and 1928, and was a team official in 1932 and 1936. After her retirement from competition, Tee, as Blanchard was affectionately known, worked tirelessly and effectively on behalf of American figure skaters, amateur and professional. She was elected to figure skating's Hall of Fame in 1976.

Florence Madeleine "Madge" Cave Syers
born England, 1881; died September 1917

A successful skater of the English "figures" school, Madge Cave was introduced to the new Austrian/International style by her coach, Edgar M. W. Syers. Naturally athletic—Cave was an award-winning swimmer and rider—she took to the new style and with Syers won the first English national pairs competition in 1899 and placed second the following year in Berlin, in one of the earliest international pairs events. The partners married that year and competed together and individually—sometimes against each other. In 1902, Cave Syers entered the world championship; no woman had previously done so, but no rule barred her. The championship was won by the great Ulrich Salchow of Sweden; second to him was Cave Syers. Officials quickly closed the world championship to women; when a separate women's event was established in 1906, the first winner was Cave Syers (who won again in 1907). In the first singles championship of Great Britain, in 1903, Cave Syers took the title, defeating Horatio Torrome; she successfully defended her title in 1904, this time defeating her husband. In 1908 she won the gold medal in singles at the London Olympics, and with her husband won the bronze medal in pairs. That was her last competition; she became ill and died of heart disease at the age of thirty-five. She is a member of figure skating's Hall of Fame.

Tiffany Chin
born Oakland, California

In 1980 Chin took the silver medal in the U.S. junior championship, and in December of that year won the junior world title at London, Ontario. A stress fracture of the ankle kept her out of the 1981 nationals; in 1982 she was fifth, in 1983 third, in 1984 she won the silver medal. (In her 1984 performance, she was first in the short and free-skating programs; only a fourth in compulsory figures kept her from the championship.) At the 1984 Olympics at Sarajevo, again the compulsory figures were the stumbling block, and Chin finished fourth. Because of a stress fracture, Chin did not compete as expected in the 1984 world championships. She has a flowing, balletic style—and the jumps in her repertoire are triple axels. Not even Elaine Zayak ever did one of those in competition, but perhaps Chin will.

Cecilia Colledge
born England, November 28, 1920

Much of the look of modern figure skating is owed to the inventiveness of Cecilia Colledge. She was the first to perform a free-skating program choreographed to a specific piece of music; the first to perform the parallel spin, or "camel," the layback, the one-foot axel; the first to perform a double jump in competition. Her career began early—at eleven she was the youngest Olympian at the 1932 Lake Placid Games (she placed eighth); the next year she was a close second to Sonja Henie for the European championship. She won the silver medal in the world championships in 1935, and that year won her first of eight consecutive national titles (1935-39 and, when competition resumed after World War II, 1946-48). In her second Olympic appearance, at the 1936 Berlin Games, she won the silver medal, her average score of 5.7 narrowly beaten by Henie's 5.8. She immigrated to the U.S. in 1951 and for more than 25 years worked for the venerable Skating Club of Boston. She was elected to figure skating's Hall of Fame in 1980.

Sjoukje Dijkstra
born The Netherlands, January 28, 1942

A few days after her fourteenth birthday, Dijkstra competed in her first Olympics, the 1956 Cortina Games; she placed twelfth. Four years later, at Squaw Valley, she won the silver medal, and two years after that she won the first of her three consecutive world championships, 1962-64. At the Innsbruck Olympics in 1964, her compulsory figures were literally unbeatable as she took a commanding lead over her competitors, and all nine judges awarded her the gold. Queen Juliana was among the spectators who saw Dijkstra win the first-ever winter gold medal for The Netherlands (and her country's first gold in any sport since 1948).

Peggy Fleming Jenkins
born San Jose, California, July 27, 1948

Fleming represents the American return to figure-skating supremacy after the disastrous 1961 airplane crash that took the lives of all 18 members of the U.S. team. She was the youngest national women's champion, holding the title 1964-68. Twice North American champion, she was world champion 1966-68. In 1967, like Tenley Albright and Carol Heiss before her, she had the figure-skating triple crown of national, North American, and world championship titles the same year. At the Innsbruck Olympics in 1964, she finished sixth; four years later, she won the gold medal— the only one for the U.S. at the Grenoble Games. She had superior compulsory figures and a romantic, graceful style that concealed great strength. Fleming had a successful professional career, performing in *Ice Follies*, *Holiday on Ice*, and in television specials. She was named to the Women's Sports Hall of Fame in 1981. A trustee of the Women's Sports Foundation, she now works actively to promote the cause of women's sports in the U.S.

Linda Fratianne
born Northridge, California

Successor to Dorothy Hamill in the national championships, Fratianne held the title four times, 1977-80. She was world champion in 1977 and 1979, alternating with East German Anett Pötzsch in a competition that would climax at the 1980 Olympics. Fratianne's first Olympic appearance was at Innsbruck in 1976, where she placed eighth. Her skating had always been athletic with fiery jumps and spins. After her loss of the world title in 1978, she worked to achieve a smoother, more "artistic" style. By the 1980 Olympics the combination seemed just right: although down in the compulsory figures, she skated brilliantly and defeated Pötzsch in the free skate. But at the end of the closest of contests she had the silver to Pötzsch's gold.

Dorothy Hamill
born Riverside, Connecticut, July 26, 1956

Hamill first tried ice skates—a Christmas present from a neighbor— on a local pond. She did all right going forward, but she reported to her mother that she wanted lessons: "I wanted to learn to skate backward." She did. Three-time U.S. champion (1974-1976), Hamill won an Olympic gold medal at Innsbruck in 1976 and was world champion as well a month later. The last national champion to win the title without a triple, she developed a new spin in the skater's repertoire, the "Hamill camel." Nearsighted and uncomfortable with contact lenses, Hamill wore glasses for her compulsory figures and did without in free skating. No matter: at the time of Innsbruck she was considered the best women's free skater in the world. After her competitve career, television and the *Ice Capades* made her known to millions.

Carol Heiss Jenkins
born New York City, New York, January 20, 1940

When Heiss won her Olympic gold medal at Squaw Valley in 1960, she had first-place votes of all nine judges. Her career falls into two parts: as second to Tenley Albright, then as her successor at the top. In 1953-56, Heiss was silver to Albright's gold in the national championships; in 1953 and 1955, for the North American; in 1955, in the world championships; and in 1956, at the winter Olympics at Cortina. Then Heiss broke through: she defeated Albright for the world championship in 1956, and held the title through 1960; she was national champion 1957-60, and North America champion in 1957 and 1959. At the 1960 Olympics at Squaw Valley, she recited the athlete's oath. In her free skating, her style was strong, athletic, spirited, fast. After her years as runner-up, Heiss had her reward: she was world champion longer than anyone but Sonja Henie, and she holds the best record to date of any North American woman in international competition.

Sonja Henie
born Oslo, Norway, April 8, 1912; died October 12, 1969

Henie received her first skates at six, won her first competition at seven, and was Norwegian champion at nine (taking the first of her six national titles). Her Olympic performance was no less remarkable: a debut (at age eleven) at the 1924 Chamonix Games, and three gold medals in three consecutive Olympiads (1928, 1932, and 1936). In the world championships, she finished second in 1926 (she was thirteen); the next year she began her unequalled streak of ten world titles (1927-36). Henie had skied before she skated, which she said helped her balance and rhythm; her ballet training gave her an understanding of the fusion of dance and skating that led to expertly choreographed programs. With Henie there were no more black boots and long skirts. She was color and light and freedom on the ice. After she left amateur competition in 1936, she had a career no less dazzling performing in her own ice show, *Hollywood Ice Revue*, and making ten 20th Century-Fox extravaganzas with co-stars like Tyrone Power and Don Ameche. Sonja Henie—and artificial ice—made skating popular with millions in the 30's. She and her third husband, Niels Onstad, had a fine collection of modern paintings, which they presented to their nation.

Anett Pötzsch
born Karl-Marx-Stadt, East Germany

When East German Gabriele Seyfert won the European title in 1966, six-year-old Pötzsch was watching on television. Ten years later Pötzsch was a champion herself, holding the East German title 1976-79. She was three times European champion, and for the world title she alternated with Linda Fratianne of the U.S., who won it in 1977 and 1979; Pötzsch took it in 1978 and 1980. In 1980 she won the Olympic gold medal at Lake Placid, the first in figure skating for East Germany. The crowd was thrilled by her as she twirled with one foot held high behind her head; they were charmed by her at the last-night festivities as, feather boa and all, she skated to Louis Amstrong's version of "Hello, Dolly."

Barbara Ann Scott
born Ottawa, Ontario, Canada, May 9, 1928

At six, Scott was skating at Ottawa's Minto Skating Club; in 1940 she was Canadian Junior Ladies Champion, and the next year (she was twelve) she was runner-up in the senior competition. Four-time Canadian champion (1944-46, 1948), she was the first North American to win a major figure-skating championship—the 1947 European title, then still open to non-Europeans. Two weeks later she won her first world championship; her second came the following year, 1948, as well as her second European title. Her Olympic gold medal came in 1948 as well, in the first Games after World War II. On ice battered by two hockey matches, she won seven of the nine first-place votes (the Austrian judge voted for the Austrian competitor, the British for the British skater).

Rosalynn Sumners
born Edmunds, Washington

Sumners won the national novice title in 1979, and in January 1980 won the world junior title at Megève, France. She was national champion 1982-84, world champion in 1983. She went into the 1984 Olympics a favorite for the gold medal, but was narrowly defeated by Katarina Witt of East Germany; she easily won the silver. Sumners did not defend her world championship title in 1984, but turned professional after the Sarajevo Games: "I'm just ready for the relaxed part of skating." Her skating, contrasted throughout her career with Elaine Zayak's, is stylish, graceful—and consistent.

Herma Szabo
born Vienna, Austria

International competition was suspended during World War I and not resumed until the 1920 Olympics; the world championships were not held again until 1922. Szabo's career, though short—1922-27—was phenomenal, eclipsed only by the rise of Sonja Henie. In 1922 Szabo won the first of her six national singles titles and the first of five consecutive world championships; in the 1927 world event, fourteen-year-old Henie, in her third attempt, defeated the twenty-five-year-old Szabo. At the 1924 Olympics at Chamonix, Szabo won the gold medal, awarded first place by all seven judges. She excelled in pairs skating as well: she and partner Ludwig Wrede were twice national champions and world champions in 1925 and 1927. Contemporary accounts describe her skating as strong and confident, with a repertoire of daring jumps and spins; there seems no doubt she would have been at home with today's triple jumps. She was named to the figure skating Hall of Fame in 1982.

Maribel Vinson Owen
born Winchester, Massachusetts, died February 15, 1961

Champion, teacher, newspaperwoman, Maribel Vinson Owen—and her daughters Laurence and Maribel, champions themselves—died when the plane carrying all 18 members of the U.S. team to the world championships crashed outside Brussels. Vinson Owen's competitive career had begun when she was eleven; the next year, 1924, she won her first national title, the junior championship. She held nine senior national championships (1928-33, 1935-37; she did not defend her title the two years she trained in Europe after college). Proficient also in pairs, she won the junior championship in 1927 with Thornton L. Coolidge, and the senior title with him in 1928 and 1929. After Coolidge's retirement, she had a new partner in George E. B. Hill, and together they won the pairs championship in 1933 and 1935-37. In international competition, she won the silver medal in the 1928 world championship (second to Sonja Henie) and the bronze medal in 1930. A member of three Olympic teams, she placed fourth at St. Moritz in 1928 and won the bronze medal at Lake Placid in 1932; in 1936 at Garmisch Partenkirchen she was fifth in singles and, with Hill, in pairs. She was North American pairs champion with Hill in 1935 and singles champion in 1937. As a teacher she wrote classic instructional books on figure skating and coached a number of national, world, and Olympic champions and medalists (among them, Tenley Albright). She was the first woman in the sports department of the New York *Times*. She was elected to figure skating's Hall of Fame in 1976.

Katarina Witt
born Karl-Marx-Stadt, East Germany
   Three-time national champion, Witt was European champion at seventeen in 1983, and again in 1984. She was five when she first wanted to learn to skate: "On that much ice there must be some space for me." There is. In 1982 she won the silver medal at the world championships, second to Elaine Zayak (Witt's style is similar to Zayak's, triples and all). In 1983 a low score in compulsory figures brought her down to fourth, but she learned: in the world championships in 1984, when she took the title, she was first place in figures. An Olympic gold medal came at Sarajevo in 1984.

Elaine Zayak
born Paramus, New Jersey
   Junior national champion in 1979, Zayak won the national title in 1981; she was fifteen, with a four-minute free-style program that included eighteen jumps, up to seven of them triples. World champion in 1982, at the 1983 world competition in March she suffered a stress fracture in her right ankle and had to withdraw. Sidelined for four months, she started skating again in the summer, carrying an additional twenty pounds and wary of injury. She lost the weight and gained confidence, and in her first full competition in a year, in December 1983, she won the Eastern regionals. The following month, at the 1984 national championships, she was third to Rosalyn Sumners's first and Tiffany Chin's surprise second. The bronze gave her a berth on the 1984 Olympic team, but in Sarajevo she was thirteenth in compulsory figures (her weakest point) and was not a contender. In her last amateur competition before signing a contract with *Ice Capades,* the world championships in March 1984, Zayak won the bronze medal. Her athletic style and the exuberance of her jumps threatened to change the nature of traditional figure skating, and her name is memorialized in the Zayak Rule limiting the repetitions of triples in the free-style program.

WORLD CHAMPIONSHIPS

Year	Gold	Silver	Bronze
1906 Davos	Madge Syers Great Britain	Jenny Herz Austria	Lily Kronberger Hungary
1907 Vienna	Madge Syers Great Britain	Jenny Herz Austria	Lily Kronberger Hungary
1908 Troppau	Lily Kronberger Hungary	Elsa Rendschmidt Germany	
1909 Budapest	Lily Kronberger Hungary		
1910 Berlin	Lily Kronberger Hungary	Elsa Rendschimdt Germany	
1911 Vienna	Lily Kronberger Hungary	Opika von Horvath Hungary	Ludowika Eilers Germany
1912 Davos	Opika von Horvath Hungary	Greenhough Smith Great Britain	Phyllis Johnson Great Britain
1913 Stockholm	Opika von Horvath Hungary	Phyllis Johnson Great Britain	Svea Noren Sweden
1914 St. Moritz	Opika von Horvath Hungary	Angela Hanka Austria	Phyllis Johnson Great Britain
1915-21	not held		
1922 Stockholm	Herma Szabo Austria	Svea Noren Sweden	Margot Moe Norway
1923 Vienna	Herma Szabo Austria	Gisela Reichmann Austria	Svea Noren Sweden
1924 Oslo	Herma Szabo Austria	Ellen Brockhöfft Germany	Beatrix Loughran USA
1925 Davos	Herma Szabo Austria	Ellen Brockhöfft Germany	Elisabeth Böckel Germany
1926 Stockholm	Herma Szabo Austria	Sonja Henie Norway	Kathleeen Shaw Great Britain
1927 Oslo	Sonja Henie Norway	Herma Szabo Austria	Karen Simensen Norway
1928 London	Sonja Henie Norway	Maribel Vinson USA	Fritzi Burger Austria
1929 Budapest	Sonja Henie Norway	Fritzi Burger Austria	Melitta Brunner Austria
1930 New York	Sonja Henie Norway	Cecil Smith Canada	Maribel Vinson USA
1931 Berlin	Sonja Henie Norway	Hilde Holovsky Austria	Fritzi Burger Austria
1932 Montreal	Sonja Henie Norway	Fritzi Burger Austria	Constance Samuel Canada

Year	Gold	Silver	Bronze
1933 Stockholm	Sonja Henie Norway	Vivi-Anne Hulten Sweden	Hila Holovsky Austria
1934 Oslo	Sonja Henie Norway	Megan Taylor Great Britain	Liselotte Landbeck Austria
1935 Vienna	Sonja Henie Norway	Cecilia Colledge Great Britain	Vivi-Anne Hulten Sweden
1936 Paris	Sonja Henie Norway	Megan Taylor Great Britain	Vivi-Anne Hulten Sweden
1937 London	Cecilia Colledge Great Britain	Megan Taylor Great Britain	Vivi-Anne Hulten Sweden
1938 Stockholm	Megan Taylor Great Britain	Cecilia Colledge Great Britain	Hedy Stenuf USA
1939 Prague	Megan Taylor Great Britain	Hedy Stenuf USA	Daphne Walker Great Britain
1940-46	not held		
1947 Stockholm	Barbara Ann Scott Canada	Daphne Walker Great Britain	Gretchen Merrill USA
1948 Davos	Barbara Ann Scott Canada	Eva Pawlik Austria	Jirina Nekolova Czechoslovakia
1949 Paris	Aja Vrzanova Czechoslovakia	Yvonne Sherman USA	Jeanette Altwegg Great Britain
1950 London	Aja Vrzanova Czechoslovakia	Jeanette Altwegg Great Britain	Yvonne Sherman USA
1951 Milan	Jeanette Altwegg Great Britain	Jacqueline du Bief France	Sonya Klopfer USA
1952 Paris	Jacqueline du Bief France	Sonya Klopfer USA	Virginia Baxter USA
1953 Davos	Tenley Albright USA	Gundi Busch Germany	Valda Osborn Great Britain
1954 Oslo	Gundi Busch Germany	Tenley Albright USA	Erica Batchelor Great Britain
1955 Vienna	Tenley Albright USA	Carol Heiss USA	Hanna Eigel Austria
1956 Garmisch	Carol Heiss USA	Tenley Albright USA	Ingrid Wendl Austria
1957 Colorado Springs	Carol Heiss USA	Hanna Eigel Austria	Ingrid Wendl Austria
1958 Paris	Carol Heiss USA	Ingrid Wendl Austria	Hanna Walter Austria
1959 Colorado Springs	Carol Heiss USA	Hanna Walter Austria	Sjoukje Dijkstra The Netherlands
1960 Vancouver	Carol Heiss USA	Sjoukje Dijkstra The Netherlands	Barbara Roles USA

Year	Gold	Silver	Bronze
1961	not held		
1962 Prague	Sjouke Dijkstra The Netherlands	Wendy Griner Canada	Regine Heitzer Austria
1963 Cortina	Sjoukje Dijkstra The Netherlands	Regine Heitzer Austria	Nicole Hassler France
1964 Dortmund	Sjoukje Dijkstra The Netherlands	Regine Heitzer Austria	Petra Burka Canada
1965 Colorado Springs	Petra Burka Canada	Regine Heitzer Austria	Peggy Fleming USA
1966 Davos	Peggy Fleming USA	Gabriele Seyfert East Germany	Petra Burka Canada
1967 Vienna	Peggy Fleming USA	Gabriele Seyfert East Germany	Hana Maskova Czechoslovakia
1968 Geneva	Peggy Fleming USA	Gabriele Seyfert East Germany	Hana Maskova Czechoslovakia
1969 Colorado Springs	Gabriele Seyfert East Germany	Beatrix Schuba Austria	Zsuzsa Almassy Hungary
1970 Ljubljana	Gabriele Seyfert East Germany	Beatrix Schuba Austria	Julie Holmes USA
1971 Lyon	Beatrix Schuba Austria	Julie Holmes USA	Karen Magnussen Canada
1972 Calgary	Beatrix Schuba Austria	Karen Magnussen Canada	Janet Lynn USA
1973 Bratislava	Karen Magnussen Canada	Janet Lynn USA	Christine Errath East Germany
1974 Munich	Christine Errath East Germany	Dorothy Hamill USA	Dianne deLeeuw The Netherlands
1975 Colorado Springs	Dianne de Leeuw The Netherlands	Dorothy Hamill USA	Christine Errath East Germany
1976 Gothenberg	Dorothy Hamill USA	Christine Errath East Germany	Dianne de Leeuw The Netherlands
1977 Toyko	Linda Fratianne USA	Anett Pötzsch East Germany	Dagmar Lurz West Germany
1978 Ottawa	Anett Pötzsch East Germany	Linda Fratianne USA	Susanna Driano Italy
1979 Vienna	Linda Fratianne USA	Anett Pötzsch East Germany	Emi Watanabi Japan
1980 Dortmund	Anett Pötzsch East Germany	Linda Fratianne USA	Dagmar Lurz West Germany
1981 Hartford	Denise Biellmann Switzerland	Elaine Zayak USA	Claudia Kristofics-Binder Austria

Year	Gold	Silver	Bronze
1982 Copenhagen	Elaine Zayak USA	Katarina Witt East Germany	Claudia Kristofics-Binder Austria
1983 Helsinki	Rosalynn Sumners USA	Claudia Leistner West Germany	Elena Vodorezova USSR
1984 Ottawa	Katarina Witt East Germany	Anna Kondrashova Soviet Union	Elaine Zayak USA

U.S. CHAMPIONSHIPS

Year	Champion	Runner-up
1924	Theresa Weld Blanchard	Ms Knapp
1925	Beatrix Loughran	Theresa Weld Blanchard
1926	Beatrix Loughran	Theresa Weld Blanchard
1927	Beatrix Loughran	Maribel Vinson
1928	Maribel Vinson	Suzanne Davis
1929	Maribel Vinson	Mrs. E. Secord
1930	Maribel Vinson	Mrs. E. Secord
1931	Maribel Vinson	Mrs. E. Secord
1932	Maribel Vinson	Ms Bennett
1933	Maribel Vinson	Suzanne Davis
1934	Suzanne Davis	Louise Weigel
1935	Maribel Vinson	Suzanne Davis
1936	Maribel Vinson	Louise Weigel
1937	Maribel Vinson	Polly Blodgett
1938	Joan Tozzer	Audrey Peppe
1939	Joan Tozzer	Audrey Peppe
1940	Joan Tozzer	Hedy Stenuf
1941	Jane Vaughn	Gretchen Merrill
1942	Jane Vaughn Sullivan	Gretchen Merrill
1943	Gretchen Merrill	Dorothy Goos
1944	Gretchen Merrill	Dorothy Goos
1945	Gretchen Merrill	Janette Ahrens
1946	Gretchen Merrill	Janette Ahrens
1947	Gretchen Merrill	Janette Ahrens
1948	Gretchen Merrill	Yvonne Sherman
1949	Yvonne Sherman	Gretchen Merrill
1950	Yvonne Sherman	Sonya Klopfer
1951	Sonya Klopfer	Tenley Albright
1952	Tenley Albright	Frances Dorsey
1953	Tenley Albright	Carol Heiss
1954	Tenley Albright	Carol Heiss
1955	Tenley Albright	Carol Heiss
1956	Tenley Albright	Carol Heiss
1957	Carol Heiss	Joan Schenke
1958	Carol Heiss	Carol Wanek
1959	Carol Heiss	Nancy Heiss
1960	Carol Heiss	Barbara Ann Roles
1961	Laurence Owen	Stephanie Westerfeld
1962	Barbara Ann Roles Pursley	Lorraine Hanlon

Year	Champion	Runner-up
1963	Lorraine Hanlon	Christine Haigler
1964	Peggy Fleming	Albertina Noyes
1965	Peggy Fleming	Christine Haigler
1966	Peggy Fleming	Albertina Noyes
1967	Peggy Fleming	Albertina Noyes
1968	Peggy Fleming	Albertina Noyes
1969	Janet Lynn	Julie Holmes
1970	Janet Lynn	Julie Holmes
1971	Janet Lynn	Julie Holmes
1972	Janet Lynn	Julie Holmes
1973	Janet Lynn	Dorothy Hamill
1974	Dorothy Hamill	Julie McKinstry
1975	Dorothy Hamill	Wendy Burge
1976	Dorothy Hamill	Linda Fratianne
1977	Linda Fratianne	Barbie Smith
1978	Linda Fratianne	Lisa-Marie Allen
1979	Linda Fratianne	Lisa-Marie Allen
1980	Linda Fratianne	Lisa-Marie Allen
1981	Elaine Zayak	Priscilla Hill
1982	Rosalynn Sumners	Vikki de Vries
1983	Rosalynn Sumners	Elaine Zayak
1984	Rosalynn Sumners	Tiffany Chin

OLYMPIC CHAMPIONSHIPS

Year	Gold	Silver	Bronze
1908 London	Madge Syers Great Britain	Elsa Rendschmidt Germany	Dorothy Greenhough Great Britain
1920 Antwerp	Magda Julin-Mauroy Sweden	Svea Noren Sweden	Theresa Weld USA
1924 Chamonix	Herma Szabo Austria	Beatrix Loughran USA	Ethel Muckelt Great Britain
1928 St. Moritz	Sonja Henie Norway	Fritzi Burger Austria	Beatrix Loughran USA
1932 Lake Placid	Sonja Henie Norway	Fritzi Burger Austria	Maribel Vinson USA
1936 Garmisch	Sonja Henie Norway	Cecilia Colledge Great Britain	Vivi-Anne Hulten Sweden
1948 St. Moritz	Barbara Ann Scott Canada	Eva Pawlik Austria	Jeannette Altwegg Great Britain
1952 Oslo	Jeannette Altwegg Great Britain	Tenley Albright USA	Jacqueline du Bief France
1956 Cortina	Tenley Albright USA	Carol Heiss USA	Ingrid Wendl Austria

Year	Gold	Silver	Bronze
1960 Squaw Valley	Carol Heiss USA	Sjoukje Dijkstra The Netherlands	Barbara Roles USA
1964 Innsbruck	Sjoukje Dijkstra The Netherlands	Regine Heitzer Austria	Petra Burka Canada
1968 Grenoble	Peggy Fleming USA	Gabriele Seyfert East Germany	Hana Maskova Czechoslovakia
1972 Sapporo	Beatrix Schuba Austria	Karen Magnussen Canada	Janet Lynn USA
1976 Innsbruck	Dorothy Hamill USA	Dianne de Leeuw The Netherlands	Christine Errath East Germany
1980 Lake Placid	Anett Pötzsch East Germany	Linda Fratianne USA	Dagmar Lurz West Germany
1984 Sarajevo	Katarina Witt East Germany	Rosalynn Sumners USA	Kira Ivanova Soviet Union

Speed Skating

Karin Enke
born Dresden, East Germany, June 20, 1961

In 1975 Enke placed fourth in the national champioships—in figure skating; in 1977 she was ninth in the European championships. But illness, injury, and her size—she's 5'9", 158 pounds—led her to try speed skating. After she learned the techniques of her new sport—the crouched stance, the knack of changing lanes—there was no doubt she was a natural. In 1980 she won the world sprint championship; a week later she won the gold medal at the Lake Placid Olympic Games in the 500 meters, setting an Olympic record of 41.78, and she was fourth in the 1000 meters. She won the world sprint championship again in 1981, in 1982 was second to Natalia Petruseva of the Soviet Union, then won again in 1983 and 1984; she won silver medals in the all-around world championships in 1981 and 1983, and the gold in 1982 and 1984. At her second Olympic appearance, at Sarajevo in 1984, she won gold medals in the 1000 and the 1500 (setting a world record with 2:03.42), and the silver medal in the 500 and 3000.

Andrea Mitscherlich Schöne
born Dresden, East Germany

Still a teenager at her first Olympics, Mitscherlich Schöne won a silver medal at Innsbruck in 1976 in the 3000 meters. The next time round, at Lake Placid in 1980, she placed fourth in the 3000 and sixth in the 1500. In 1982 she won the silver medal in the all-around world championships; in 1983 she won the gold, and took the European championship as well. By the time of the 1984 Sarajevo Games, she had become a nurse, married, and had a three-year-old child. She took the gold medal in the 3000 meters, setting an Olympic record of 4:24.79, and silver medals in the 1500 and

1000. A month later, in a competition between East Germany and the Soviet Union, she set a world record in the 1500 of 2:03.34 and in the 3000 of 4:20.91.

Leah Poulos Mueller
born Berwyn, Illinois, October 5, 1951

"I learned the basic principles by trial and error—falling down and getting up." At her first Olympics, Sapporo in 1972, she was seventeenth in the 3000, twenty-fourth in the 1500; at Innsbruck in 1976, she was sixth in the 1500, fourth in the 500, and won the silver medal in the 1000. After the games she married teammate Peter Mueller, who had won the gold medal in the men's 1000 meters. She left competitive skating for two years to help support her husband's training program; she returned to training in 1978, and in 1979 took the world sprint championship. At Lake Placid in 1980, Poulos Mueller competed in the 500 meters and the 1000 meters, winning silver medals in both events.

Lydia Skoblikova
born Zlatoust, Chelyabinsk, Soviet Union, March 8, 1939

Skoblikova was a psychology student when she competed in the 1960 Olympics at Squaw Valley. She took two gold medals, in the 3000 meters and in the 1500 meters (in which she broke the world record with 2:52.2); she was fourth in the 1000 meters. In 1963 she won the world championship in all four events (500, 1000, 1500, 3000), and was world champion again in 1964. By the time of the next Olympics, she was a teacher; at the 1964 Innsbruck Games she swept all four races, taking a gold medal each day for four days straight. Her times in three events broke Olympic records: 500 meters in 45 seconds flat, 1000 in 1:33.2, 1500 in 2:22.6. The last event, the 3000, was run on slushy ice; Skoblikova set no record but nonetheless came in 3.6 seconds ahead of second-place Pil-Hwa Han of North Korea. Her achievement earned Skoblikova full membership in the Communist Party, of which she was notified directly by Premier Nikita Khrushchev. Her last Olympic competition was in 1968 at Grenoble, when she finished eleventh in the 1500 meters.

Sheila Young Ochowicz
born Detroit, Michigan, October 14, 1950

In 1973, Young held a unique double: she was world sprint champion, in speed skating *and* cycling. Three years later, she did it again. No other athlete, man or woman, has been a world champion in two sports. Her Olympic competition of course was all in speed skating, since there were no Olympic cycling events for women until 1984, and then only a road race. At the Sapporo Games in 1972 Young was fourth in the 500 meters. At Innsbruck in 1976 she went down the line: the gold medal in the 500, the silver in the 1500, and the bronze in the 1000. In the 500-meter event, on "slow" ice, she set an Olympic record of 42.76; the week before she had set a world record at that distance of 40.91, and in March of that year she brought her time down to 40.68, achieving an average speed of 27.47 miles per hour.

OLYMPIC SPEED SKATING RECORDS

Event	Skater	Country	Time	Date/Place
500M	Christa Rothenberger	East Germany	41.02	1984/Sarajevo
1000M	Karin Enke	East Germany	1.21.61	1984/Sarajevo
1500M	Karin Enke	East Germany	2.03.42	1984/Sarajevo
3000M	Andrea Schöne	East Germany	4.24.79	1984/Sarajevo

WORLD SPEED SKATING RECORDS

Event	Skater	Country	Time	Date
500M	Christa Rothenberger	East Germany	39.69	1983
1000M	Natalia Petruseva	U.S.S.R.	1.19.31	1983
1500M	Andrea Schöne	East Germany	2.03.34	1984
3000M	Andrea Schöne	East Germany	4.20.91	1984

U.S. SPEED SKATING RECORDS

Event	Skater	Time	Date
500M	Sheila Young Ochowicz	40.63	1976
1000M	Leah Poulos Mueller	1.23.07	1980
1500M	Beth Heiden	2.07.87	1980
3000M	Sarah Docter	4.28.05	1982

LUGE

The Vikings used sleds, and luge (the French word for sled) is the oldest known winter sport. The first international luge competition was held in 1883 on the four-kilometer road from St. Wolfgang to Klosters, Switzerland. There were 21 competitors from 7 countries; the winning time was 9:15. There were no U.S. entries—the sport was unknown to Americans until after World War II. The first American lugers were skiers (including some women) who learned the sport in Austria, and U.S. soldiers stationed in West Germany. In the 50's and early 60's women competed in singles and mixed doubles; today, especially since luge was recognized as an Olympic event in 1964, women compete internationally only in singles events. The twisting luge track of modern women's competition is a minimum of 700 meters (the course at Sarajevo in 1984 was 993 meters, considered long), and the sleds attain speeds of 70 to 80 miles per hour. The hallmarks of a good luger are those of a good small-plane pilot: ability of the body to handle and recover from stress; good reaction speed; acute vision; good equilibrium. On the straightaway, the heavier competitor tends to be faster, since her greater momentum will enable her to maintain her starting speed; and if the track is snow-covered, her greater weight will push her sled's runners down through the friction-creating snow to the ice below. On curves, however, the advantage is to the lighter competitor.

East German women have been in command throughout the history of the sport. At the 1983 world championships, the four East German women entered took the top four places. The gold medal went to an economics student from Schlema, **Steffi Martin,** who is tall (6' 0"), strong, and fast. Martin was competing in her first world championships; at her first Olympics, the 1984 Sarajevo Games, she led another East German sweep: she won the gold, the silver medal went to **Bettina Schmidt,** heavy, powerful, and experienced in international competition, and the bronze to **Ute Weiss,** a relative newcomer, who is small and light for a luger, and has perhaps the smoothest and most elegant style.

From left: Toni Damigella, 1984 U.S. Olympian; Erica Terwillegar; Donna Burke, 1980 U.S. Olympian; Bonny Warner

Erica Terwillegar
born Nelsonville, New Jersey, April 8, 1963

Terwillegar grew up in the capital of U.S. luge (Lake Placid has a refrigerated track, built for the 1980 Olympics), and she grew up in the sport—the only American to have done so. She began at thirteen, and won a silver medal in an international junior event in 1982, the first and to date the only American to win a medal in world competition. In the world championships in 1983 she finished fifth, the best American performance ever, by a man or a woman; that year she was North American champion. So far, she's had no Olympic luck: in 1980 she finished fourth in the trials, just missing a berth on the team, and in 1984 she had trouble the day of the trials and again just missed a spot. Still, as Jim Moriarty, head of the U.S. Luge Association, has remarked, "She is so smooth that even the East Germans stop to watch her in the gate."

Bonny Warner
born Mount Baldy, California, April 7, 1962

Goalie on Stanford University's field hockey team, Warner was introduced to luge when she watched it at the 1980 Lake Placid Olympics; she stayed on to train there and, later, in West Germany. A member of the U.S. luge team and defending national champion, she came in seventh in the 1983 world championships. She continues to play field hockey, believing that the two sports complement each other in developing skills. She qualified easily in January 1984 for the U.S. Olympic team, winning all twelve heats. At Sarajevo she was making a more than respectable showing against the favored East Germans, hoping to finish sixth in the event, when in the third of four runs her sled hit the wall and flipped. She was unhurt, but after the fourth run she ranked fifteenth overall, with 2:51.910.

OLYMPIC SINGLES CHAMPIONSHIPS

Year	Gold	Silver	Bronze
1964 Innsbruck	Ortrun Enderlein East Germany	Ilse Geisler East Germany	Helene Thurner Austria
1968 Grenoble	Erica Lechner Italy	Christa Schmuck West Germany	Angelika Dunhaupt West Germany
1972 Sapporo	Anna-Maria Muller East Germany	Ute Ruhrold East Germany	Margit Schumann East Germany
1976 Innsbruck	Margit Schumann East Germany	Ute Ruhrold East Germany	Elisabeth Demleitner West Germany
1980 Lake Placid	Vera Zozulia USSR	Melitta Sollmann East Germany	Ingrida Amantova USSR
1984 Sarajevo	Steffi Martin East Germany	Bettina Schmidt East Germany	Ute Weiss East Germany

WORLD SINGLES CHAMPIONS

Year	Champion	Country
1955	Karla Kienzl	Austria
1956	not held	
1957	Maria Isser	Austria
1958	Maria Semozyszak	Poland
1959	Elly Lieber	Austria
1960	Maria Isser	Austria
1961	Elisabeth Nagele	Switzerland
1962	Ilse Geisler	East Germany
1963	Ilse Geisler	East Germany
1964	Ortrun Enderlein	East Germany
1965	Ortrun Enderlein	East Germany
1966	not held	
1967	Ortrun Enderlein	East Germany
1968	Erica Lechner	Italy
1969	Petra Tierlich	East Germany
1970	Barbara Piecha	Poland
1971	Elisabeth Demleitner	West Germany
1972	Anna-Maria Muller	East Germany
1973	Margit Schumann	East Germany
1974	Margit Schumann	East Germany
1975	Margit Schumann	East Germany
1976	Margit Schumann	East Germany
1977	Margit Schumann	East Germany
1978	Vera Sosulja	USSR
1979	Melitta Sollmann	East Germany
1980	Vera Zozulia	USSR
1981	Melitta Sollmann	East Germany
1982	not held	
1983	Steffi Martin	East Germany
1984	Steffi Martin	East Germany

ROWING

Vassar's Daisy Chain and Barnard's Greek Games never really achieved national significance, but rowing for women in America did get a gentle push from Wellesley's Float Night (very gentle—the crew were selected for their ability to sing). But it was Wellesley that had the first rowing program for women in the U.S. (1875), restrained as it was. Similar clubs were formed in other Eastern colleges, and there was some club racing on the West Coast in the years before World War I. There was no serious competition until the founding of the Philadelphia Girls' Rowing Club in 1938, whose members were the wives and girlfriends of men who rowed for the clubs on Boat House row. But for almost thirty years they had no one to race against except each other. Then the National Women's Rowing Association was formed in California in 1962 and sponsored the first national championship regatta in 1966. That year, 45 boats were entered. Women have competed for world championships since 1974, and various classes of women's rowing have been included in the Olympics since the Montreal Games in 1976, all rowed on a 1000-meter course.

East European and Soviet women have dominated rowing: the world champion single sculler in 1982 was **Irina Fetissova** of the Soviet Union, in 1983 **Jutta Hampe** of East Germany (Fetissova was second). Because of the Soviet-led boycott neither competed at the Los Angeles Olympics in 1984; the single scull champion at those Games was **Valeria Racila** of Romania, and the silver medal went to **Charlotte Geer** of the U.S.; **Ann Haesebrouck** of Belgium was third. **Joan Lind**, five times U.S. national singles champion, won the silver medal in single scull at the Montreal Olympics in 1976; eight years later she came out of retirement to row on the silver-winning U.S. quad scull at the Los Angeles Olympics. At the International Rowing Regatta at Lucerne in June 1984, the U.S. eight scored a surprising and impressive victory over East Germany, and set a course record. U.S. women had their first chance at an Olympic gold medal in the Los Angeles Games, and they took it, winning the eight-oar shell event (Romania was second, The Netherlands third).

Carol Brown
born Philadelphia, Pennsylvania

"Looking back over all these years, I'm just glad I wandered down to the boathouse." That was at Princeton in 1971, where Brown decided to go out for the newly formed women's crew. Brown was in the open eight U.S. crew at the 1975 world championships, when the U.S. gained its first medal, the silver to East Germany's gold. The following year the Olympics opened rowing to women's events, and Brown was on the U.S. crew that placed third in eight-oared shell at Montreal. Taking a year out for graduate school in 1977, Brown was on the U.S. team again, 1978-81. The U.S. eight were a close third at the 1979 world championships, and their 1980 Olympic prospects were good—only to be thwarted by the boycott. In 1980 the team had faced the East Germans twice, and, for the first time, in one of those contests had defeated them; the East Germans went on to win at Moscow. The next year, 1981, at the world championships, the U.S. was second— to the Soviet Union. After a year's layoff, Brown returned to training in 1983, but for the first time did not make the eight for the world championships; instead, she stroked the coxed four to a fifth-place finish.

Virginia Gilder

Her rowing coach at Yale said she was "too small" for the crew he was putting together to tour Europe in 1978. Nor did Gilder make the team for the 1979 world championships. She redoubled her efforts and made the U.S. Olympic team as a sweep rower—in 1980, when the U.S. boycotted the games. In 1982 she rowed in quad sculls in the world championships, finishing fourth. By then based in Boston and working for a computer firm, Gilder switched from team rowing to single sculling. Rowing with the Boston Rowing Club, she came in second in the national championship in 1982 in the elite single, in 3:59.9; in 1983 she won the class, in 3:55.8. Also in 1983, she and Ann Strayer (Gilder at stroke, Strayer in the bow) took the elite double for the Boston Rowing Club in 3:39 flat. At the 1983 world championships, Gilder won the bronze medal in single scull (the first medal for the U.S. women in international competition since Joan Lind's silver at the 1976 Olympics). Three weeks later Gilder was a close second to world champion Jutta Hampe of East Germany at the Lake Casitas International Regatta, held on the Olympic course for the 1984 Games. There was one slot on the U.S. Olympic team for single scull: Gilder wanted to be the one to fill it, but a broken rib two weeks before the trials ended that hope. She did make the team, though, and she (and Lind, who had come out of retirement) rowed on the silver-winning quad scull in the 1984 Olympics.

SKIING

Where there's snow, there are sleds; where there are sleds, there are skis—and that includes the Scandinavia of 7000 B.C. The earliest skiers were hunters; over the years skiing lost neither its utility nor its appeal, and when descendants of those first skiers immigrated to the U.S. in the mid-nineteenth century, skiing came too. In the 1920's the Lake Placid Club organized skiing events for college women: a two- or three-mile cross-country race, a slalom, and a downhill. The International Ski Congress was founded in 1910; at the first winter Olympic Games (1924), it reorganized as the International Ski Federation, which sponsors the world ski championships in downhill, slalom, cross-country, and, for men, jumping; women have competed in all the other events since 1931. Cross-country, or nordic, skiing has been an Olympic event for men since the Chamonix Games in 1924; a women's event (at 10K) was included for the first time as Oslo in 1952. Men and women competed in separate "alpine combined"—downhill plus slalom—events at the Garmisch Partenkirchen Games in 1936; since then, the two segments are distinct competitions, scored separately, and a third has been added: the giant slalom, a variant first skied in 1934, when a downhill race on the Marmolada glacier in Italy was considered too dangerous and the competitiors asked for gates to control their speed. Not surprisingly, Scandinavians (and, later, the Russians) are great nordic skiers; more surprisingly, Americans, including and sometimes especially women, have done extremely well in alpine events, with an impressive record in international competition.

Alpine Skiing

Deborah Armstrong
born Seattle, Washington

Armstrong went straight from regional races to her first World Cup event in December 1981. Six weeks later she was named for the downhill competition for the world championship, but broke her leg in a training run. After her recovery she skied five World Cup giant slalom and downhill races in 1982-83, her best finish fifth place in the downhill at Le Diablerets, Switzerland. In early 1984 she was third in a World Cup supergiant slalom and fifth in a giant slalom. Named to the U.S. team for the 1984 Sarajevo Olympics, she won the first gold medal in the Games with a combined time of 2:02.98 in the two runs of the giant slalom. Asked by reporters what she had sacrificed for this moment, Armstrong said, "Nothing. Skiing is my life. That's what I love to do. It's fun." Her father said, "This is a sweet spot in time."

Barbara Ann Cochran
born Claremont, New Hampshire, January 4, 1951
   Cochran's first race was the Lollipop Slalom in Vermont—she was six. The Cochrans were the ultimate skiing family: by 1973 all four children were on the U.S. ski team, and their father was head coach. Cochran was 1966 junior national champion in the giant slalom. Her World Cup performance in 1970 was fifth overall, second in slalom, and third in giant slalom; the next year she won two World Cup races (slalom and giant slalom) back to back. At the 1970 world championships she won the silver medal in slalom, and at the 1972 Olympics at Sapporo—in which her brother, Robert, and her sister Marilyn also competed—she won the gold medal slalom. Her medal was the first American gold in skiing since Andrea Mead Lawrence's two in 1952, and there would not be another until Debbie Armstrong's victory in 1984.

Christin Cooper
born California
   Cooper began skiing after her family moved to Idaho; at fifteen she won the Canadian-American title, at sixteen she was national slalom champion and had three World Cup finishes in the top ten. At the 1980 nationals she was first in slalom, giant slalom, and overall. Her first Olympics was Lake Placid in 1980, where her seventh and eighth place showing in giant slalom and slalom were the best American finishes. In 1981 she was second in World Cup slalom and fourth overall; in 1982 she was third in slalom and overall. At the 1982 world championships she took the silver medal in both slalom and giant slalom and the bronze in combined. A broken leg that required delicate surgery took her out of the 1983 season, but she was racing well in World Cup events in the month preceding the 1984 Sarajevo Games, where she won the silver medal in the giant slalom. Cooper was 1984 national champion in giant slalom. Her 1984 World Cup season was her last in competition; she finished sixth in the overall standings. Not a perfect technician, Cooper was a strong competitor and a dynamic racer—on her day nothing could stop her.

Gretchen Fraser
born Tacoma, Washington, February 11, 1919
   Fraser began skiing at seventeen, and the same year (1936) won several novice races. She married Don Fraser, a member of the 1936 Olympic ski team, in 1939; the couple lived at Sun Valley. Both made the U.S. team for the 1940 Olympics that were never held. In 1940 and 1941, Gretchen Fraser won every major event she entered, including the 1941 national

downhill and combined championships, and in 1942 the national slalom title. In 1942 Don Fraser joined the Navy and Sun Valley became a military rehab center; Gretchen Fraser did little skiing during the war. Nonetheless, at the trials for the 1948 Olympics, she won the number-one position on the team. At the St. Moritz Games she won the first Olympic skiing medals ever won by an American: the gold in the slalom and the silver in the alpine combined. In the slalom, she posted the fastest time in the first run; as she was about to lead off the second, the telephone connection to the bottom of the run went dead, and she had to stand in the starting gate—in numbing cold—for 17 minutes while technicians looked for the break in the wires. The repair made, she won the second run as well. In February 1984, on the occasion of the Sarajevo Olympics, she wrote a short piece for the New York *Times*, which appeared the week before her sixty-fifth birthday. The editor's note read: "Gretchen Fraser skis downhill in the morning and cross-country in the afternoon."

Marielle Goitschel
born Ste. Maxime, France, September 28, 1945
The youngest gold medalist at the Innsbruck Olympics in 1964, Goitschel had already been world champion in her sport for two years, winning her first of three consecutive overall world titles (1962, 1964, 1966) at the age of sixteen. Her sister Christine, the elder by fifteen months, also competed at Innsbruck, and the pair had one-two finishes in both slalom and giant slalom (Christine winning the gold medal, Marielle the silver in slalom the reverse order in the giant slalom). Marielle's best event was the slalom, but seeing her sister's excellent performance, she chose to ski a sure and cautious race and kept both medals in the family. Her turn came two days later, in the giant slalom. Christine and Jean Saubert of the U.S. were tied for first at 1:53.11. Hearing that, Marielle, the fourteenth competitor to ski the course, went all out and won the gold by .47 of a second. Christine did not compete at the Grenoble Olympics in 1968; there Marielle won the gold medal in slalom, with 1:25.86.

Erika Hess
born Switzerland
In slalom, Hess is supreme. At seventeen she won the slalom bronze medal at the Lake Placid Olympics in 1980; the next year she was World Cup slalom champion. In 1982 she won everything in sight: World Cup overall, World Cup slalom, and gold medals in the world championships in slalom, giant slalom, and overall. In 1983, she was again World Cup slalom champion. At the 1984 Sarajevo Olympics she was, surprisingly, fifth in the slalom and seventh in the giant slalom. Hess has flawless technique and perfect balance—and six weeks later she again had the World Cup overall title.

Tamara McKinney
born Lexington, Kentucky, October 16, 1962
Like Beth Heiden and Sheila Young Ochowicz, McKinney excells in two sports: she was 1983 Kentucky Sportswoman of the Year as skier and horsewoman. McKinney is from a skiing and riding family. On skis since

earliest childhood, she raced in her first World Cup event at fifteen, in 1978. Small (5'4", 117 pounds) and fearless, she has a light touch and tremendous speed, which she has had to develop the strength to control: at the 1980 Olympics she fell in both the slalom and giant slalom. But in 1981 she was World Cup giant slalom champion, and after a 1982 season in which she skied for three months with her arm in a cast taped to her pole, in 1983 she was the first American to win the World Cup overall. At the Sarajevo Games in 1984 she was the favorite to win the giant slalom, but she came in fourth, .43 of a second behind the bronze medalist, Perrine Pelen of France, and in the slalom her ski hooked a gate and she did not finish. Six weeks later she had won the World Cup slalom title and was third in the 1984 overall standings. She was 1984 national champion in slalom.

Andrea Mead Lawrence
born Rutland, Vermont, April 19, 1932

Growing up at Pico Peak, her parents' ski center, Mead Lawrence was on skis by the time she learned to walk. She began serious competition at eleven and at fourteen won her first major event—the slalom trial for the 1948 Olympics. At the St. Moritz Games she placed thirty-fifth in the downhill (going too fast, she took a bad fall), twenty-first in the combined alpine, and eighth in the slalom. She swept the national championships in 1949, winning downhill, slalom, and combined. In 1951, she raced exclusively on the international circuit for the U.S. Ski Association and entered 16 international races, placing first in ten of these events and second in four others. At the 1952 Olympics at Oslo, she won gold medals in slalom and giant slalom, and finished seventeenth in the downhill (she was in the lead when she took a fall). Before the Games she married skier David Lawrence; the third of their five children was born four months before the 1956 Olympics at Cortina. She made the team and tied for fourth in the giant slalom (.10 of a second behind the bronze medalist), and placed twenty-fifth in the slalom and thirtieth in the downhill. Her last Olympic appearance, though not in competition, was at Squaw Valley in 1960, when she skied the Olympic flame into the stadium. Mead Lawrence is the only American skier to have won two gold medals in a single Olympics. She was named to the Women's Sports Hall of Fame in 1983.

Rosi Mittermaier
born Reit im Winkel, West Germany, August 5, 1950

When twenty-five-year-old Mittermaier won a gold medal in the downhill at the Innsbruck Games in 1976, she was in her tenth season of competition, and she was known fondly by her fellow skiers as "Omi," that is, "Granny." It was her first Olympic medal, and her first downhill victory in a major race. Three days after that win, she took another gold medal, in the slalom, and two days after that she missed sweeping all three Olympic alpine events by .12 of a second, coming in second to Kathy Kreiner of Canada in the giant slalom. Innsbruck was her third Olympic appearance (in 1968 at Grenoble she was twenty-fifth in downhill, disqualified in slalom, and twentieth in giant slalom; at Sapporo in 1972 she

was sixth in downhill, seventeenth in slalom, and twelfth in giant slalom).
A hotel waitress in the off-season, she was a popular competitor.

Annemarie Moser-Pröll
born Austria, March 27, 1953

The youngest winner of the overall World Cup, Moser-Pröll took it in
1971 and again in 1972. A favorite in the 1972 Sapporo Olympics, she
won a silver medal in the downhill (she was out of first place by .32 of
a second) and another silver in the giant slalom, losing in both events to
Marie-Thérèse Nadig of Switzerland; she was fifth in the slalom. She was
bitterly disappointed, and though she won races again after the Games,
she retired from competition in 1975 and did not seek to enter the 1976
Olympics. Her competitors missed her: Cindy Nelson of the U.S. said,
"I'd rather be second to Annemarie than win without her. . . . it wasn't the
same. You knew you weren't up against the best." But Moser-Pröll did
start skiing again later in 1976, and going into the 1980 Moscow Olympics
she held six World Cup titles; all she lacked in her career was an Olympic
gold medal. In the giant slalom at Moscow she came in sixth, but she won
her gold in the downhill, defeating Nadig (third place) by 30 seconds.

Marie-Thérèse Nadig
born Tanneboden, Switzerland, March 8, 1954

When Nadig at seventeen won an Olympic gold medal in downhill at
the Sapporo Games in 1972, she defeated a two-time World Cup champion,
Annemarie Moser-Pröll of Austria; Nadig herself had never won a World
Cup race. Three days later she had her second gold of the Games, winning
the giant slalom in 1:29.9 and again defeating Moser-Pröll. The attention
(and the pressure) was on Moser-Pröll, and Nadig has said her ability to
go in relaxed since nothing was expected of her gave her the victories. At
the 1976 Innsbruck Games she had flu; she was too sick to compete in
the downhill and was fifth in the giant slalom five days later. Her last
Olympic appearance was at Moscow, in 1980. In the World Cup 1980
season, Nadig had won six downhill races, Moser-Pröll only one. But this
time the pressure was on Nadig, and she had to settle for third in the
Olympic event while Moser-Pröll got the gold. These two were the best
of their generation.

Cynthia Nelson
born Lutsen, Minnesota

Twenty-eight years old at the 1984 Olympics, Nelson was affectionately
known in Europe as "die alte Amerikanerin." Possibly the best ever U.S.
downhill racer, she has been a member of the U.S. World Cup team since
she was fifteen and has four World Cup victories. She was five times
national champion (downhill in 1973 and 1978, slalom in 1975 and 1976,
combined in 1978). Chosen for the 1972 Olympic team, she did not compete because of a dislocated hip. Four years later at the Innsbruck Games
she won the bronze medal in the downhill. In 1980, at Lake Placid, she
competed in all three events (her best finish was a tie for seventh in the
downhill); that year she won the silver medal for the world combined

championship, and finished the 1983 season seventh overall in World Cup standings and second in giant slalom. Two months before the 1984 Olympics at Sarajevo she had a bad injury to her right knee that forced her to withdraw from the downhill event. Skiing with a brace, she was nineteenth in the slalom. A superb technical skier, she has had to work to develop a looser, glider style suitable for the straighter and faster courses of the 1980's.

Hanni Wenzel
born Germany, December 14, 1956

A small woman (5'4", 125 pounds) who grew up in a small country (Liechtenstein), Wenzel was a great skier in all three events. In 1974 she won the world slalom championship at St. Moritz, in 1976 she took the bronze medal in slalom at the Innsbruck Olympics, in 1978 the world championship. At the Lake Placid Olympics in 1980 she won the silver medal in the downhill and gold medals in the giant slalom and the slalom. (These were not Liechtenstein's only medals: Hanni's brother, Andreas, won the silver in the men's giant slalom.) In 1980 Wenzel also won the world championship gold medal in slalom, giant slalom, and combined. In 1982 injury kept her from competing in the world championships, but in 1983 she was runner-up to Tamara McKinney of the U.S. Ineligible for the 1984 Olympics because she had signed a commercial contract, she was second to Erika Hess of Switzerland in 1984 World Cup overall. At the end of the 1984 season, Wenzel announced her retirement after a 13-year career in which she won 32 World Cup titles.

OLYMPIC CHAMPIONSHIPS
Downhill

Year	Gold	Silver	Bronze
1948 St. Moritz	Hedy Schlunegger Switzerland	Trude Beiser Austria	Resi Hammer Austria
1952 Oslo	Trude Beiser Austria	Annemarie Buchner West Germany	Giuliana Minuzzo Italy
1956 Cortina	Madeleine Berthod Switzerland	Frieda Danzer Switzerland	Lucile Wheeler Canada
1960 Squaw Valley	Heidi Biebl West Germany	Penelope Pitou USA	Traudl Hecher Austria
1964 Innsbruck	Christl Haas Austria	Edith Zimmermann Austria	Traudl Hecher Austria
1968 Grenoble	Olga Pall Austria	Isabelle Mir France	Christl Haas Austria
1972 Sapporo	Marie-Thérèse Nadig Switzerland	Annemarie Pröll Austria	Susan Corrock USA
1976 Innsbruck	Rosi Mittermaier West Germany	Brigitte Totschnigg Austria	Cynthia Nelson USA

Year	Gold	Silver	Bronze
1980 Lake Placid	Annemarie Moser-Pröll Austria	Hanni Wenzel Liechtenstein	Marie-Thérèse Nadig Switzerland
1984 Sarajevo	Michela Figni Switzerland	Maria Walliser Switzerland	Olga Charvatova USSR

Slalom

Year	Gold	Silver	Bronze
1948 St. Moritz	Gretchen Fraser USA	Antoinette Meyer Switzerland	Erika Mahringer Austria
1952 Oslo	Andrea Mead Lawrence USA	Ossi Reichert West Germany	Annemarie Buchner West Germany
1956 Cortina	Renee Colliard Switzerland	Regina Schopf Austria	Evgenia Sidorova USSR
1960 Squaw Valley	Anne Heggtveit Canada	Betsy Snite USA	Barbara Henneberger West Germany
1964 Innsbruck	Christine Goitschel France	Marielle Goitschel France	Jean Saubert USA
1968 Grenoble	Marielle Goitschel France	Nancy Greene Canada	Annie Famose France
1972 Sapporo	Barbara Cochran USA	Danielle Debernard France	Florence Steurer France
1976 Innsbruck	Rosi Mittermaier West Germany	Claudia Giodani Italy	Hanni Wenzel Liechtenstein
1980 Lake Placid	Hanni Wenzel Liechtenstein	Christa Kinshofer West Germany	Erika Hess Switzerland
1984 Sarajevo	Paoletta Magoni Italy	Perrine Pelen France	Ursula Konzett Liechtenstein

Giant Slalom

Year	Gold	Silver	Bronze
1952 Oslo	Andrea Mead Lawrence USA	Dagmar Rom Austria	Annemarie Buchner West Germany
1956 Cortina	Ossi Reichert West Germany	Josefine Frandl Austria	Dorothea Hochleitner Austria
1960 Squaw Valley	Yvonne Ruegg Switzerland	Penelope Pitou USA	Giuliana Chenal-Minuzzo Italy

Year	Gold	Silver	Bronze
1964 Innsbruck	Marielle Goitschel France	Christine Goitschel France	Jean Saubert USA
1968 Grenoble	Nancy Greene Canada	Annie Famose France	Fernande Bochatay Switzerland
1972 Sapporo	Marie-Thérèse Nadig Switzerland	Annemarie Pröll Austria	Wiltrud Drexel Austria
1976 Innsbruck	Kathy Kreiner Canada	Rosi Mittermaier West Germany	Danielle Debernard France
1980 Lake Placid	Hanni Wenzel Liechtenstein	Irene Epple West Germany	Perrine Pelen France
1984 Sarajevo	Deborah Armstrong USA	Christin Cooper USA	Perrine Pelen France

WORLD CHAMPIONS
Downhill

Year	Champion	Country
1931	Esme MacKinnon	Great Britain
1932	Paula Wiesinger	Italy
1933	Inge Wersin-Lantschner	Austria
1934	Anny Ruegg	Switzerland
1935	Christel Cranz	Germany
1936	Evelyn Pinching	Great Britain
1937	Christel Cranz	Germany
1938	Lisa Resch	Germany
1939	Christel Cranz	Germany
1940-47	not held	
1948	Hedy Schlunegger	Switzerland
1950	Trude Jochum-Beiser	Austria
1952	Trude Jochum-Beiser	Austria
1954	Ida Schopfer	Austria
1956	Madeleine Berthod	Switzerland
1958	Lucile Wheeler	Canada
1960	Heidi Biebl	West Germany
1962	Christl Haas	Austria
1964	Christl Haas	Austria
1966	Erika Schinegger	Austria
1968	Olga Pall	Austria
1970	Anneroesli Zyrd	Switzerland
1972	Marie-Thérèse Nadig	Switzerland
1974	Annemarie Pröll	Austria
1976	Rosi Mittermaier	West Germany
1978	Annemarie Moser-Pröll	Austria
1980	Annemarie Moser-Pröll	Austria
1982	Gerry Sorensen	Canada
1984	Michela Figini	Switzerland

Slalom

Year	Champion	Country
1931	Esme MacKinnon	Great Britain
1932	Rosli Streiff	Switzerland
1933	Inge Wersin-Lantschner	Austria
1934	Christl Cranz	Switzerland
1935	Anny Ruegg	Switzerland
1936	Gerda Paumgarten	Austria
1937	Christl Cranz	Germany
1938	Christl Cranz	Germany
1939	Christl Cranz	Germany
1940-47	not held	
1948	Gretchen Fraser	USA
1950	Dagmar Rom	Austria
1952	Andrea Mead Lawrence	USA
1954	Trude Klecker	Austria
1956	Renee Colliard	Switzerland
1958	Inger Bjornbakken	Norway
1960	Anne Heggtveit	Canada
1962	Marianne Jahn	Austria
1964	Christine Goitschel	France
1966	Annie Famose	France
1968	Marielle Goitschel	France
1970	Ingrid Lafforgue	France
1972	Barbara Cochran	USA
1974	Hanni Wenzel	Liechtenstein
1976	Rosi Mittermaier	West Germany
1978	Lea Solkner	Austria
1980	Hanni Wenzel	Liechtenstein
1982	Erika Hess	Switzerland
1984	Paoletta Magoni	Italy

Giant Slalom

Year	Champion	Country
1950	Dagmar Rom	Austria
1952	Andrea Mead Lawrence	USA
1954	Lucienne Schmith-Coultet	France
1956	Ossi Reichert	West Germany
1958	Lucile Wheeler	Canada
1960	Yvonne Ruegg	Switzerland
1962	Marianne Jahn	Austria
1964	Marielle Goitschel	France
1966	Marielle Goitschel	France
1968	Nancy Greene	Canada
1970	Betsy Clifford	Canada
1972	Marie-Thérèse Nadig	Switzerland
1974	Fabienne Serrat	France
1976	Kathy Kreiner	Canada
1978	Maria Epple	West Germany
1980	Hanni Wenzel	Liechtenstein
1982	Erika Hess	Switzerland
1984	Deborah Armstrong	USA

Combined

Year	Champion	Country
1932	Rosli Streiff	Switzerland
1933	Inge Wersin-Lantschner	Austria
1934	Christl Cranz	Germany
1935	Christl Cranz	Germany
1936	Evelyn Pinching	Great Britain
1937	Christl Cranz	Germany
1938	Christl Cranz	Germany
1939	Christl Cranz	Germany
1940-47	not held	
1948	Trude Jochum-Beiser	Austria
1950-52	not held	
1954	Ida Schopfer	Austria
1956	Madeleine Berthod	Switzerland
1958	Frieda Danzer	Switzerland
1960	Anne Heggtveit	Canada
1962	Marielle Goitschel	France
1964	Marielle Goitschel	France
1966	Marielle Goitschel	France
1968	Nancy Greene	Canada
1970	Michelle Jacot	France
1972	Annemarie Pröll	Austria
1974	Fabienne Serrat	France
1976	Rosi Mittermaier	West Germany
1978	Annemarie Moser-Pröll	Austria
1980	Hanni Wenzel	Liechtenstein
1982	Erika Hess	Switzerland

Nordic Skiing

Judy Rabinowitz Endestad
born Fairbanks, Alaska

Despite her Alaskan background Endestad started skiing relatively late, and despite her small size (5'1", 121 pounds), she's good at it. She had been skiing only two years when she came East to college at Harvard; in another two years she knew she missed the sport and that college could wait. Giving herself six years, she started skiing seriously in 1978. In her fifth season she was regularly finishing in the top 20 in World Cup races. In 1982 she won the U.S. national championship in 5K and 10K; she is now the number-one racer on the U.S. women's team. Both she and her husband, Audun Endestad, qualified for the 1984 Olympic squad (Judy Endestad placed twenty-seventh in the 10K at Sarajevo, the best U.S. finish).

Marja-Liisa Hamalainen
born Simpele, Finland

Hamalainen first skied the hilly countryside of her father's farm. In her first year of competition, 1971, she finished fifth in the 5K European junior championship. In the 1980 Olympics at Lake Placid, she finished nineteenth in the 5K, eighteenth in the 10K. After ten racing seasons she had not won a world championship medal, and she almost quit. With the support of her fiancé, Harri Kirvesniemi, a skier on the Finnish Olympic team in 1980 and again in 1984, she stayed with it—and won the World Cup title in 1983. At the Sarajevo Games in 1984, cross-country was hers: tall, strong, and quick, Hamalainen won gold medals in the 5K, the 10K, and the 20K and anchored Finland's bronze-winning relay team.

Raisa Smetanina
born Soviet Union, February 29, 1952

A medal winner at each of her three Olympics, Smetanina, a teacher (and national champion) at home, won the gold in the 10K and the silver in the 5K at Innsbruck in 1976 and was a member of her country's gold-winning 20K relay team; won the gold medal in the 5K and silver in the relay at Lake Placid in 1980; and took two silvers in the 10K and 20K at Sarajevo in 1984. She won the 1981 World Cup championship (winning six of her eight races) and the gold medal for the 20K in the 1982 world championships. Her last racing season was 1983-84; she was a great competitor and a true sportswoman.

Lynn Spencer-Galanes
born Anchorage, Alaska

An alpine skier until she was eighteen, Spencer-Galanes tried the junior nationals in nordic in 1972—and came in second in the 10K. A nordic skier ever since, she marked her ninth season on the U.S. team in 1983-84. She has competed in three Olympics; in 1984 at Sarajevo she had the best American finishes in the 5K (twenty-seventh) and the 20K (thirty-third). National champion in the 5K, 10K, and 20K in 1983, she had three top-twenty World Cup finishes, one of them in the top ten.

SOFTBALL

Indoor-outdoor is what it was first called; then kitten ball, diamond ball, playground ball . . . mush ball came closer . . . but what it was, was softball. Developed in 1887 by George Hancock of the Chicago Board of Trade as an event for the Thanksgiving Day festivities for the Farragut Boat Club, Hancock's version used a broomstick for a bat and the ball was an old boxing glove. The Amateur Softball Association was formed in 1933, in a decade of terrific national interest. After World War II, the sport continued to grow, with hundreds of thousands of local teams across the country. Until the 60's softball was mostly a fast-pitch game, in which the pitcher dominated. In the U.S., slow-pitch has made considerable inroads, but on the international scene fast-pitch is the game that's played. The first international world championship was the women's tournament held in Melbourne in 1965, at which Australia beat the U.S. in the finals, 1-0. Fast-pitch softball is likely to be an Olympic sport in 1988. In June and July 1984 eight countries (the U.S., represented by the Raybestos Brakettes, Mexico, Canada, Puerto Rico, The Netherlands, China, Japan, and Taiwan) competed for the first Women's International Cup at Los Angeles. In the 33-game round-robin tournament, the U.S. was strongly challenged by China and Japan. Japanese pitcher **Kazue Yamakoshi** did not allow a run in the 25 innings she pitched; she was backed up by catcher **Chitomi Kymishima** and center fielder **Midori Suzuki.** China owed much to the batting of **Mei Ying Wang,** who hit or drove home 9 of her team's 19 runs. But the U.S. prevailed 1-0 against China in the final game, on the strength of superb pitching by **Kathy Arendsen** and **Barbara Reinalda.** Reinalda had led the Brakettes to their eighteenth national title in August 1983, and in this competition she gave up one earned run in the 22 innings she pitched. Arendsen, twice on the U.S. team in the Pan American Games, was blazing; she too allowed only one run—in 38 innings—and she won all five games she pitched.

Betty Evans Grayson
born Portland, Oregon, October 9, 1925; died July 9, 1979
    Originally an outfielder, Evans Grayson was a star player in the Portland City League at thirteen. She wanted to be a pitcher and, coached by her

father, became a good one; two years later she was pitching for Erv Lind's Florists. In 1943 she pitched the Florists to the world title, and in 1944 to the national championship. In her 17-year amateur career with the Florists, "Bullet Betty" had a record of 465 wins and 91 losses; she pitched three perfect games and 125 consecutive scoreless innings. As a pro she played three seasons with the Chicago Queens, where in 1950 she had a 35-5 record. Oregon Woman Athlete of the Year in 1944, she was elected to the National Softball Hall of Fame in 1959.

Joan Joyce
born Waterbury, Connecticut, August 1, 1940

Some say she was one of the greatest all-around athletes since Babe Didrickson Zaharias; Joyce was playing top basketball as a teenager in addition to volleyball and softball. A three-time AAU basketball All-American, she averaged 25 points per game. An accomplished bowler, she sported a 180 average. But it was as a pitcher in softball that Joyce became a legend. During 20 years of amateur competition, Joyce won 509 games and lost a mere 33. She threw an astounding 105 no-hitters and 33 perfect games during her 17 years with the Raybestos Brakettes. Named an All-American 18 years in a row, she was MVP (outright or shared) eight times. A solid hitter and first baseman when not pitching, Joyce's 17-year batting average was a more than respectable .327. In 1983, Joan Joyce was named to the National Softball Hall of Fame. Though she retired from softball in 1975, she continues her career as a golf touring pro.

Joan Joyce   Bertha Tickey

Mickey Stratton
born Meriden, Connecticut, July 12, 1938

Catcher for the Raybestos Brakettes of Stratford, Connecticut, Stratton batted .300 or better in seven of her fourteen seasons with the team. Three times she led the team in batting (with .320 in 1959, .324 in 1961, and .370 in 1965); her lifetime average is .314. She played in four national championships, including 1958, the year the Brakettes won the first of their 18 national titles (in 1983 they defeated the California Blazers for the title). Retiring after the 1965 season, Stratton was named to the National Softball Hall of Fame in 1969.

Bertha Tickey
born Dinuba, California, March 13, 1925

"Blazing Bertha" had a 23-year career in which she pitched 757 winning games and lost 88. She played for the Raybestos Brakettes for 13 years and never lost more than five games in a season. A member of 11 national championship teams (the Orange, California, Lionettes 1950-52 and 1955; the Raybestos Brakettes 1958-60, 1963, 1966-68), she was eight times tournament Most Valuable Player. Possibly her greatest season was 1950, when, playing for the Lionettes, she won 65 of 73 games, struck out 795 batters, gave up 143 hits and had 143 consecutive scoreless innings. In her lifetime record she had 162 no-hitters, one of them a 13-inning game against Fresno in 1967—the year before she retired. She was named to that National Softball Hall of Fame in 1972, to the Connecticut Hall of Fame in 1973.

M. Marie Wadlow
born St. Louis, Missouri, April 12, 1917; died April 6, 1979

Pitcher Wadlow's career began in 1929 with the Tabernacle Baptist Church team in St. Louis; she retired in 1950, after seven seasons with the Caterpillar Dieselettes of Peoria. Her Dieselette record was 103 wins and 18 losses; her lifetime record was 341 and 51, including 42 no-hitters.

Hall of Famers pitcher Marjorie Law (left) and catcher Dorothy Wilkinson of the Phoenix, Arizona, Ramblers

The first woman elected to the National Softball Hall of Fame (1957), Wadlow was, according to Dieselette manager Charles McCord, "one of the greatest competitors I've seen anywhere."

INTERNATIONAL SOFTBALL FEDERATION WORLD CHAMPIONSHIPS—WOMEN'S DIVISION

Year	Champion	Location	Number of Entries
1965	Australia	Melbourne	5
1970	Japan	Osaka	9
1974	United States	Stratford	15
1978	United States	San Salvador	15
1982	New Zealand	Taipei	23

WOMEN'S MAJOR FAST PITCH CHAMPIONSHIPS

Year	Champion Team	Team City	Location
1933	Great Northern	Chicago, IL	Chicago, IL
1934	Hart Motors	Chicago, IL	Chicago, IL
1935	Bloomer Girls	Cleveland, OH	Chicago, IL
1936	National Mfg. Co	Cleveland, OH	Chicago, IL
1937	National Mfg. Co.	Cleveland, OH	Chicago, IL
1938	J. J. Krieg's	Alameda, CA	Chicago, IL
1939	J. J. Krieg's	Alameda, CA	Chicago, IL
1940	Arizona Ramblers	Phoenix, AZ	Detroit, MI
1941	Higgins "Midgets"	Tulsa, OK	Detroit, MI
1942	Jax Maids	New Orleans, LA	Detroit, MI
1943	Jax Maids	New Orleans, LA	Detroit, MI
1944	Lind & Pomeroy	Portland, OR	Cleveland, OH
1945	Jax Maids	New Orleans, LA	Cleveland, OH
1946	Jax Maids	New Orleans, LA	Cleveland, OH
1947	Jax Maids	New Orleans, LA	Cleveland, OH
1948	Arizona Ramblers	Phoenix, AZ	Portland, OR
1949	Arizona Ramblers	Phoenix, AZ	Portland, OR
1950	Orange Lionettes	Orange, CA	San Antonio, TX
1951	Orange Lionettes	Orange, CA	Detroit, MI
1952	Orange Lionettes	Orange, CA	Toronto, ONT
1953	Betsy Ross Rockets	Fresno, CA	Toronto, ONT
1954	Leach Motor Rockets	Fresno, CA	Orange, CA
1955	Orange Lionettes	Orange, CA	Portland, OR
1956	Orange Lionettes	Orange, CA	Clearwater, FL
1957	Hacienda Rockets	Fresno, CA	Buena Park, CA
1958	Raybestos Brakettes	Stratford, CT	Stratford, CT
1959	Raybestos Brakettes	Stratford, CT	Stratford, CT
1960	Raybestos Brakettes	Stratford, CT	Stratford, CT

Year	Champion Team	Team City	Location
1961	Gold Sox	Whittier, CA	Portland, OR
1962	Orange Lionettes	Orange, CA	Stratford, CT
1963	Raybestos Brakettes	Stratford, CT	Stratford, CT
1964	Erv Lind Florists	Portland, OR	Orlando, FL
1965	Orange Lionettes	Orange, CA	Stratford, CT
1966	Raybestos Brakettes	Stratford, CT	Orlando, FL
1967	Raybestos Brakettes	Stratford, CT	Stratford, CT
1968	Raybestos Brakettes	Stratford, CT	Stratford CT
1969	Orange Lionettes	Orange, CA	Tucson, AZ
1970	Orange Lionettes	Orange, CA	Stratford, CT
1971	Raybestos Brakettes	Stratford, CT	Orlando, FL
1972	Raybestos Brakettes	Stratford, CT	Tucson, AZ
1973	Raybestos Brakettes	Stratford, CT	Stratford, CT
1974	Raybestos Brakettes	Stratford, CT	Orlando, FL
1975	Raybestos Brakettes	Stratford, CT	Salt Lake City, UT
1976	Raybestos Brakettes	Stratford, CT	Stratford, CT
1977	Raybestos Brakettes	Stratford, CT	Hayward, CA
1978	Raybestos Brakettes	Stratford, CT	Allentown, PA
1979	Sun City Saints	Sun City, AZ	Springfield, MO
1980	Raybestos Brakettes	Stratford, CT	Lansing, MI
1981	Orlando Rebels	Orlando, FL	Houston, TX
1982	Raybestos Brakettes	Stratford, CT	Binghamton, NY
1983	Raybestos Brakettes	Stratford, CT	Salt Lake City, UT

WOMEN'S MAJOR FAST PITCH NATIONAL TOURNAMENT BATTING CHAMPIONS

Year	Player	Home City	Average
1950	Margaret Dobson	Portland, OR	.615
1951	Mary Gilpin	Cleveland, OH	.545
1952	Loretta Chushuk	Kansas City, KS	.500
1953	Mary Baker	Regina, SASK	.500
1954	Marg Grant	Olympia, WA	.500
1955	Kay Rich	Fresno, CA	.611
1956	Chick Long	Lancaster, PA	.600
1957	Delores Price	Portland, OR	.416
1958	Jo Day	Orange, CA	.467
1959	Eleanor Rudolph	Pekin, IL	.454
1960	Dot Wilkinson	Phoenix, AZ	.444
1961	Pam Kurrell	Redwood City, CA	.471
1962	Janet Dicks	Reading, PA	.429
1963	Carol Lee	Whittier, CA	.438
1964	Joy Peterson	Salt Lake City, UT	.545
1965	Jan Berkland	Minneapolis, MN	.455
1966	Edwina Bryan	Atlanta, GA	.571
1967	Jane Hughes	Salt Lake City, UT	.471
1968	Toni Swartout	Orlando, FL	.500
1969	Carol Lichtenberger	Plainfield, NJ	.600
1970	Cathy Benedetto	Portland, OR	.412

Year	Player	Home City	Average
1971	Joan Joyce	Stratford, CT	.467
1972	Donna Lopiano	Stratford, CT	.429
1973	Judy Jungwirth	Bloomington, MN	.438
1974	Diane Kelliam	Santa Clara, CA	.444
1975	Diane Kelliam	Santa Clara, CA	.632
1976	Barbara Reinalda	Stratford, CT	.429
1977	Kathy Toppi	Bridgeport, CT	.571
1978	Reatha Stucky	Wichita, KS	.533
1979	Cindy Anderson	West Allis, WI	.500
1980	Marilyn Rau	Sun City, AZ	.520
1981	Patty Cutright	Macomb, IL	.391
1982	Venus Jennings	Parsippany, NJ	.533
1983	Pat Guenzler	Stratford, CT	.562
1984	Sue Lewis	Los Angeles, CA	.421

SWIMMING

Benjamin Franklin advised the beginning swimmer to stand in chest-deep water and try to retrieve an egg from the bottom: thus would a novice be convinced of buoyancy. (Like Gertrude Ederle and Donna de Varona, Franklin is a member of the International Swimming Hall of Fame.) The first national swimming competition was held in England in 1837; swimming (for men) was an Olympic sport at the first modern games in 1896. Women (no Americans, though) competed at Stockholm in 1912. At the first postwar Olympics, in 1920, American women did take part, and their performance was the beginning of a golden decade: that year, at Antwerp, U.S. women took four of the five events, at Paris in 1924 they won six of seven, and five of seven in 1928 in Amsterdam. Part of the reason for the Americans' success was their use of the six-beat kick. Some had felt that the six-beat would be too tiring, but Claire Galligan and Charlotte Boyle of the Women's Swimming Association of New York agreed to train with it, and in 1918 they took first and third in the national 500-yard championship, and broke the existing U.S. records for the 880 and the mile.

Through much of the nineteenth century, diving—or "plunging"—was simply the most direct way into the water to swim. But by the 1890's the activity had attracted notice for its own sake, and the first plunging championships were held in 1893 (they continued through 1937). Early diving was "plain," the header or the swan dive. Then, German and Swedish gymnasts realized that performing their routines from a height over water gave them more exciting acrobatic possibilities (since they would no longer have to land on their feet) and a better landing surface, and they erected springboards and scaffolds with trapezes and rings. As their new version of gymnastics was refined, the trapeze and rings were abandoned and the gymnasts were in fact now using springboards and platforms to do both plain and "fancy" dives, that is, "dives with somersaults or twists." The first women's plain high diving Olympic event was in 1912; fancy springboard diving entered the women's Olympic program in 1920.

One of the only two Olympic sports without a men's class (the other is rhythmic gymnastics), synchronized swimming demands tremendous strength, flexibility, lung capacity, and fine timing and coordination—and it must look effortless, as well. Annette Kellerman developed "ornamental swimming" in Australia in the 1900's, a team called the Modern Mermaids performed at the Chicago World's Fair in 1934, Billy Rose produced a "water ballet" for the 1939 New York World's Fair, and Esther Williams was a household name in the 40's. Still, it is only recently that synchronized swimming is recognized as a serious competitive sport, not an exhibition. Although world championships have been held since 1955, the supremacy of the U.S. (which took the world title in individual, duet, and team events for twenty years in a row) perhaps discouraged the development of the sport elsewhere. American coaches went abroad to promote and develop synchronized swimming in other countries, and today there are serious challengers to America's domination of the sport, particularly Canada and Japan. Synchronized swimming was an Olympic event (with duet and solo competition) for the first time in Los Angeles in 1984.

On the other hand, no one ever said marathon swimming had to look easy—and it doesn't. It is more than endurance, it is physical combat. There is no set distance for a marathon swim; championships are awarded by a point system that factors in length and difficulty. Marathon, in swimming, means nonstop; in open-water marathons, the most difficult, there are no river currents to ride and no shoreline to offer protection from wind or waves. The longest unaided open-water swim made to date is the 89 miles from Florida to Cuba, achieved by Diana Nyad; in August 1984 Stacy Chanin, a physical education major at the University of Maryland, swam three laps around Manhattan, 83 miles, in 33:29. Other notable swims, each with its own hazards of temperature, weather, and sometimes sharks, are the 60 miles across Lake Michigan from Chicago to Benton Harbor, Lake Ontario (32 miles), the Bay of Naples (22 miles), Catalina Island to the California coast (22 miles), the 40-degree waters of the Juan de Fuca Strait between Washington state and Vancouver Island (15 miles), and the 21 cold miles, accompanied by sharks, from the nearest of the Farallon Islands to San Francisco. The 21-mile English Channel, by no means the most difficult, holds a unique appeal for both athlete and public. In 1926, when nineteen-year-old Gertrude Ederle was the first woman to swim it, New York gave her a tickertape welcome after her feat. The great Danish Olympic gold medalist, Greta Andersen—who beat every man she swam against at least once—did the crossing six times.

Racing

Ethelda Bleibtrey
born Waterford, New York, February 27, 1902; died May 6, 1978

To counteract the effects of polio, Bleibtrey began swimming; to keep a friend company (that was Charlotte Boyle, third-place winner in the 500-yard national championship in 1918), she began competing. In an undefeated amateur career she won every national championship, from 50 yards up. The 1920 Antwerp Olympics came at the end of her second year of competition: she won gold medals in the 100-meter freestyle, the 300-meter (as it then was) freestyle, and the 2 × 100-meter freestyle relay. Had there been an Olympic backstroke event for women then, she would undoubtedly have won that, too; she was at the time world record holder in the backstroke. The races were held in a tidal estuary, and Bleibtrey recalled that the competitors swam "in mud and not water." Nonetheless, her 1:13.6 in the 100-meter freestyle set a world record. Another notable citation in Bleibtrey's career came from the police: in 1919 at Manhattan Beach she received a summons for "nude swimming" when she removed her stockings before going in the water. The resulting popular outcry in her favor spelled the end of stockings as an essential part of women's swimwear. Bleibtrey was elected to the International Swimming Hall of Fame in 1967.

Tracy Caulkins
born Winona, Minnesota, January 11, 1963

Proficient in all four strokes, Caulkins had just turned fourteen when she won her first national title; at fifteen, she took five gold medals and a silver at the 1978 world championships and won that year's Sullivan Award (she was the youngest winner to date). At the 1979 Pan American Games she took another two golds (in 200- and 400-meter individual medley) and two silvers (in 100-meter breaststroke and 400-meter free-style), and she was superlatively ready for the 1980 Olympics, where she was confidently expected to win several gold medals. The U.S. boycotted. Caulkins was hit hard. She continued to win: she was named Sportswoman of the Year in 1981 by the Women's Sports Foundation, and by 1982 she had won more national titles than Johnny Weissmuller; she won the 1982 Broderick Cup for outstanding college female athlete. But she finished no higher than third in any event in the 1982 world championships, her times were slower, and she was simply not swimming so well. She won the gold medal in the 400-meter individual medley at the 1983 Pan American Games, but her time (4:51.82) was 11 seconds slower than it had been five years earlier at the world championships; she also won the 200-meter individual medley, in 2:16.22. The U.S. Swimming International meet in January 1984 seemed to signal a turnaround: Caulkins won the 200-meter and 400-meter individual medleys by defeating powerful East German swimmers whom she had not previously been able to hold off. After that meet she said, "I think a lot of people have counted me out. They better watch out." Two months later, at the national indoor championships, she won the 200-meter individual medley, and that summer, at the Los Angeles Olympics, won three gold medals and placed fourth in the 100-meter breaststroke. Her victory—by 15 meters—in the 400-meter individual medley set an American record of 4:39.24, and her 200-meter individual medley in 2:12.64 was an Olympic record. She was also a member of the winning U.S. team in the 4 × 100-meter medley relay. Captain of her team, Caulkins was respected and admired by her teammates for her understanding and compassion as well as for her talents. She retired after the Los Angeles Games, having won 48 national titles and set 61 American and 5 world records in her career.

Tiffany Cohen
born Culver City, California, June 11, 1966

At 5' 8" and 120 pounds, Cohen is slightly built for a swimmer, but she can go the distance—specifically, 1650 yards freestyle, in which she set an American record of 15:46.54 at the 1983 indoor national championships. At that competition she also won freestyle gold medals at 200 yards, 500 yards, 1000 yards, and 800-yard relay. She was at the top in overall point standing, surpassing Tracy Caulkins, who had been top scorer since 1977. Two months later, at the outdoor nationals, Cohen was again high scorer, winning gold medals in freestyle at 400, 800, and 1500 meters. At the 1983 Pan American Games she won the 400 and 800 meters, and did the same at the Pan Pacific Games. That year she was ranked first in the world in the 400-meter and 1500-meter freestyle. Her earlier years of competition were less consistent, but no less impressive: she had her first national title at fifteen, winning the gold medal in the 400 meter at the outdoor nationals, and taking the silver medal in 1500 meters as well. At the 1982 world championships her best place was third in the 400 meters, but she won the U.S. title in that event that year. Her 1983 season was a knockout, and her only challenger in distance freestyle competition is Astrid Strauss of East Germany, who narrowly defeated Cohen in January 1984 at the U.S. Swimming International meet at 400, 800, and 1500 meters. Cohen won the gold in the 200 meters, and in March at the national indoor championships won the 400 and 800. At the 1984 Los Angeles Olympics (at which East Germany did not compete) Cohen won the gold medal in the 400 meters (in 4:07.10, an American record) and the 800 meters, in which her time was 8:24.95, an Olympic record and only .33 of a second short of a world record.

Donna de Varona
born San Diego, California, April 26, 1947

Thirteen at her first Olympics (Rome, 1960), and the youngest member of the U.S. team, over the next five years de Varona set eight long-course (50-meter pool) world records and ten short-course (25-yard pool) American records (which would have been world records if the International Aquatics Federation had not ceased to record 25-yard pool times in 1957). In her career de Varona won 37 individual national championships, in three different strokes—freestyle, backstroke, and butterfly; thus she was not only often the fastest but also the best all-around swimmer. At the 1964 Olympic Games in Tokyo, she won gold medals in the 400-meter individual medley and the 4 × 100-meter freestyle relay. After her retirement from competition in 1965, de Varona became the first woman sportscaster on network television, and has worked actively to advance women's sports. A founding member and president of the Women's Sports Foundation, she was a consultant to the U.S. Senate on the Amateur Sports Act. She was elected to the International Swimming Hall of Fame in 1969, and to the Women's Sports Hall of Fame in 1983.

Fanny Durack
born Australia, 1892; died 1956

When it was announced that women's swimming events were to be included in the Olympics for the first time in 1912, Australian officials (male) were not impressed; they thought it would be a waste of time to send a team to the Stockholm Games. Durack, already an established swimmer in Australia, thought otherwise. She gathered popular support, and finally the officials gave way. Her gold medal, for the 100-meter freestyle, was the first for a woman in any sport—and in the course of winning it she set a world record of 1:19.2 in one of the heats (her final averaged time was 1:22.2). Swimming the true Australian crawl with its two-beat kick, she held 11 world records between 1912 and 1918. She swam—magnificently—distances from 50 yards to a mile; she held the 100-yard freestyle record 1912-21, the 100-meter freestyle 1912-20, the 220-yard freestyle 1915-21, the 500-meter freestyle 1915-17, and the mile record 1914-26. She was elected to the International Swimming Hall of Fame in 1967.

Kornelia Ender
born Halle, East Germany, October 25, 1958
Ender first swam as orthopedic therapy; by the time she was thirteen she was swimming in the Olympics, at the 1972 Munich Games. She won three silver medals, in the 200-meter individual medley, the 4 × 100-meter freestyle relay, and the 4 × 100-meter medley relay. Four years later, at the Montreal Games, she improved on that performance, winning four gold medals (100- and 200-meter freestyle, 100-meter butterfly, and 4 × 100-meter medley relay), and a silver in the 4 × 100-meter freestyle relay. Her time in the 100-meter freestyle (55.65) broke the world record; in the previous three years she had new world records in that event nine times. At the 1973 world championships she won the silver medal in the 200-meter individual medley and the gold medals in the 100-meter free-style, 100-meter butterfly, and freestyle and medley relays; in the 1975 competition she won gold medals again in the same events as two years before, and a silver in the 200-meter freestyle. In the 1974 European championships she won gold medals in the 100-meter and 200-meter free-style and medley relays. The holder of ten East German championships, Enders was the first woman to swim the 200-meter freestyle in less than 2 minutes. Not surprisingly, she was World Swimmer of the Year in 1973, 1975, and 1976. She was elected to the International Swimming Hall of Fame in 1981.

Dawn Fraser, O.B.E.
born Balmain, New South Wales, Australia, September 4, 1937
"I have my fun—and I think I am a better swimmer because of it." Fraser's fun often meant breaking the rules, but there is no doubt about the caliber of her swimming. She did not compete until she was sixteen; at seventeen she won the Australian national championship in the 100-meter freestyle with a world record time of 1:04.5. At an age when many women swimmers retire, Fraser was just beginning. The 1956 Olympics were held in Melbourne: Fraser, swimming in her first international competition, won a silver medal in the 400-meter freestyle and a gold medal in the 4 × 100-meter freestyle relay. Her individual gold medal was in the 100-meter freestyle, which she won with a world record time of 1:02 flat. She was the world record-holder at that distance for the next 15 years, lowering the time on nine occasions. At the 1960 Rome Games, Fraser successfully defended her 100-meter freestyle title with another gold medal,

and won two silvers as well, in the 4 × 100-meter freestyle relay and the 4 × 100-meter medley relay. In October 1962 (she had turned twenty-five), Fraser swam 110 yards freestyle in 59.9 seconds, thus becoming the first woman to do 100 meters in less than a minute. Six months before the Tokyo Olympics in 1964, Fraser was seriously hurt in an automobile accident in which her mother was killed. She recovered from her injuries and depression to compete, and won her third gold medal in the 100-meter freestyle with a time of 59.5; at those Games she also won silvers as a member of the second-place 4 × 100-meter freestyle and medley relay teams. Throughout her career, Fraser fought with officials, argued with teammates, indulged in pranks, and after the 1964 Olympics was suspended from competition by the Australian Amateur Swimming Association; she was also named Australian Athlete of the Year, which more accurately reflected her countrymen's views. She was elected to the International Swimming Hall of Fame in 1965.

Shane Gould
born Brisbane, Queensland, Australia, November 23, 1956

Each time she won a gold medal at the 1972 Munich Olympics, Gould waved her toy kangaroo in triumph. She got to wave it three times, as she won three events, each in world-record time: the 200-meter freestyle in 2:03.56, the 400-meter freestyle in 4:19.04 (lowering her own previous world record of 4:21.2), and the 200-meter individual medley in 2:23.07. At those Games she also won the silver medal in the 800-meter freestyle and the bronze in the 100-meter freestyle. Her 100-meter time was 59.06; she had previously set a world record time of 58.5, which stood after the event was over, even though the winner, Sandra Neilson of the U.S., had set an Olympic record with her time of 58.59. When she was fourteen, Gould had equalled her countrywoman Dawn Fraser's world-record 58.9 in the 100-meter freestyle, and set another world record—the next day—in the 200, doing 2:06.5. By the end of the year—that is, in the six months between July 1971 and January 1972—Gould set world records at 100, 200, 400, 800, and 1500; she was the first woman to achieve that sweep. It is no wonder that at the Munich Games the U.S. team, in an attempt to boost their morale, wore T-shirts that read, "All that glitters is not Gould"—and indeed, two Americans did beat her in the 100 meters, Neilson and Shirley Babashoff. Gould retired a year after the 1972 Olympics, at sixteen wanting more in her life than the all-consuming discipline of competitive swimming. But at Munich in 1972, Gould glittered very brightly indeed. She was named to the International Swimming Hall of Fame in 1977.

Nancy Hogshead
born Iowa City, Iowa, April 17, 1962

When Hogshead won the gold medal in 100-meter freestyle at the 1984 national indoor championships—and the silver in 200 meters, beaten by inches by Mary T. Meagher—the New York *Times* headlined its story, "'Good Loser' a Success." A competitive swimmer since 1976, specializing in butterfly and individual medley, Hogshead had gathered a number of national silver and bronze medals, but only three gold, all in butterfly: 1977, 100 yards and 200 meters; 1978, 200 yards. She was named to the

1980 Olympic team, but the U.S. boycotted the Moscow Games. She stayed out for 1981 and 1982, returning to competition in 1983; at the national indoor championships, she won the bronze medal in 200-yard butterfly (and was named Comeback Swimmer of the Year), and at the outdoor nationals she won the bronze in 200-meter butterfly. Her coach, Mitch Ivey, encouraged her to work on her freestyle, and at the U.S. Swimming International meet in January 1984 she won bronze medals in both 100- and 200-meter freestyle and was high-point scorer. Three months later were the indoor nationals, and Hogshead had her gold in a national freestyle event. She was a success that night, and a success at the Los Angeles Olympics that August. She and teammate Carrie Steinseifer tied for the gold medal in 100-meter freestyle, and Hogshead picked up two more gold medals for her participation in the first-place 4 × 100-meter medley relay and 4 × 100-meter freestyle relay teams, and won the silver medal in the 200-meter individual medley. In the freestyle relay, she swam the last—and fastest—leg in 55.18.

Eleanor Holm
born New York, New York, December 6, 1913
   In the 20's and 30's, swimming and show business had a certain affinity: Esther Williams, Johnny Weissmuller, Buster Crabbe—and Eleanor Holm. In 1928 (she was fourteen) Holm placed fifth in the 100-meter backstroke at the Amsterdam Olympics. Within four years, she held the world record in the event (1:18.2) and at the next Olympiad (Los Angeles, 1932) won the gold medal in 1:19.4. The following year she married musician Art Jarrett and sang with his band, but she was still a swimmer and set another 100-meter backstroke world record in 1935. Although Hendrika Mastenbroek of The Netherlands had broken that record the February before the 1936 Berlin Games, Holm was still the Olympic champion and a favorite. She never defended her title. On the ship going over from the U.S., she broke rules and broke training (there are different versions of the story, all of them involving parties and champagne). Possibly to her surprise, she was dropped from the team. When she returned to the U.S., she toured with Jarrett's band and in 1938 made a movie (she was Jane to 1936 decathlon gold medalist Glenn Morris's Tarzan in *Tarzan's Revenge*). Divorced from Jarrett, she married impresario Billy Rose and swam in his Aquacade in 1939-40 at the New York's World Fair. In a New York *Times* interview just before the 1984 Los Angeles Olympics, she told reporter Dave Anderson, "I don't swim at all anymore, I just play tennis. But I still have my 1932 Olympic bathing suit." She was elected to the International Swimming Hall of Fame in 1966.

Ragnild Hveger
born Denmark, December 10, 1920
   Hveger's career was out of sync with history: a great stylist with world-record speed, she undoubtedly would have swept the freestyle events in the Olympics of 1940 and 1944—Games that were never held. She was fifteen at her first Olympic appearance, Berlin in 1936, where she won the silver medal in the 400-meter freestyle, outdistanced by Hendrika Mastenbroek's powerful finishing kick, which gave the Dutch competitor

the victory by one meter. Over the next six years, Hveger broke more than 40 world records at various distances; in 1941 she held 19. Her world records at 200, 400, 800, and 1500 stood for fifteen years, 1938-53. After the war, Olympic competition did not resume until 1948; Hveger, who had retired in 1945, did not attempt to make the Danish team. But four years later she was competing for Denmark at the 1952 Helsinki Games; she swam on the fourth-place Danish team in the 4 × 400-meter relay. She was thirty-one, and while her style was still remarkable she simply no longer had the endurance at speed: in the 400-meter freestyle she led for almost three-quarters of the way, then was passed by four competitors, to finish fifth. But when the race was over, her world record of 5:00.1 still stood. She was elected to the International Swimming Hall of Fame in 1966.

Annette Kellerman
born Sydney, Australia, July 6, 1888; died November 5, 1975

Racer? She was Swim Champion of New South Wales (100 yards in 1:18) and set a women's world record for the mile of 32:29, which she later lowered to 28 minutes. Diver? She performed from a 50-foot board at Cavills Bath in Sydney. Synchronized swimmer? Her "ornamental swimming" shows toured England and the U.S., and she made smash Hollywood movies—*Neptune's Daughter* (1914), followed by *A Daughter of the Gods*, *Diving Venus*, and *Queen of the Mermaids*. Distance swimmer? Kellerman swam the Thames from Putney Bridge to Blackwall in 3½ hours, made it three-quarters of the way across the English Channel, and won a 22-mile race in the Danube from Tuln to Vienna. Crippled as a child, Kellerman was introduced to swimming as therapy for her legs. Her legs grew stronger, and she was able to abandon braces and crutches, but she never abandoned the water. Forty years after her prime, Hollywood made *Million Dollar Mermaid,* another "Annette Kellerman" movie—this time, the Australian swimmer was played by her American successor, Esther Williams. She was named to the International Swimming Hall of Fame in 1974.

Hendrika Mastenbroek
born Rotterdam, The Netherlands, February 26, 1919

There was nothing like the Dutch women's swimming team at the 1936 Berlin Olympics. They won four gold medals, and Mastenbroek was responsible for three of them: the 100-meter freestyle (in which she set an Olympic record of 1:05.9), the 400-meter freestyle (another Olympic record, 5:26.4), and the 4 × 100-meter freestyle relay, in which Mastenbroek's last-leg finishing sprint gave her team the victory. She missed a fourth gold medal in the 100-meter backstroke (which was won by her teammate, Dina Senff, by .3 of a second. Mastenbroek's determination was as good as her style: in both her individual gold medal events, she came from behind to win. The first year she competed at a level above Rotterdam regional contests was 1934; she won that year's European championship. In her short career, she held nine world records, three in freestyle and six in backstroke. She was elected to the International Swimming Hall of Fame in 1968.

Mary T. Meagher

Mary T. Meagher
born Louisville, Kentucky, October 27, 1964

The most difficult of swimming strokes is the butterfly, and that's Meagher's specialty. A swimmer since childhood, she set her first world record at the 1979 Pan American Games in the 200-meter butterfly, and the following April she set a world record in the 100 meter. She qualified for the 1980 Olympics in five events, but did not get to swim because of the U.S. boycott. At the time of the Moscow Games she held world records in butterfly at 200 meters (2:07.01) and 100 meters (59.26). These records stood after the Games were over; indeed, the next week Meagher lowered her 200-meter time to 2:06.37 and since to 2:05.96 (East Germany's Ines Geissler won the gold medal at Moscow in 2:10.44). At the nationals in 1981, Meagher dropped her 100-meter time to 57.93, another world record. But, much like Tracy Caulkins, she was deeply disappointed by the 1980 boycott and her concentration and performance suffered: at the 1982 world championships she lost to Geissler (by 1.1 seconds) in the 200 meter. But five months later she in turn defeated Geissler, and also like Caulkins, looked very good at the U.S. Swimming International meet in January 1984, where she took the 100-meter butterfly in 59.63 and the 200 meter in 2:07.88. In March, at the national indoor championships, she won the 200-meter freestyle, the 100-meter butterfly, and the 200-meter butterfly. Still, she was not swimming up to her own high standard at the Olympic trials in June. But at the Los Angeles Games it was another story: she won gold medals in 100-meter butterfly, 200-meter butterfly, and as a member of the winning U.S. 4 × 100-meter medley relay team. She won her 100-meter butterfly gold medal in 59.26—having earlier that day swum the qualifying heat in 59.05, the closest anyone had yet come to her 1981 world record.

Deborah Meyer
born Annapolis, Maryland, August 14, 1952

In 1967 Meyer was named Woman Athlete of the Year—by TASS, the news agency of the Soviet Union. The West agreed: in 1968 she won the Sullivan Award. Winner of two gold medals at the 1967 Pan American Games, Meyer set world records at the trials for the 1968 Olympics in the 200 meter, 400 meter, and 800 meter. At the Mexico City Games, the altitude and dysentery slowed her times—but she still finished with a gold medal in each race, setting an Olympic record of 4:31.8 in the 400. She was the first woman to swim 1500 meters in less than 18 minutes, and 400 meters in under 4:30. World Swimmer of the Year 1967-69, she was elected to the International Swimming Hall of Fame in 1977.

Aileen Riggin. See Diving.

Cynthia "Sippy" Woodhead
born Riverside, California, February 7, 1964

Like several of her teammates at the 1984 Olympics, Woodhead had been a very likely candidate for gold at the 1980 Moscow Games—which the U.S. boycotted. In 1978 and 1979 she was, simply, the world's best freestyle swimmer: in 1978 she won the world championship gold medal in the 200 meters and silvers in 400 and 800, and at home won national titles in 500 yards, 1650 yards, 100 meters, and 200 meters; in 1979 she swam a world-record 200 meters in 1:58.23 and an American-record 100 in 55.63 (the latter still stood in mid-1984). Her 1979 victories included gold medals at the indoor nationals in 100 and 200 yards; at the outdoor nationals and the Pan American Games the distances—100, 200, and 400—were meters, but the medals were still gold. But the 1980 boycott seemed to signal a downturn in Woodhead's career, marked by illness, injury, and dissatisfaction with her training. Still, in 1981 she was never far from the top: she won silver medals in the indoor nationals in 200 yards, 500 yards, and 1000 yards; in the outdoors she was second in the 200-meter individual medley and third in the 100- and 200-meter freestyle. She had more of a slump in 1982, her only gold a first-place finish in the 200 yards in the indoor nationals. In 1983 she was second both in 200 and 400 meters at the outdoor nationals, and at the Pan American and Pan Pacific Games she won gold medals in the 200 meters. By 1984 her training was solid, and going into competition at the Los Angeles Olympics she was relaxed—so relaxed that when she put aside her novel to get ready for her preliminary heat in the 200-meter freestyle she realized she had forgotten her swimsuit. Borrowing one from a teammate in another heat, she proceeded to win her own, and went on to win the silver medal in the event, only a foot and a half behind the first-place winner, teammate Mary Wayte.

U.S. SWIMMING RECORDS

Event	Swimmer	Time	Date
100M Freestyle	Cynthia Woodhead	55.63	1979
200M Freestyle	Cynthia Woodhead	1:59.36	1979
400M Freestyle	Tiffany Cohen	4:07.10	1984
800M Freestyle	Kim Linehan	8:24.70	1979
1500M Freestyle	Kim Linehan	16:04.49	1979
100M Backstroke	Sue Walsh	1:02.48	1982
200M Backstroke	Sue Walsh	2:13.86	1983
100M Breastroke	Tracy Caulkins	1:10.40	1980
200M Breastroke	Tracy Caulkins	2:32.48	1981
100M Butterfly	Mary T. Meagher	57.93	1981
200M Butterfly	Mary T. Meagher	2:05.96	1981
200M Medley	Tracy Caulkins	2:14.18	1981
400M Medley	Tracy Caulkins	4:39.24	1984
4 × 100M Freestyle Relay	Habernigg, Major, Woodhead, Williams	3:45.68	1981
4 × 200M Freestyle Relay	Linzmeier, Habernigg, Cohen, Woodhead	8:07.44	1981
4 × 100M Medley Relay	Carlisle, Rhodenbaugh, Meagher, Elkins	4:11.59	1980

WORLD SWIMMING RECORDS

Event	Swimmer	Country	Time	Date
100M Freestyle	Barbara Krause	East Germany	54.79	1980
200M Freestyle	Kristin Otto	West Germany	1:57.75	1984
400M Freestyle	Tracey Wickham	Australia	4:06.28	1978
800M Freestyle	Tracey Wickham	Australia	8:24.62	1978
1500M Freestyle	Kim Linehan	USA	16:04.49	1979
100M Backstroke	Rica Reinisch	East Germany	1:00.86	1980
200M Backstroke	Cornelia Sirch	East Germany	2:09.91	1982
100M Breaststroke	Ute Geweniger	East Germany	1:08.51	1983
200M Breaststroke	Lin Kaciusyte	USSR	2:28.36	1979
100M Butterfly	Mary T. Meagher	USA	57.93	1981
200M Butterfly	Mary T. Meagher	USA	2:05.96	1981
200M Medley	Ute Geweniger	East Germany	2:11.73	1981
400M Medley	Petra Schneider	East Germany	4:36.10	1982
4 × 100M Freestyle Relay	Krause, Metschuk, Huisenbeck, Diers	East Germany	3:42.71	1980
4 × 200M Freestyle Relay	Otto, Strauss, Surch, Meineke	East Germany	8:02.27	1983
4 × 100M Medley Relay	Kleber, Geweniger, Geissler, Meineke	East Germany	4:05.79	1983

OLYMPIC SWIMMING RECORDS

Event	Swimmer	Country	Time	Date/Place
100M Freestyle	Barbara Krause	East Germany	54.79	1980/Moscow
200M Freestyle	Barbara Krause	East Germany	1:58.33	1980/Moscow
400M Freestyle	Tiffany Cohen	USA	4:07.10	1984/Los Angeles
800M Freestyle	Tiffany Cohen	USA	8:24.95	1984/Los Angeles
100M Backstroke	Rica Reinisch	East Germany	1:00.86	1980/Moscow
200M Backstroke	Rica Reinisch	East Germany	2:11.77	1980/Moscow
100M Breaststroke	Petra Van Staveren	Netherlands	1:09.88	1984/Los Angeles
200M Breaststroke	Lin Kaciusyte	USSR	2:29.54	1980/Moscow
100M Butterfly	Mary T. Meagher	USA	59.26	1984/Los Angeles
200M Butterfly	Mary T. Meagher	USA	2:06.90	1984/Los Angeles
200M Medley	Tracy Caulkins	USA	2:12.64	1984/Los Angeles
400M Medley	Petra Schneider	East Germany	4:36.29	1980/Moscow
4 × 100M Freestyle Relay	Krause, Metschuk, Huisenbeck, Diers	East Germany	3:42.71	1980/Moscow
4 × 100M Medley Relay	Reinisch, Geweniger, Metschuk, Pollack	East Germany	4:06.67	1980/Moscow

Diving

Maxine "Micki" King Hogue
born Pontiac, Michigan

A fourth-place Olympic springboard finish isn't bad—especially if you've got a broken arm. In 1968 at the Mexico City Games, King was in first place after eight of her ten dives; on her ninth, she hit the board. She took her tenth dive with a broken left forearm, and finished fourth. Four years later, at the Munich Games, King got her gold—with the same reverse one-and-a-half somersault. She was Diver of the Year in springboard in 1965, 1969, and 1972; in 1969 she was platform Diver of the Year as well. She holds nine U.S. national diving titles, and four Canadian ones (two each in 1-meter and 3-meter); she was also a water-polo player (with two national titles), an Air Force officer, and the first woman coach at the Air Force Academy. A founding member of the Women's Sports Foundation, she was elected to the International Swimming Hall of Fame in 1978 and the Women's Sports Hall of Fame in 1983.

Ulrika Knape
born Sweden

Blonde and beautiful, Knape had an equally stunning coach in the late Gunnel Weinas, and between them they dominated world diving in the first half of the 70's. Knape held 38 national Swedish titles. In two European championships, two world championships, and two Olympics, she won more total medals than any other diver, male or female. She was World Platform Diver of the Year 1972-74. In the 1972 Munich Olympics she won the gold medal in platform, silver in springboard; four years later, at the Montreal Games, she won the silver in platform. At the world championships in 1973 she won the gold medal in platform and silver in springboard; in 1975 she won the bronze in platform. She won gold medals in both springboard and platform at the 1974 European championships, and gold European diving cups in both springboard and platform in 1975. Knape was the first Swedish diver to be an Olympic gold medalist in 60 years, since the days of Swedish diving supremacy. She was elected to the International Swimming Hall of Fame in 1982.

Ingrid Kramer
born Dresden, Germany, July 29, 1943

In number of Olympic gold medals and length of time as leading woman diver, Kramer is surpassed only by Patricia McCormick of the U.S. Kramer was fourth in springboard and eighth in platform at the 1958 European championships; two years later, at the Rome Olympics, she won the gold medal in springboard (breaking a U.S. streak of eight consecutive victories), and the gold medal in platform as well. At the 1962 European championships she was first in both springboard and platform, performing perhaps the greatest dives of her career. At Tokyo in the 1964 Olympics Kramer again won the gold medal in springboard, the silver in platform. At the 1968 Mexico City Olympics, she placed fifth in springboard. Kramer was elected to the International Swimming Hall of Fame in 1975, the first East German so honored.

Kelly McCormick
born Anaheim, California, February 13, 1960

Born four years after Patricia Keller McCormick, her mother, won her second Olympic double gold at the Melbourne Games, Kelly McCormick was a first-time Olympian at Los Angeles in 1984. A member of the U.S. national team since 1977, she was national springboard champion in 1-meter 1979-81 and in 3-meter in 1983 and 1984; she won the gold medal in 3-meter springboard at the 1983 Pan American Games. At the 1984 Olympic trials she performed brilliantly, accumulating top points in the finals. At the Los Angeles Games, she won the silver medal with 527.46 points; Sylvie Bernier of Canada, with 530.70, won the gold. Despite the pressure of her mother's accomplishments and of her own reputation for a lack of consistency in her otherwise stunning diving, McCormick was gracious throughout. When it was over, she embraced Bernier warmly and told a New York *Times* reporter, "I had a great time, it was an honor to be here."

Patricia Keller McCormick
born Seal Beach, California, May 12, 1930

After her first three years in diving competition, a physician who examined McCormick said of her accumulated cracked bones and scars, "I've seen worse casualty cases, but only where a building caved in." But practice—80-100 dives a day, six days a week—made just about perfect. In 1949 McCormick won the national platform title; she successfully defended it in 1950 and took the springboard national championship as well. In 1951 she won all five U.S. indoor and outdoor championships, and at the Pan American Games won the gold medal in platform diving and the silver in springboard. At the 1952 Olympics in Helsinki, McCormick won gold medals in three-meter springboard and in platform. Over the next four years she won 77 national championships, and at the 1955 Pan American Games took the gold medal in both platform and springboard. At the 1956 Olympics in Mexico City, McCormick repeated her gold-winning performances in both springboard and platform, achieving a unique "double double." The Melbourne Games were held eight months after her first child was born—she had continued her training through her pregnancy. She was 1956 AP Athlete of the Year and winner of the Sullivan Award, and was elected to the International Swimming Hall of Fame in 1965; she was named to the Women's Sports Hall of Fame in 1984.

Cynthia Potter
born August 27, 1950

The head diving coach at the University of Arizona, Tucson (and before that at Southern Methodist University) can share considerable first-hand experiences with her divers: the holder of 28 national diving championships, Potter was a member of four U.S. Olympic diving teams (1968-80) and World Diver of the Year in 1970, 1971, and 1977. In her years of national competition, 1968-79, she won at least a title a year; in international competition, 1967-80, she won more than 20 golds. Her specialty was springboard, but at the 1970 World University Games she won the silver medal in platform as well as the springboard gold. At the 1975 Pan American Games she won the bronze medal in springboard, and at the 1978 world championships won the silver. She finished seventh at the 1972 Munich Olympics; four years later, at the Montreal Games, she won the bronze medal (in 1980 the U.S. did not compete). During and after her competitive career, Potter worked actively in behalf of her sport, as a member of the U.S. Olympic Diving Committee since 1972, and in support of women's athletics. Her expertise has added much to television's coverage of national diving championships in the years since her retirement from competition.

Aileen Riggin
born Newport, Rhode Island, May 2, 1906

Tiny Aileen Riggin—she is always described that way—was fourteen when she won the first Olympic women's springboard event, at Paris in 1924. At her next Olympic appearance, four years later in Amsterdam, she won the silver medal in springboard *and* the bronze medal in the 100-

meter backstroke. In her amateur career she had one indoor and three outdoor titles in the U.S. springboard championships, and swimming for the great Women's Swimming Association of New York, she shared in two 800-meter relay championships and one 400-yard relay title. A fine natural athlete and a beautiful stylist, in 1922 she made the first motion pictures of underwater swimming and slow-motion swimming and diving. Turning professional in 1926, she played the Hippodrome, toured with Gertrude Ederle, starred in Billy Rose's first Aquacade, made movies, and wrote. She was named to the International Swimming Hall of Fame in 1967.

Christina Seufert
born Sacramento, California, January 13, 1957

Seufert and Kelly McCormick, both springboard specialists on the national team since 1977, are great friends, competitors, and were the two U.S. springboard divers at the 1984 Los Angeles Olympics. Seufert had made the U.S. Olympic team in 1980, but did not compete because of the U.S. boycott. Her national titles are few and far between (1980, the 3-meter outdoor championship, and again in 1983), but she has consistently placed in the top three or four. She won the Swedish Cup title in 1981 and 1983, and the silver medal in the 1982 world championships. At the 1984 Olympic trials, Seufert was the oldest competitor and, at 5' 9", the tallest (a mixed blessing in diving—the line looks good, but the extra inches have to be coordinated and aligned). In Los Angeles, she was seventh after making the four required dives; she came from behind in her optionals to win the bronze medal. Her last dive—last in the competition, and the last before her retirement—merited the highest score awarded in the event.

Kelly McCormick

Christina Seufert

Wendy Wyland
born Jackson, Michigan, November 25, 1964

When Wyland won her world championship platform title in 1982, the wind was so strong as she stood 33 feet above the water that the flags were in tatters. Nevertheless, her performance—typically—was strong, consistent, controlled. Platform is Wyland's specialty, but she is proficient in springboard as well (she is a former junior trampoline champion). At the 1983 Pan American Games she won the gold medal in platform and the silver in springboard. She was U.S. indoor platform champion 1981-84, outdoor champion as well in 1982, and won the platform title at the 1983 National Sports Festival; she has been several times runner-up in 1- and 3-meter springboard in national competition. At the July 1984 Olympic trials she unexpectedly placed second to Michele Mitchell, and she was second to Mitchell again at the Los Angeles Games: Zhou Jihong of China won the gold medal, Mitchell the silver, Wyland the bronze. After her low-scoring required dives, Wyland stood fifth in the competition; in her optionals, she forged ahead to accumulate enough points for third place. She told New York *Times* reporter Lawrie Mifflin, "At the world championships I was an unknown, and afterward I felt at first like it was a fluke. But this medal means a lot, because I've grown up a lot more. It's been a long time since 1982." At the 1984 U.S. outdoor championships, two weeks after the Olympics, Mitchell won the gold and Wyland the silver.

Wendy Wyland

U.S. CHAMPIONS
Springboard

Year	Champion
1921	Helen Meany
1922	Helen Meany
1923	Aileen Riggin
1924	Aileen Riggin
1925	Aileen Riggin
1926	Helen Meany
1927	Helen Meany
1928	Lillian Fergus
1929	Georgia Coleman
1930	Georgia Coleman
1931	Georgia Coleman
1932	Katherine Rawls
1933	Katherine Rawls
1934	Katherine Rawls
1935	Mary Hoerger
1936	Claudia Eckert
1937	Marjorie Gestring
1938	Marjorie Gestring
1939	Helen Crienkovich
1940	Marjorie Gestring
1941	Helen Crienkovich
1942	Ann Ross
1943	Ann Ross
1944	Ann Ross
1945	Helen Crienkovich Morgan
1946	Zoe Ann Olsen
1947	Zoe Ann Olsen
1948	Zoe Ann Olsen
1949	Zoe Ann Olsen
1950	Patricia McCormick
1951	Patricia McCormick
1952	not held
1953	Patricia McCormick
1954	Patricia McCormick
1955	Patricia McCormick
1956	Patricia McCormick
1957	Paula Jean Myers
1958	Paula Jean Myers
1959	Irene MacDonald
1960	Patsy Willard
1961	Joel Lenzi
1962	Barbara McAlister
1963	Jeanne Collier
1964	Barbara Talmage
1965	Micki King
1966	Sue Gossick
1967	Micki King
1968	Jerrie Adair
1969	Micki King
1970	Micki King

Year	Champion
1971	Cynthia Potter
1972	Cynthia Potter
1973	Carrie Irish
1974	Christine Loock
1975	Cynthia Potter McIngvale
1976	Cynthia Potter McIngvale
1977	Christine Loock
1978	Jennifer Chandler
1979	Michele Hain
1980	Christina Seufert
1981	Megan Neyer
1982	Kelly McCormick
1983	Christina Seufert
1984	Wendy Williams

Platform

Year	Champion
1916	Evelyn Burnett
1917	Aileen Allen
1918	Josephine Bartlett
1919	Betty Grimes
1920	not held
1921	Helen Meany
1922	Helen Meany
1923	Helen Meany
1924	not held
1925	Helen Meany
1926	Esther Foley
1927	not held
1928	Helen Meany
1929	Georgia Coleman
1930	Georgia Coleman
1931	Georgia Coleman
1932	not held
1933	Dorothy Poynton
1934	Dorothy Poynton Hill
1935	Dorothy Poynton Hill
1936	Ruth Jump
1937	Ruth Jump
1938	Ruth Jump
1939	Marjorie Gestring
1940	Marjorie Gestring
1941	Helen Crienkovich
1942	Margaret Reinholdt
1943	Jeanne Kessler
1944	not held
1945	Helen Crienkovich Morgan
1946	Victoria Draves
1947	Victoria Draves
1948	Victoria Draves
1949	Patricia McCormick

Year	Champion
1950	Patricia McCormick
1951	Patricia McCormick
1952	not held
1953	Paula Jean Myers
1954	Patricia McCormick
1955	June Stover Irwin
1956	Patricia McCormick
1957	Paula Jean Myers
1958	Paula Jean Myers
1959	Paula Jean Myers
1960	Juno Stover Irwin
1961	Barbara McAlister
1962	Linda Cooper
1963	Barbara M. Talmadge
1964	Patsy Willard
1965	Leslie Bush
1966	Shirley Teeples
1967	Leslie Bush
1968	Ann Peterson
1969	Micki King
1970	Cynthia Potter
1971	Cynthia Potter
1972	Janet Ely
1973	Deborah Keplar
1974	Teri York
1975	Janet Ely
1976	Barb Weinstein
1977	Christine Loock
1978	Melissa Briley
1979	Kit Salness
1980	Barb Weinstein
1981	Debbie Rush
1982	Wendy Wyland
1983	Michele Mitchell
1984	Michele Mitchell

OLYMPIC CHAMPIONSHIPS
Springboard

Year	Gold	Silver	Bronze
1920 Antwerp	Aileen Riggin USA	Helen Wainwright USA	Thelma Payne USA
1924 Paris	Elizabeth Becker USA	Aileen Riggin USA	Caroline Fletcher USA
1928 Amsterdam	Helen Meany USA	Dorothy Poynton USA	Georgia Coleman USA
1932 Los Angeles	Georgia Coleman USA	Katherine Rawls USA	Jane Fauntz USA

Year	Gold	Silver	Bronze
1936 Berlin	Marjorie Gestring USA	Katherine Rawls USA	Dorothy Poynton Hill USA
1948 London	Victoria Draves USA	Zoe Ann Olsen USA	Patricia Elsener USA
1952 Helsinki	Patricia McCormick USA	Madeleine Moreau France	Zoe Ann Olsen USA
1956 Melbourne	Patricia McCormick USA	Jeanne Stunyo USA	Irene McDonald Canada
1960 Rome	Ingrid Kramer East Germany	Paula Jean Myers Pope USA	Elizabeth Ferris Great Britain
1964 Tokyo	Ingrid Kramer East Germany	Jeanne Collier USA	Mary "Patsy" Willard USA
1968 Mexico City	Sue Gossick USA	Tamara Pogoscheva USSR	Keala O'Sullivan USA
1972 Munich	Micki King USA	Ulrika Knape Sweden	Marina Janicke East Germany
1976 Montreal	Jennifer Chandler USA	Christa Kohler East Germany	Cynthia Potter USA
1980 Moscow	Irina Kalinina USSR	Martina Proeber East Germany	Karin Guthke East Germany
1984 Los Angeles	Zhou Jihong China	Michelle Mitchell USA	Wendy Wyland USA

Platform

Year	Gold	Silver	Bronze
1912 Stockholm	Greta Johansson Sweden	Lisa Regnell Sweden	Isabelle White Great Britain
1920 Antwerp	Stefani Fryland-Clausen Denmark	Eileen Armstrong Great Britain	Eva Ollivier Sweden
1924 Paris	Caroline Smith USA	Elizabeth Becker USA	Hjordis Topel Sweden
1928 Amsterdam	Elizabeth Becker Pinkston USA	Georgia Coleman USA	Lala Sjoquist Sweden
1932 Los Angeles	Dorothy Poynton USA	Georgia Coleman USA	Marion Roper USA
1936 Berlin	Dorothy Poynton Hill USA	Velma Dunn USA	Kathe Kohler West Germany
1948 London	Victoria Draves USA	Patricia Elsener USA	Birte Chistoffersen Denmark

Year	Gold	Silver	Bronze
1952 Helsinki	Patricia McCormick USA	Paula Jean Myers USA	Juno Irwin Stover USA
1956 Melbourne	Patricia McCormick USA	Juno Irwin Stover USA	Paula Jean Myers USA
1960 Rome	Ingrid Kramer East Germany	Paula Jean Myers Pope USA	Ninel Krutova USSR
1964 Tokyo	Lesley Bush USA	Ingrid Kramer East Germany	Galina Alekseyeva USSR
1968 Mexico City	Milena Duchkova Czechoslovakia	Natalya Lobanova USSR	Ann Peterson USA
1972 Munich	Ulrika Knape Sweden	Miena Duchkova Czechoslovakia	Marina Janicke East Germany
1976 Montreal	Elena Vaytsekhovskaya USSR	Ulrika Knape Sweden	Deborah Wilson USA
1980 Moscow	Martina Jaschke East Germany	Servard Emirzyan USSR	Liana Tsotadze USSR
1984 Los Angeles	Sylvie Bernier Canada	Kelly McCormick USA	Christina Seufert USA

Synchronized Swimming

Candy Costie
born Seattle, Washington, March 12, 1963
Tracie Ruiz
born Honolulu, Hawaii, February 4, 1963

Unlike several pairs of synchronized swimmers, Ruiz and Costie are not identical twins. They don't even look particularly alike—until they get into the pool, where they have been partners since 1975. At the 1982 world championships, Ruiz won the gold medal in solo and she and Costie took the silver in duet. In August 1983, at both the American Cup competition and the Pan American Games, Ruiz again won the gold medal in solo and the two won the duet event (their American Cup gold medals were presented by Esther Williams). Their style is powerful, precise, and acrobatic—the quintessence of the American approach. They gained their berth for the 1984 Olympics at the national championships held in April, at which Ruiz was first in solo, Costie runner-up, and the pair first in duet. Sarah Josephson, third in solo, was named Olympic alternate. At an international meet in May, the Rome Open II, Ruiz and Costie were respectively first and second in compulsory figures and solos, and had six out of a possible seven tens in duet to take the gold medal. They went on to win the duet gold medal at the 1984 Los Angeles Games, and Ruiz was first in the solo competition (Carolyn Waldo of Canada won the silver and Miwako Motoyoshi of Japan the bronze.)

Sharon Hambrook
born Canada
Kelly Kryczka
born Canada

Hambrook and Kryczka are world champion in pairs, their title won in 1982. At the Pan Pacific Games in Melbourne in March 1983, Hambrook was first in solo and she and her partner took the duet crown. In August Hambrook was second to Tracie Ruiz of the U.S. in solo, and she and Kryczka were second to Ruiz and Candy Costie in duet in the American Cup competition. Their difference in height (Kryczka is four inches taller than Hambrook) is least apparent in their superb compulsory figures, which are performed individually. At the Los Angeles Olympics in 1984 they were a very close second indeed to Candy Costie and Tracie Ruiz of the U.S.

Karen Josephson
born Bristol, Connecticut, January 10, 1964
Sarah Josephson
born Bristol, Connecticut, January 10, 1964

Identical twins, the Josephsons are 1983 national collegiate champions; they placed second in the 1983 Pan American trials and the Rome international championship. They have been swimming together since they were eight, and work in possibly the most comprehensive training program ever developed (ranging from distance and interval swimming to dance, Nautilus, visualization, and yoga). Just behind Tracie Ruiz and Candy Costie in U.S. competition, they are catching up. At the national championships in April 1984 (which served as Olympic trials), Sarah Josephson, who came in third in solo, was selected as alternate to train with Ruiz and Costie for the Los Angeles Games.

Tracie Ruiz

Esther Williams

She was the Million Dollar Mermaid, and also the 100-meter freestyle national champion in 1939, with a time of 1:09, swimming for the Los Angeles Athletic Club. Williams was ready for the 1940 Olympics, but World War II intervened. The 1940 San Francisco World's Fair Aquacade needed a female lead to appear opposite Johnny Weissmuller. Weissmuller had previously worked with Eleanor Holm, but wanted someone taller and picked Williams at an open call. Her many M-G-M movies did much to popularize synchronized swimming, and after her performing career she continued to encourage young swimmers and promote the sport, and has made instructional films and videos on teaching infants to swim. Interestingly, while today's star American synchronized swimmers are gymnastic and acrobatic, Williams's more balletic and extravagant style is apparent in the look of the Canadian swimmers. Williams was elected to the International Swimming Hall of Fame in 1966.

Distance Swimming

Greta Andersen
born Copenhagen, Denmark, May 1, 1927

Although a healthy and active child, Andersen was not particularly interested in sports. Her father, a national gymnastics champion, took a dim view of this, and enrolled his teenage daughter in a swimming school; within six months she was the second fastest in Denmark. Over the next two years she broke all Danish girls' records; she qualified easily for the 1948 London Olympics, where she won the gold medal in 100-meter freestyle relay. After the Games she set a world record for 100 yards— 58.2—that stood for seven years. When she left amateur competition she held 24 national titles and 4 European championships. Andersen had visited California in 1950, liked it, and returned to live in the U.S. in 1953, eventually becoming a citizen. She worked as a swimming instructor, and in 1956 entered a professional distance race in the Salton Sea. Several men beat her, but she was the first woman to finish, doing 10½ miles in 4:25. She continued to race in the U.S., Canada, and Mexico, and a pattern was developing: she was always the first woman, and usually second overall. But she knew she could beat the men. In 1957 she did, in an English Channel race in which 24 swimmers started, 2 finished, Andersen winning in 13:53, Ken Wray of Great Britain second in 16:00. That year she swam 26 miles along the coast at Guaymas, Mexico, finishing second to Tom Park of the U.S.; in 1958, Andersen's greatest year, 27 swimmers, including Park, entered the race, and Andersen beat all of them. She swam the English Channel again, coming in ahead of four men with a time of 11:01; also in 1958 she swam the 18-mile Lake St. John in Quebec in 8:17, again defeating all competition. That year, too, she made a double crossing of the Catalina Channel. Andersen's route was a total of 38 miles: she pushed too hard going over, doing 19 miles in an incredible 10:49, but nonetheless was able to finish the return swim, for a total time of 26:53. The following year, 1959, saw a third successful English Channel crossing, and a swim from the mainland to Catalina Island in 11:07, a time that broke the record set by Florence Chadwick. In 1962 she swam Lake Michigan, 50 miles—farther than anyone else, man or woman, had ever done. Andersen made three solo attempts at a double crossing of the English Channel in 1964 and 1965; each time she was successful in the first leg, but could not complete the return. In her October 1964 attempt, which was thwarted by gales on the return, she swam England-to-France, the more difficult crossing, in a record 13:14; she was thirty-seven. Andersen believed she could compete on equal terms with men, and she proved it: in her professional career she beat every man she swam against at least once. She was elected to the International Swimming Hall of Fame in 1969.

Florence Chadwick
born San Diego, California, November 9, 1918

When in 1950 the London *Daily Mail* ran a contest swim across the English Channel, the paper regretfully rejected Chadwick's entry: she had no previous record nor reputation. She had swum since she was ten in San Diego Bay, and won a number of regional contests. But her best in national competition was a second place—once—when she was fourteen, and in 1936 she hadn't made the U.S. Olympic team, having placed fourth in the trials. And even that was a long time ago. But Chadwick wanted to swim, and realized she was an ocean swimmer, a distance swimmer. She took a job with Aramco and practiced in the Persian Gulf for a Channel attempt. When the *Daily Mail* wouldn't sponsor her, she made the try at her own expense. She didn't succeed in that attempt, in July; but she certainly did a month later, on August 8, in a record 13:23. Reaching Dover, she observed, "I feel fine. I am quite prepared to swim back." (Back, in this case, means against the tides.) The following year, on September 11, 1951, she became the first woman to swim the Channel England-to-France, in 16:22; she repeated her feat on September 4, 1953 (in 14:42) and October 12, 1955 (in 13:55). She was the first woman to swim the Catalina Channel; she did it in 13:47, a record time. Her swim across the Straits of Gibraltar in 1953 (in 5:06) also beat all previous times, men's or women's. After her 1950 English Channel swim, San Diego had welcomed her wildly, but she was broke from the expenses she had incurred. Only later did she begin to realize financial reward for her accomplishments, through radio and TV appearances, endorsements, and exhibitions. She encouraged the teaching of swimming to children, and in her public appearances promoted the value of sport and fitness for everyone. She became a stockbroker in 1969, but continued to invest in swimming as well as the market, coaching promising young distance swimmers of another generation. She was elected to the International Swimming Hall of Fame in 1970.

Gertrude Ederle
born New York, New York, October 23, 1906

The first woman to swim the English Channel, in 1927 Ederle took two hours off the existing record with her time of 14:31—which means of course that she swam it considerably faster than any man had ever done. Her record stood until 1964, when it was broken by another woman, Denmark's Greta Andersen, in 13:14. As an amateur, Ederle held world records at every distance from 100 to 800 meters. In 1922, in the course of a single 500-meter swim at Brighton Beach, New York, she broke seven world records at various distances along the way. Also in 1922 she held national championships in 220 and 440 (yards), and had her first taste of distance swimming: although at the time she had never done more than 220 yards, she defeated a field of 50 and upset Hilda James of Great Britain in an international competition for the J. P. Day Cup, swimming three miles in New York Bay. At the Paris Olympics in 1924, she won bronze medals in the 100- and 400-meter freestyle, and a gold in the 4 × 100-meter freestyle relay. According to her coach, although Ederle was a fine competitor when challenged, she lacked confidence; her older sister, Margaret, also a swimmer, encouraged and supported her. Ederle received a tumultuous New York tickertape welcome after her Channel swim, but was left with another memento of her feat—deafness. After her own career was over, she taught swimming to deaf children. She was elected to the International Swimming Hall of Fame in 1965 and to the Women's Sports Hall of Fame in 1980.

Diana Nyad
born New York, New York

The embodiment of her Greek name, Nyad began swimming as a child in Ft. Lauderdale, Florida, where she grew up. By the time she was twelve she was state champion in 100-meter and 200-meter backstroke. After a promising early career, viral endocarditis and the effects of three months' bedrest put training for the 1968 Olympics out of the question and the rest of her amateur career in doubt. Still determined to swim, she was introduced to marathon swimming by Buck Dawson, director of the International Swimming Hall of Fame (located in Ft. Lauderdale). Physically right and psychologically attuned to distance swimming, Nyad trained at Dawson's camp in Ontario and entered her first professional race in July 1970, ten miles in Lake Ontario. She finished tenth overall (out of 60), and broke the women's world record with a time of 4:22. Over the next five years (during which she finished college and graduate school) she entered races all over the world. She set a world record (8:11) in the 22-mile Bay of Naples race in June 1974, and was world champion that year. But lack of organization—and decent compensation—on the pro circuit led Nyad to solo attempts. Her first was a two-way crossing of Lake Ontario (only five swimmers had previously done it one-way, south to north; the north-south route meant fighting the currents of the Niagara River). Nyad completed the first half, 32 miles north to south, in water whose temperature unexpectedly dropped ten degrees, in 18:20. Allowed by marathon rules no more than ten minutes' rest, she returned to the water to swim back and lost consciousness at 20:30. Her first attempt to swim around Manhattan in September 1975 was thwarted by tides—because of hurricanes in the southeast, the rivers were flowing faster and the tides were off. Nyad was caught at the Battery, unable to gain a yard; after treading water for two hours, fighting not to drop back, she found the tide coming down the East River was still too strong. It would probably not change for another two hours and Nyad had to quit. She tried again on October 6, and completed the circuit in the remarkable record time of 7:57. Surprisingly, the English

Channel—not the most difficult of swims—defeated her three times in 1976. In the summer of 1977, after training for a year, she tried and failed to finish a 130-mile swim from Havana to Marathon Key, Florida, in a shark-proof cage, but her 89-mile swim from Florida to Cuba still stood as a world distance record in mid-1984. Nyad has swum thousands of miles under all kinds of conditions. Not the least of her accomplishments is her book, *Other Shores,* which gives a vivid and immediate picture of what it's like to do that.

TABLE TENNIS

You probably first knew it as Ping-Pong, and the Chinese still do—the onomatopoetic sound of the trade name is pleasing to them. In its present form, the game is about as old as the century. The International Table Tennis Federation was formed in 1926, and the first world championship was held in London that year. Nine nations (Austria, Czechoslovakia, Denmark, England, Germany, Hungary, India, Sweden, and Wales) competed—85 nations participated in the 1983 world championships, held in Tokyo. When the championships were held in Asia for the first time (Bombay, 1952), the Japanese players, particularly in men's singles, made a terrific showing. Not only did they use the new penholder grip, they played with sponge rubber racquets, making possible new and unpredictable loop drives, spins, and smashes. These innovations changed the very nature of table tennis: it became a fast and aggressive game of attack, not defense. The Asian players—first the Japanese, then the Chinese—played this game brilliantly. When the world championships were held in Peking in 1961, the Chinese took first place in women's singles, men's singles, and men's team events; 15,000 spectators watched each session, and thousands more stood in line outside the stadium. Table tennis will be an Olympic sport for the first time at the Seoul Games in 1988, with women's and men's singles and doubles (no team events or mixed doubles).

As of 1984, **Ruth Hughes Aarons** is the only American, man or woman, to have won the world championship singles title (women play for the G. Geist Prize); her victory was in 1936, and the next year she played on the U.S. team that won the Corbillon Cup, the trophy for the team world championship. She won the world mixed doubles title 1934-37 with, respectively, Sam Silberman, Sidney Hertner, Victor Barna, and Robert Blattner. She was U.S. women's singles champion as well in those years, and doubles champion (with Anne Sigman) in 1936. She never lost a match in organized tournament play.

Angelica Rozeanu of Romania won six consecutive world singles titles, 1950-55, a record that stood in 1984. (She was also mixed doubles champion in 1952 and 1953, playing with Ferenc Sido.) **Maria Mednyanszky** of Hungary was world singles champion five times, 1927-31. World championship women's doubles have been played for the W. J. Pope Trophy since 1928, and Mednyanszky won the first title, playing with Erika Flamm;

133

she won six more (1930-35) with **Anna Sipos,** who was singles champion in 1932 and 1933. In mixed doubles, Mednyanszky won the world title six times, with three different partners: 1927 and 1928 with Zoltan Mechlovits; 1930, 1931, and 1934 with Miklos Szabodos; and 1933 with Istvan Kelen.

The top American player of the 50's was **Leah Thall Neuberger,** known as "Ping": in her career she won more than 500 tournaments. She was national singles champion 9 times (1947, 1949, 1951-53, 1955-57, and 1961), and won the Canadian singles title as well 11 times. In U.S. championship women's doubles, Neuberger took the title 12 times: in 1941 with Mary Baumback; 1943 with Mae Clothier; 1944 with Helen Baldwin; 1947-49 with her sister, Thelma J. Thall; 1951, 1952, 1954, and 1956 with Mildred Shahian; and 1953 and 1955 with Peggy Folke. In mixed doubles she won in 1942 and 1943 with Bill Holzrichter, in 1951 with Douglas Cortland, in 1952 and 1956-58 with Sol Schiff, and in 1953 with Tibor Hazi. In world competition, Neuberger played on the winning U.S. Corbillon Cup team in 1949 and won the mixed doubles title in 1956, playing with Erwin Klein; her sister had won the same title in 1948 with Richard Miles.

In the 60's, Californian **Patty Martinez** was three times national singles champion, in 1965, 1967, and 1969; in doubles, she won in 1967 with Priscilla Hirschkowitz and in 1969 and 1970 with Wendy Hicks. She was twice national mixed doubles champion, in 1967 with Billie Bergstrand and in 1969 with Dal Joon Lee.

Across the Atlantic, **Diana Rowe** and her twin sister, **Rosalind,** were formidable players: Diana was lefthanded, her sister righthanded. They used wooden paddles, and were excellent defensive players; they also had fine attacking forehands. The pair won the world doubles title in 1951 and 1954, and were runners-up in 1952, 1953, and 1955.

Overall, in world competition the Asian nations have dominated; notable players are China's **Lin Hui-ching** and **Cheng Min-chih,** who won the world doubles championship in 1965 and 1971 (in 1971 Lin won the world singles title as well, and the mixed doubles with Chang Shih-lin). The Chinese players had a superb technique with strokes; defensive players, they never used the loop drive, but relied on quick response and speed of play.

In this generation of players, **Insook Bhushan** is the top American and a competitor of world class. Originally from South Korea, Bhushan was captain of the world champion South Korean team that won the title in 1973. After coming to the U.S., she began competing internationally for her adopted country in 1977; she has been six times national champion (1976-78, 1981-83). In 1983 she had a particularly fine year, taking four gold medals at the National Sports Festival (singles, doubles with Diana Gee, mixed doubles with Brian Masters, and team), and another four in the Pan American Games (singles, doubles with Gee, mixed doubles with Sean O'Neill, and team). In December she swept the 1983 national championships: without losing a game in the course of the tournament, she won singles, doubles with Gee, and mixed doubles with Danny Seemiller. Not surprisingly, she was named the U.S. Table Tennis Association's Amateur Athlete of the year.

TENNIS

Mary Outerbridge, of Staten Island, New York, on a visit to Bermuda in 1874, was intrigued by the game popular among British officers stationed there. She returned to New York with a net, balls, and rackets, and had some difficulty with customs officials, who had never seen such equipment before. She then arranged through her brother, a director of the Staten Island Cricket and Baseball Club, for a court to be set up on the club's grounds. In this way was the game of tennis brought to America by a woman. Within 15 years, lawn tennis clubs were popular throughout the city, and the 7-year-old U.S. National Lawn Tennis Association (later the USLTA) voted to include "Lady Lawn Tennis Players" in its organization. Across the Atlantic, women were admitted to the championship at Wimbledon in 1884. But for almost another century, women amateurs lacked the sponsorship available to men, and women professionals played for discounted purses. The Davis Cup for men in international competition was established in 1900; not until 1963 was the comparable Federation Cup for women offered by the International Lawn Tennis Federation. In 1973, for the first time, the prize money—$25,000—was the same for men and women competing for the U.S. national singles championships. The turning point was the establishment of the Women's Professional Tour, sponsored by Virginia Slims, in 1970; the players who put their careers on the line to participate in the tour in the face of considerable political opposition were Jane "Peaches" Bartkowicz, Rosemary Casals, Nancy Richey Gunter, Julie M. Heldman, Billie Jean King, Kristy Pigeon, Valerie Zeigenfuss (all Americans) and the Australians Judy Tegart Dalton and Kerry Melville Reid. Since 1973, women's professional tennis has been organized by the Women's Tennis Association, which administers an international series of tours. Tennis was discontinued as an Olympic sport after the 1924 Games; 60 years later it reappeared at the Los Angeles Games as an exhibition, and is expected to have full competitive status in 1988.

Tracy Austin
born Rolling Hills, California, December 12, 1962
  Austin was sixteen years old in 1979—the year she defeated first Martina

Navratilova and then Chris Evert Lloyd to win the U.S. Open (the next day she returned to California to begin her junior year at Rollings Hills High). Austin seems to have been playing championship tennis from the cradle, winning national age group titles by the time she was ten; she holds a record 25 national junior titles. She won the Italian Open in 1979 (breaking Evert Lloyd's 125-match clay streak), and the U.S. Open again in 1981. Playing with her brother John, she won Wimbledon mixed doubles in 1980. She won the New York Avon Circuit Championship in 1980 and 1981, Eastbourne in 1980 and 1981, and the Canadian Open in 1981. On the Federation Cup team 1978-1980, the Wightman Cup team in 1978, 1979, and 1981; she was WTA Player of the Year in 1980. Beginning in 1981, a series of injuries called a halt to a remarkable career; sciatic nerve damage, a stress fracture in the back, a shoulder injury. She did not play for ten months in 1981 and 1982, and had to withdraw from Wimbledon in June 1983, not to play for eight months. She returned to competitive tennis in February 1984, winning her first match in an early round of the U.S. indoor championship, but then was upset by Pam Casale. Austin recognized that her concentration had been impaired by her forced layoff, but was determined to fight through: "I'll be where I was before if I work at it." But it will be a difficult road: in April, Austin pulled a hip muscle during the first round of the Carta Blanca Invitational and lost the match 4-6, 6-1, 6-2 to Bettina Bunge.

Carling Bassett
born Toronto, Ontario, Canada, October 9, 1967
   Top-ranked junior player in 1982, WTA Most Impressive Newcomer and *Tennis* magazine Newcomer of the Year in 1983, Bassett took a set from Chris Evert Lloyd at the Lipton Championships at Amelia Island, Florida, in April 1983 (the first set Evert Lloyd lost on her home court in

Tracy Austin   Carling Bassett

five years of tournament play). She "slumped" in early 1984, eliminated in early rounds of tournaments; then, by "playing, not thinking," began reaching quarterfinals and semifinals again. By the summer she was ranked sixteenth in the world; but in July she had to withdraw from the Canadian national championships, and in August from the tennis exhibition at the Los Angeles Olympics, because of mononucleosis. After a six-week layoff, she returned to competition with a strong game, more varied, she believed, than before her illness. She defeated Hana Mandlikova in the quarterfinals of the U.S. Open in September before losing to Evert Lloyd in the semifinals.

Pauline Betz Addie
born Dayton, Ohio, August 6, 1919
In 1946, Betz was ranked number one by the USLTA, and unofficially was listed as the top woman player in the world—and immediately thereafter her name disappears from the records. In 1947, she was suspended for her public support of a women's professional tour. She was U.S. singles champion 1942-44 and 1946; runner-up (to Sarah Palfrey Cooke) in 1941 and 1945. The first postwar Wimbledon champion (1946), she took her title without losing a set. The same year, she won the French mixed doubles (with Budge Patty), and in her Wightman Cup play won her two singles matches and her doubles (with Doris Hart). Ranked in the top ten 1939-46, number one in 1942-44 and 1946. She was both strong and agile, and BBC commentator Max Robertson said of her Wimbledon performance, "She played like a ballerina." She was named to the International Tennis Hall of Fame in 1965.

A. Louise Brough Clapp
born Oklahoma City, Oklahoma, March 11, 1923
One of the great postwar American players, Brough Clapp was Wimbledon singles champion 1948-50 and 1955 (runner-up three times) and U.S. singles champion in 1947 (runner-up five times). She was a tremendous doubles player: with Margaret Osborne du Pont, she won the Wimbledon doubles 1946, 1948-50, and 1954, the U.S. doubles twelve times (1942-50, 1955-57), and the French doubles in 1946, 1947, and 1949. With Doris Hart, she won the Australian doubles in 1950. In mixed doubles, she won Wimbledon four times (1946, with Thomas P. Brown, Jr.; 1947 and 1948 with John Bromwich; 1950, with Eric Sturgess). In the U.S. mixed doubles she was also a four-time winner (1942 with Frederick R. Schroeder, Jr., and 1947-49 with Bromwich, Brown, and Sturgess in that order). In Wightman Cup play, 1946-57, she won all 22 of her matches. She was ranked in the top ten 1941-50 and 1952-57. She and partner Osborne du Pont represented the old school of tennis. Playing in 1949 at Wimbledon against Gussie Moran and Pat Todd of the U.S., they disapproved entirely of Moran's costume and the furor surrounding it. But when they walked out to center court, Louise, in tennis historian Ted Tinling's words, "bent nearly double" to see the famous lace panties. She and Osborne du Pont were made members of the International Tennis Hall of Fame in 1967.

Maria Bueno
born São Paulo, Brazil, October 11, 1939

The first year Bueno won the Wimbledon singles championship, Alex Olmedo, born in Peru, took the men's title, and for the first time in fifty years, the "lap of honor" at the Wimbledon Ball in 1959 was not a waltz, but a cha-cha-cha. Bueno was Wimbledon singles champion again in 1960 and 1964; she took the doubles title in 1958 (with Althea Gibson), 1960 and 1963 (with Darlene Hard), 1965 (with Billie Jean Moffitt), and 1966 (with Nancy Richey). She was U.S. singles champion 1959, 1963, 1964, and 1966; doubles champion 1960 and 1962 (with Hard), 1966 (with Richey). In 1968 the team of Bueno and Margaret Smith Court took both the U.S. doubles championship and the U.S. Open doubles. In 1960, Bueno took the French doubles championship with Hard and mixed doubles with Robert Howe. A magnificent competitor, Bueno had ground strokes as powerful as her volleys; her performance made her a national hero, with a postage stamp and a statue to honor her. In 1978 she was named to the International Tennis Hall of Fame.

Rosemary Casals
born San Francisco, California, September 10, 1948

No question about it: the premiere doubles team of the late 60's and early 70's was Casals and Billie Jean King. Together they won Wimbledon five times (1967, 1968, 1970, 1971, 1973) and the U.S. Open doubles twice (1967 and 1974). Casals also took the U.S. doubles title in 1971 with Judy Tegart Dalton and in 1982 with Wendy Turnbull; also in 1982, she won the U.S. indoor doubles, again with Turnbull. In mixed doubles, she took the U.S. title in 1975 with Richard Stockton. In singles she was finalist twice in the U.S. Open, losing in 1970 to Margaret Smith Court and in 1971 to King; in 1973 she won the Family Circle Cup. She holds eight titles in the Virginia Slims circuit, 1970-78. She played on the Wightman Cup team 1967, 1976-81 (in 1977, 1979, and 1980 she was coach as well); she captained the Federation Cup team in 1980 and 1981 (she was on the team 1976-81).

Maureen Connolly Brinker
born San Diego, California, September 17, 1934; died June 21, 1969

"Little Mo" loved horses, but riding is expensive. So she took to playing tennis on the concrete public courts in San Diego. She came to the attention of coach Eleanor Tennant, and was national junior champion at thirteen. In 1950, she was ranked number ten among senior players, and number one 1951-53. She was the youngest American Wightman Cup player (1951-54), and in 1953 was the first woman to achieve the grand slam of the French, Wimbledon, U.S., and Australian championships in the same year—a feat unequalled until 1970 and not again since. (Martina Navratilova won the four events successively over two calendar years, 1983-84.) In 1954 Connolly was the Italian singles champion and won the French women's doubles (with Nell Hopman) and mixed doubles (with Lew Hoad); she was U.S. clay court singles champion in 1953 and 1954, and doubles champion (with Doris Hart) in 1954. She was only nineteen, and she still loved horses, and two weeks after her third Wimbledon title she had a bad riding accident that severely damaged her right leg; she could never again play competitive tennis. A baseline player, she had tremendous flat drives and brilliant accuracy that overcame even great serve-and-volley players like Doris Hart. In the years after her accident, before her death from cancer, she coached and worked, through the Maureen Connolly Brinker Foundation, to advance the cause of junior tennis. She was named to the International Tennis Hall of Fame in 1968.

Chris Evert Lloyd
born Ft. Lauderdale, Florida, December 21, 1954

Clay is her surface—Evert had 125 consecutive wins on clay, August 1973-May 1979, breaking her streak with a loss to Tracy Austin in the Italian championships. As of her 1984 victory in the Family Circle Cup tournament (which she also won in 1974-78 and in 1981), Evert had a clay court career record of 281-7. At sixteen, she won the U.S. eighteen-and-under singles title; three years later she had her first Wimbledon. She has a flawless baseline game, and made the two-handed backhand famous. Her style is not dramatic, but her cool play, her concentration, and her reserved manner—reminiscent of Helen Wills Moody—make her fascinating, and inexorable; she was WTA Player of the Year in 1981. Her great obstacle is her one-time doubles partner, Martina Navratilova, who in the early 80's is number one player in the world to Evert Lloyd's number two. Going into the Wimbledon tournament in the summer of 1984, Navratilova had defeated Evert Lloyd 11 consecutive times, but their later matches had been more competitive: after the 1984 Virginia Slims Championship final, Evert Lloyd said frankly, "The way I played today I probably would have killed anybody else." Although she lost to Navratilova in the 1984 Wimbledon finals, she played brilliantly in 7-6, 6-2 matches and Navratilova had to work for her victory. At the U.S. Open in September, their sixty-first meeting (they had been tied 30-all), Evert Lloyd lost to Navratilova 4-6, 6-4, 6-4. Evert Lloyd holds 15 grand slam singles titles (and more than 100 career singles titles); she won the French singles championship the same year she first took Wimbledon (1974) and again in 1975, 1979, 1980, and 1983. She won the U.S. Open 1975-78, 1980, and 1982, Wimbledon again in 1976 and 1981, and the Australian championship in 1982 and 1984. In doubles, Evert Lloyd took Wimbledon in 1976, playing with Olga Morozova in 1974 and Navratilova in 1975. Evert Lloyd won the Colgate series in 1977 and 1978, and the Virginia Slims circuit championship in 1972, 1973, 1975, 1977. She played on the Wightman Cup team 1971-73, 1975, 1977-82 and for the Federation Cup 1977-80 and 1982. In 1981 she was named Women's Sports Foundation Sportswoman of the Year and inducted into the Women's Sports Hall of Fame.

Zina Garrison
born Houston, Texas, November 16, 1963

A product of Houston's public parks tennis program, Garrison was 1982's WTA Most Impressive Newcomer, having won both the Wimbledon and U.S. Open junior championships in 1981. She took the American Tennis Association championship in 1979 and 1980, the youngest winner ever, and is the first black woman to be ranked number one in the Texas region. She was a quarterfinalist in her first pro event, the 1982 French Open. In the 1983-84 season she was a semifinalist in the Australian Open and runner-up for the U.S. clay court title.

Althea Gibson
born Silver, South Carolina, August 25, 1927

"Nothing was easy for Althea in those days." So said Mary Harwick Hare, the English player who practiced with Gibson before a tournament in Chicago because no American would. Women's singles champion of the black American Tennis Association 1947-57 and (with R. Walter Johnson) mixed doubles champion in 1948-50 and 1952-55, Gibson first played Forest Hills in 1950, losing to Louise Brough in an early round. Two years later she was ranked in the top ten (and would be another five times; she was number one in 1957 and 1958). She won both French and Italian championships in 1956, was runner-up to Shirley Fry for U.S. title, and (with Angela Buxton) won French and Wimbledon doubles. In 1957, with Shirley Fry, she took the Australian doubles. A strong serve-and-volleyer, Gibson had her greatest years in 1957 and 1958, when she won the U.S. championship and the Wimbledon singles and (with Darlene Hard in 1957 and Maria Bueno in 1958) doubles titles; she was also a member of the Wightman Cup team, winning all but one of her matches. She was the first black U.S. champion, the first black Wimbledon champion; in perhaps a less well known first, Althea Gibson was the first champion of any color who, at her Wimbledon Ball, took the microphone and sang. She was named to the International Tennis Hall of Fame in 1971, and to the Women's Sports Hall of Fame in 1980.

Evonne Goolagong Cawley
born Griffith, New South Wales, Australia, July 31, 1951

An eighteen-year-old aboriginal girl whose surname in English meant "tall trees by still waters" was not much noticed at Wimbledon in her first appearance; she was defeated in her first round. The next year, 1971, Goolagong was Wimbledon singles champion. She had already won 42 regional and national age-group titles in Australia; in 1971, her second year of major international competition, she was also French champion and (with Margaret Court) Australian doubles champion. She played on the Federation Cup team 1971-76 and 1982 (Australia was victorious in 1973 and 1974). In 1973, she won the Italian championship; she took the Australian championship 1974-76 and December 1977 (she was pregnant earlier in 1977) and the Virginia Slims championship in 1974 and 1976. She was Wimbledon singles champion again in 1980, matching Bill Tilden for longest gap (nine years) between singles titles. Her second child was born in May 1981; returning to competition in 1982, she was ranked twenty-ninth that year in the international rankings of the WTA. Her style has been described as natural, graceful, effortless, instinctive; her "walka-bouts," lapses in concentration, have led to inconsistency in her record. Nonetheless, she has been consistent enough to have defeated all the great players of her time.

Doris J. Hart
born St. Louis, Missouri, June 20, 1925

As a small child learning to walk, Hart suffered what was probably polio. Her leg muscles atrophied, and for exercise her brother took her to the park to play tennis, but she never fully regained mobility. It hardly mattered: with a flowing style, fast serve, and an all-court game, she grew up to win the four major singles titles (Australian, 1949; French, 1950 and 1952; Wimbledon, 1951; U.S., 1954 and 1955), as well as the championships of Italy (1951 and 1953) and South Africa (1952). A great doubles player, she won the Wimbledon title in 1947 with Patricia Todd, and another three times with Shirley Fry (1951-53). Fry was also her partner in winning the U.S. doubles championship 1951-54. In 1954 Hart swept the U.S. tournament, winning singles, doubles, and (with Vic Seixas) mixed doubles. Other U.S. mixed doubles victories with Seixas were in 1953 and 1955; in 1951 and 1952 she had won with Frank Sedgman. Hart and Sedgman also took the Wimbledon and French mixed doubles in 1951 and 1952; with Seixas, she won the Wimbledon mixed doubles again and the French title in 1953. Hart played on the Wightman Cup team 1946-55, during which time she lost only one match. She ranked in the top ten 1942-55 (number one in 1954 and 1955). She was named to the International Tennis Hall of Fame in 1969.

Kathy Jordan

Andrea Jaeger

Kathleen Horvath
born Chicago, Illinois, August 25, 1965

Martina Navratilova had one defeat in 84 matches in 1983; that one loss was inflicted by Horvath, in the French Open. An outstanding junior, Horvath was the youngest player to win the U.S. under-twenty-one title (she was thirteen years and eleven months old), and the only one to win all four age-group titles in consecutive years. In 1980 she won the Pepsi Junior, the Orange Bowl Junior, and the French Open Junior. By 1982 she was ranked number 27, but a back injury slowed her advance. In her 1983 season, however, she won the Ginny of Nashville and took the Ginny championship; she made the quarterfinals of the French, U.S. clay, and Canadian titles, the semifinals of the Italian Open, and the finals of the German Open, finishing the year ranked 15. In 1984 she was runner-up to Bonnie Gadusek for the Avon Cup and was named to the Federation Cup team.

Helen Hull Jacobs
born Berkeley, California, August 8, 1908

"They are far more sensible," remarked the Duchess of York (now Queen Mother Elizabeth). Jacobs agreed; she was the first woman to wear shorts at Wimbledon. She was U.S. girls' singles champion 1924, 1925. Ranked number one by the USLTA 1932-35, number two ten times, she was national singles champion 1932-35, runner-up in 1928 (to Helen Wills Moody), in 1936-1938, 1939 (to Alice Marble). She took the national doubles title (with Sarah Palfrey Danzig) in 1932, 1934, 1935; mixed doubles (with George Lott) in 1934. She played on the Wightman Cup team 1927-37 and 1939. A Wimbledon runner-up five times (1929, 1932, 1934, 1935, 1938), she lost four times to Moody. A determined, sportsmanlike player with a friendly and unpretentious manner, when Jacobs did win the Wimbledon title in 1936, she was one of the most popular champions ever. Jacobs never quite caught up with Moody, defeating her only once, by default, for the U.S. women's singles title in 1933. She had a precise serve, a strong and accurate backhand, and excellent volley—and a devoted following. She was made a member of the International Tennis Hall of Fame in 1972.

Andrea Jaeger
born Chicago, Illinois, June 4, 1965

One of the top players of the 80's, her rank ranging from number seven to number two, Jaeger has yet to win a major championship. But to be defeated by Martina Navratilova is no disgrace. Jaeger was 1980's Most Impressive Newcomer, winning the Avon Futures of Las Vegas, and the next year she was U.S. clay court champion. In 1982 she defeated Mima Jausovec in the Avon championship of Detroit and Chris Evert Lloyd in the Avon championship of Oakland, and was runner-up to Navratilova in the French Open. Navratilova was her nemesis again in 1983, narrowly defeating her in the Wimbledon final; Jaeger defeated Hana Mandlikova in January 1984 to win the Avon Cup at Marco Island, Florida, but injury plagued her later in the year, forcing her to withdraw from the French Open and Wimbledon. She played on the Wightman Cup team 1980 and 1981 and was named to the 1984 Federation Cup team.

Kathy Jordan
born Bryn Mawr, Pennsylvania, December 3, 1959

The Most Impressive Newcomer and *Tennis* magazine's Rookie of the

Year in 1979, in 1980 Jordan was ranked ninth. A fine doubles player, in 1980 she and Anne Smith won Wimbledon, the French Open, and Eastbourne (the pair was 1980 Doubles Team of the Year); together they have won all the grand-slam doubles titles, the French and Wimbledon in 1980, the Australian and U.S. in 1981. Jordan's first major singles title was the Avon Futures of San Antonio in 1979, which she won by taking 13 matches in a row; she went on to win the Avon Futures championship that year. Overcoming shoulder difficulties, she had a very good year in 1983, reaching the finals in major tournaments (Virginia Slims of Detroit, Richmond, Virginia Slims of Detroit, Sydney, and the Australian championship). At Eastbourne in 1984, she reached the final by defeating Chris Evert Lloyd; she and Smith were runners-up in doubles at Wimbledon to Martina Navratilova and Pam Shriver. In the U.S. Open in September, she was unexpectedly defeated in the second round by Helena Sukova of Czechoslovakia, 6-3, 6-3. Jordan was on the Wightman Cup team 1979 and 1980, the Federation Cup team in 1980 and 1984.

Billie Jean Moffitt King
born Long Beach, California, November 22, 1943

"Records are made to be broken," Elizabeth Ryan said of her 19 Wimbledon titles. "If mine is to go, I would like Billie Jean to have it, because she has so much guts." And the day after Ryan's death at the age of eighty-seven, King did it: her 1979 Wimbledon doubles victory with Martina Navratilova gave her 20 Wimbledon titles, an all-time record. King was singles champion 1966-68, 1972, 1973, 1975; doubles champion 1961 and 1962 (with Karen Hantze Susman), 1965 (with Maria Bueno), 1967, 1968, 1970, 1971, 1973 (with Rosemary Casals), 1972 (with Betty Stove), 1979 (with Navratilova); playing with Owen Davidson, she won mixed doubles in 1967, 1971, 1973, and 1974. At home, she was U.S. singles champion in 1967, 1971, 1972, and 1974, and doubles champion in 1964 (with Susman), 1967 and 1974 (with Casals), and 1978 and 1980 (with Navratilova). She won the U.S. mixed doubles with Davidson in 1967, 1971, and 1973, and in 1976 with Phil Dent. She is the only woman to have won her singles championships on grass, clay, carpet, and hard courts. King also holds singles titles in the Australian Open (1968), the French Open (1972), and the German Open (1971). On the Virginia Slims circuit, she won 29 titles in the years 1970-78. She was a member of the Wightman Cup team 1961-67, 1970, 1977, 1978, and in Federation Cup competition (1963-67, 1976-79), King was unbeaten in her 27 doubles. Her strong serve-volley game was reinforced by her determination—and ability—to rise to the occasion in match play. And as well as prodigious talent and willingness to work, King has a keen knowledge and love of the history and traditions of her sport. In March 1984, King announced that after the Bridgestone doubles tournament in Japan (which she and partner Sharon Walsh won for the second year in a row), she had no further plans for playing competitive tennis, but intended to coach and give seminars. In 1984 she worked to organize Team Tennis, the first professional sports league in which women would compete on a completely equal basis with men. She has been a member of the Women's Sports Hall of Fame since 1980.

Chris Evert Lloyd   Billie Jean Moffitt King

Suzanne Lenglen
born Compiègne, France, May 24, 1899; died July 4, 1938
"Voulez vous jouer avec ma fille?" Thus Charles Lenglen invited established tennis players on the Riviera to play with his precocious twelve-
year-old daughter Suzanne—who in 1914, before her fifteenth birthday,
became world singles champion (and, playing with Elizabeth Ryan, world
doubles champion as well). After the Armistice, she played at the reopened
Wimbledon, and took the singles title (her first of six, 1919-23 and 1925)
from seven-time champion Dorothea Lambert Chambers in 46 games—
the longest women's final match until that between Margaret Court and
Billie Jean King in 1977. In partnership with Elizabeth Ryan, Lenglen
was also women's doubles champion in those years, and won the mixed
doubles in 1920 (with Gerald Patterson), 1922 (with Pat O'Hara Wood),
and in 1925 (with Jean Borotra). Lenglen was French singles, doubles,
and mixed doubles champion in 1914, 1920-23, 1925, and 1926. In 1920
she was Olympic singles champion (losing only four games in ten sets)
and, with Max Decugis, mixed doubles champion. With her bobbed hair
and silk headbands, and her contempt for corsets, Lenglen was the ultimate
flapper and the ultimate star—she was also an aggressive player who
rushed the net and was both agile and fast. Her most celebrated confron-
tation came in 1926 in an otherwise minor tournament at the Carlton Club
in Cannes: after much speculation and jockeying for posititon, she faced
off with Helen Wills. Although Lenglen won (even after having to return
to play after a wrong call—from the stands—had led her to believe the
match was over), the queen of tennis had met her successor. She was
named to the International Tennis Hall of Fame in 1978, and to the Wom-
en's Sports Hall of Fame in 1984.

Manuela Maleeva
born Sofia, Bulgaria, February 14, 1967

"She is an all-around athlete. She's got all of the shots, and the desire to win." From Martina Navratilova, that's not bad. Maleeva's first year of serious competition was 1982; she won the European eighteen-and-under and the French Open junior titles. In 1983 she reached the third round of the U.S. Open (as she had in 1982) and the third round of the French Open. In 1984 she was runner-up at the Virginia Slims of Houston, and at the U.S. women's indoor championship she advanced to the semifinals before being beaten by Chris Evert Lloyd. Says Maleeva's mother, "She plays much better than I did"; her mother was nine times champion of Bulgaria. Later in the year, Manuela won the Swiss Open, and she defeated Evert Lloyd to win the Italian Open, 6-3, 6-3; she also took the U.S. clay court title. Also in 1984 she was a member of Bulgaria's Federation cup team. She is a modest and sportsmanlike competitor who has earned the respect of older and more experienced players.

Hana Mandlikova
born Prague, Czechoslovakia, February 19, 1962

When Martina Navratilova was playing at the Sparta Club in Prague, Mandlikova watched her. In 1984, Mandlikova was the one to hold Navratilova's winning streak at 54 games when she defeated her in the final of the Virginia Slims of California in January. Five years earlier, the WTA named Mandlikova Most Impressive Newcomer, in 1980 the Most Improved Player. She has made it to the finals of all four grand slam events, and has won the Australian (1980) and the French (1981) championships. In 1982 she was runner-up in the U.S. Open, the Italian Open, and Eastbourne. The following year she was more erratic, with unexpected losses in early rounds. Her performance on the Virginia Slims circuit in

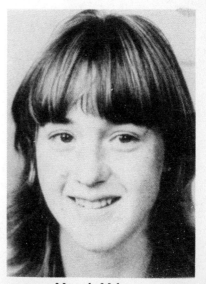

Hana Mandlikova   Manuela Maleeva

1984 was impressive: as well as the California title, she won Houston (which she had previously won in 1981) and Washington. During the Wimbledon tournament that summer, she openly expressed her view that she would meet Navratilova in the final; however, she was soundly defeated by Chris Evert Lloyd in the semifinal, 6-1, 6-2. At the U.S. Open in September, she lost to Carling Bassett in the quarter finals. She was a member of Czeckoslovakia's Federation Cup team in 1978-80 and 1982-84.

Alice Marble
born Beckworth, California, September 28, 1913

Active in sports as a child, at the age of eight Marble was picking up baseballs for the San Francisco Seals. "She had a pretty good arm," recalled one of the players—Joe Di Maggio. She began playing tennis on the city courts at Golden Gate Park. As a beginner, she had natural aptitude and excellent coordination but little technique; therefore, unlike most novices, she rushed the net to avoid having to use ground strokes. Thus she developed the aggressive serve-volley game that changed the nature of women's tennis. She was first in California junior rankings and runner-up in the 1931 under-eighteen girls' nationals; the next year, she achieved USLTA ranking in the top ten (in seventh position). She played on four winning Wightman Cup teams, 1933, 1937, 1938, 1939, and was national champion four times in five years (1936, 1938, 1939, 1940). At Wimbledon, she won in mixed doubles (with Don Budge) in 1937 and 1938 and (with Bobby Riggs) in 1939; she took the women's doubles title in 1938 and 1939 with Sarah Palfrey Fabyan. In 1939 Marble was also Wimbledon singles champion, thus in one year sweeping all three events. During her early career, she battled ill health, variously diagnosed as anemia, gall bladder, and tuberculosis. In 1934, she collapsed on the court during the French championships. A long and inactive sanitarium "convalescence" in California only further weakened her condition, as she gained weight and lost strength. Finally, with the aid and support of her coach, Eleanor Tennant, Marble left the sanitarium and began a program of diet and exercise that led to recovery—and the first of her national championships two years later. From 1936-1940, Marble was ranked number one. She was named to the International Tennis Hall of Fame in 1964.

René Simone Mathieu
born Neuilly-sur-Seine, France, January 31, 1908

"When I was first brought to see Elizabeth in my pram," said Mathieu, "I didn't think we should be winning Wimbledon together." They did: Mathieu and Elizabeth Ryan won the Wimbledon doubles (and the French doubles as well) in 1933 and 1934. Mathieu won the Wimbledon doubles again in 1937 with A. M. "Billie" Yorke, and the French doubles with Yorke in 1936 and 1938, with Jadwiga "Jed" Jedrzejowska in 1937 and 1939. In 1937 and 1938 Mathieu also won the French mixed doubles (with Yvan Petra and D. Mitic), and was French singles champion in 1938 and 1939. Ted Tinling, designer and chronicler of women's tennis, believes she had one of the "most classic continental forehands ever seen in the game."

Helen Wills Moody Roark
born Berkeley, California, October 6, 1905

"Up, up—where would the ball go if it didn't come down?" The small child who wondered grew up to hold the all-time record of eight Wimbledon singles championships (1927-30, 1932, 1933, 1935, 1938). Helen Wills won her first national championship at fifteen; two years later, in 1923, she won the U.S. women's singles title at Forest Hills, the first of seven such triumphs. A member of the U.S. Olympic team in 1924, she won Olympic singles and doubles. In 1928, she took the French, Wimbledon, and U.S. titles without losing a set—and repeated that remarkable performance in 1929. In her 15-year rivalry with Helen Jacobs, Moody's only possible defeat (at Forest Hills in 1933) was forestalled by her controversial default in the last set at 0-3. In her signature eyeshade, Moody was an elegant figure on the court, self-possessed and expressionless; she was known as "Miss Poker Face." A hard hitter, Moody had a powerful serve and a superb baseline game; she was not an instinctive volleyer. Her aim in competition was to conserve her strength, playing with an economy of effort brilliantly matched to her opponent's game. She was named to the International Tennis Hall of Fame in 1959.

Martina Navratilova
born Prague, Czechoslovakia, October 8, 1956

The powerhouse of modern women's tennis, Navratilova's lefthanded serve has been timed at 93 miles an hour. National champion of Czechoslovakia 1972-75, Navratilova defected while on tour in the U.S. in 1975 and became a U.S. citizen in 1981. She played on the Federation Cup team for Czechoslovakia in 1975, for the U.S. in 1982. She was WTA Player of the Year in 1978, 1979, 1982, 1983. She was five times Wimbledon singles (1978, 1979, 1982-84) and six times doubles champion (1976 with Chris Evert Lloyd, 1979 with Billie Jean King, and 1981-84 with Pam Shriver). In the French championships, Navratilova won the doubles with Evert Lloyd in 1975, with Anne Smith in 1982, and with Shriver in 1984; in 1982 and 1984 she was singles champion as well. She won the Australian Open singles in 1981 and 1983, doubles with Shriver in 1982 and 1983. In her eleventh try, she won the U.S. Open singles in 1983; she was doubles champion in 1977 (with Betty Stove), in 1978 and 1980 (with King) and 1983 and 1984 (with Pam Shriver). In 1982, Navratilova's match record was 90-3; in 1983, it was 86-1, marred only by her defeat by Kathy Horvath in the French Open. Navratilova's 54-match winning streak (second only to Evert Lloyd's 56, in 1974) was ended in January 1984 by Hana Mandlikova at the Virginia Slims of California. Six weeks later Navratilova won the U.S. women's indoor championship, and in March became Virginia Slims champion in singles and (with Pam Shriver) in doubles. An aggressive serve-and-volleyer, Navratilova has always been a strong player; in the last two or three years, she has become more at ease and sure of herself. When she won the French Open in June 1984, defeating Evert Lloyd in straight sets, she became the third woman to win the grand slam of tennis. Maureen Connolly Brinker had done it in 1953, Margaret Smith Court in 1970. While Navratilova's victories, unlike her predecessor's, did not occur in one calendar year, the International Tennis Federation recognizes consecutive wins in the French, Wimbledon, U.S. and Australian championships as a grand slam. In September 1984 she defeated Evert Lloyd for the U.S. Open championship, Navratilova's sixth grand slam title in a row. Three weeks later she won her sixty-fifth straight match when she won the Virginia Slims of New Orleans. Navratilova was Women's Sports Foundation Sportswoman of the Year 1982-84 and was named to the Women's Sports Hall of Fame in 1984.

Martina Navratilova

Candy Reynolds, 1983 French Open Doubles Champion

Margaret Osborne du Pont
born Joseph, Oregon, March 4, 1918,

A terrific volleyer with a backhand smash, Osborne du Pont ranked in the top ten 14 times in her career, number one in 1948. Three-time U.S. singles champion (1948-50), she was Wimbledon champion in 1947 and French champion in 1946 and 1949. She formed a superb doubles partnership with her friend Louise Brough; together they won the U.S. doubles title twelve times (1942-50, 1955-57), the Wimbledon doubles in 1946, 1948-1950 and 1954, and the French doubles in 1946, 1947, and 1949. (Du Pont also won the U.S. doubles in 1941, with Sarah Palfrey Cooke, and in 1958, with Jeanne Arth.) She was a member of the Wightman Cup team in 1946-49, 1950, 1954, 1955, 1957, 1961, and 1962. In 1962, playing with Neale Fraser, du Pont took the Wimbledon mixed doubles title—16 years after her first Wimbledon victory. She was named to the International Tennis Hall of Fame in 1967, along with Brough Clapp.

Barbara Potter
born Waterbury, Connecticut, October 22, 1961

Potter's accomplishments aren't only in tennis: she is also an award-winning skier and a fine student. Accepted by Princeton University, she delayed entrance while she learned just how good a tennis player she is—and that is very good. In 1980 she had a 7-7 match record on the Avon circuit, which included a victory over Andrea Jaeger. The next year as well she was often in the quarterfinals and semifinals of major tournaments, and in 1982 she won the U.S. indoor championship, defeating Tracy Austin. In doubles, playing with Sharon Walsh, she has won Kansas City (1981, 1982), Oakland and Tampa (both in 1982), the Murjani Cup in Palm Beach Gardens (1983), and Virginia Slims of Washington (1984); the pair were semifinalists at Wimbledon in 1983. Potter is known for her determination, and for what is usually described as a blistering serve.

Elizabeth Ryan
born Anaheim, California, February 5, 1891; died 1979

No woman had volleyed like Elizabeth Ryan—but many would after her, in the line of aggressive players from Alice Marble to Martina Navratilova. As a doubles player, Ryan won 19 Wimbledon titles, a record that stood until 1979. The first time Ryan and Suzanne Lenglen played as partners, they were beaten—it was a handicap event and they gave their opponents points. But they were never beaten again, and they took the Wimbledon double championship six times (1919-23 and 1925). Ryan's other Wimbledon doubles victories were 1914 (with A. M. Morton), 1926 (with Mary K. Browne), 1927 and 1930 (with Helen Wills Moody) and 1933 and 1934 (with René Simone Mathieu). In mixed doubles at Wimbledon, Ryan won in 1919, 1921, and 1923 with Randolph Lycett, in 1927 with Francis Hunter, in 1928 with Pat Spence, in 1930 with Jack Crawford, and in 1932 with Enrique Majer. In the U.S. Ryan was doubles champion in 1926 (with Eleanor Goss) and won mixed doubles in 1933 (with Ellsworth Vines). Ryan was French doubles champion in 1930 and 1932 (with Wills Moody), 1933 and 1934 (with Mathieu). In her career, Ryan took over 650 titles, including four events of the championships held in St. Petersburg in the weeks before World War I, the last tournament of imperial Russia. She never won a major singles title (she defeated Lenglen the first time they played singles, but never beat her again, although she tried, thirty-six times)—and was possibly the greatest woman doubles player the game has known. In 1972 she was named to the International Tennis Hall of Fame.

Pam Shriver
born Baltimore, Maryland, July 4, 1962

Shriver was voted Most Impressive Newcomer of the Year by the WTA in 1978—it's certainly impressive to make the finals of the U.S. Open at sixteen—and has been ranked in the top ten every year since; in 1980 she was Comeback Player of the Year, after recovery from shoulder trouble. She played on the Wightman Cup team in 1978 and 1981. A brilliant doubles player, Shriver and partner Martina Navratilova won Wimbledon four times (1981-84), the Australian doubles (1982-1984), the U.S. Open doubles (1983 and 1984), the Virginia Slims championship doubles (1984), the Avon Circuit championship doubles (1981 and 1982), and the Bridgestone doubles (1982). When the pair took the French doubles championship in June 1984, they became the first women partners to win the four grand slam doubles titles in succession. Not surprisingly, Shriver and Navratilova have been Doubles Team of the Year in 1981, 1982, and 1983 (in 1983 the team won 11 of the 12 tournaments they played). In singles, Shriver's record is less consistent, and her nemesis is her partner, whom she has not defeated since the semifinals of the U.S. Open in 1982. But after her loss to Navratilova in the semifinals of the Virginia Slims championships in 1984, Shriver said, "It's the first time I played her in a year and half when I felt I had a chance." With a fine serve-and-volley game and a powerful serve, her style is right for the job: it may well yet happen.

Margaret Smith Court
born Albury, New South Wales, Australia, July 16, 1942

A player of great courage, yet subject to nervousness in competition that cost her more than one key match; a well-coordinated, strong, fast player (at 5'10" and 145 pounds, splendidly built for tennis), yet she was never regarded as a "great" player. But however you count them Court holds more major titles than anyone else in the game: eleven Australian singles championships (1960-66, 1969-71, 1973), five French (1962, 1964, 1969, 1970, 1973), three Wimbledon (1963, 1965, 1970) and U.S. national titles in 1962, 1965, 1969, 1970, and 1973. In 1966, after her seventh Australian title, she retired from competitive tennis—the grand slam had eluded her (twice she had won three of the four titles, in 1962, 1965) and she was exhausted from touring. She went into business in Perth, married world-class sailor Barry Court—and returned to tennis in 1968, more relaxed, more confident. Again in 1969 she won three of the four grand slam victories, then made the sweep in 1970, playing the longest final in the history of Wimbledon, defeating Billie Jean King in 46 games. Court announced her pregnancy at the end of 1971, returning to play in 1973, winning her eleventh Australian championship and defeating two rising— and younger—players, Chris Evert for the French championship and Evonne Goolagong at Forest Hills. After the birth of her second child, Court won the U.S. Open doubles title (with Virginia Wade) in 1975. Court holds a string of doubles championships, including the grand slam in mixed doubles with Kenneth Fletcher in 1963. At Wimbledon, she won doubles in 1964 with Lesley Turner and in 1969 with Judy Tegart Dalton, and mixed doubles with Fletcher in 1963, 1965, 1966, 1968. In the French championships, Court won with Turner in 1964 and 1965 and Tegart Dalton in 1966, and in mixed doubles she won with Fletcher 1963-65, in 1969 with Martin Riessen. She holds U.S. doubles titles for 1963 (with Robyn Ebbern), 1968 (with Maria Bueno), and 1969 (with Wade), and mixed doubles titles in 1963 (with Fletcher), 1964 (with John Newcombe), and 1965 (with Fred Stolle); in the U.S. Open she won doubles with Bueno in 1968, Tegart Dalton in 1970, and Wade in 1973 and 1975, and mixed doubles with Riessen in 1969 and 1970. Her Australian doubles titles were won with Mary C. Reitano in 1961, Ebbern in 1962 and 1963, Turner in 1965, Tegart Dalton in 1969 and 1970, Goolagong in 1971, and Wade in 1973; she won mixed doubles in 1963 with Fletcher and in 1964. Court also won Italian singles 1962-64, Canadian singles 1970, German singles 1964-66, Irish singles 1968, South African singles 1968-71, and the Welsh singles in 1969. She played for the Federation Cup 1963-65, 1967, 1968, 1971; her singles record in that competition is 22-0. She was named to the International Tennis Hall of Fame in 1979.

Hilda Krahwinkel Sperling
born Essen, Germany, March 26, 1908

With Gottfried von Cramm, Sperling won the Wimbledon mixed doubles championship in 1933. Although she never won the Wimbledon singles title (she was runner-up in 1931 and 1936), she had the distinction of taking seven games from Helen Moody in the semifinal round in 1933. Sperling was French singles champion in 1935; she was six times German singles champion (1933, 1934, 1935, 1937-39), and doubles champion in 1932 (with A. Peitz) and in 1937 (with Mrs. M. Rollin Conquerque). Partnered by von Cramm, she won the German mixed doubles championship 1932-34.

Katherine Stammers Menzies
born St. Albans, Hertfordshire, England, April 3, 1914

Lefthanded, attractive, and popular, Kay Stammers was Wimbledon doubles champion with Freda James in 1935 and 1936, and French doubles champion with Margaret Scriven in 1935. She played on the Wightman Cup team 1935-39, 1946-48. In 1939, she lost the Wimbledon singles final to Alice Marble, who played through to the championship without losing a set.

Sarah Virginia Wade
born Bournemouth, Hampshire, England, July 10, 1945

Fifteen times Wade had tried for the Wimbledon singles title, and fifteen times had missed, losing in early rounds to weaker opponents. In 1977, the pressure, especially on an English player, was tremendous—it was the Wimbledon centenary and Elizabeth II's Silver Jubilee; for the first time since 1962 the Queen was in the Royal Box. In a fairy-tale triumph, Wade, against the odds, achieved the ambition of her career, and England had her champion. Wade won the first U.S. Open title in 1968, defeating Billie Jean King; with Margaret Court, she won the U.S. Open doubles title in 1969 and 1975. She won the Italian championship in 1971, the Australian in 1972. On the Virginia Slims circuit, she holds five titles, 1971-77; she was 1977 WTA Player of the Year. A member of the Wightman Cup team 1965-68 and the Federation Cup team 1967-82, Wade ranked number one in Great Britain for a record ten consecutive years. In 1982, she was the first woman elected to the Wimbledon Committee. Although she competed rarely in 1983 and 1984, she was always warmly received. In 1983 she was a quarterfinalist at Wimbledon and, with Virginia Ruzici, won the Italian Open doubles title; in 1984 she was at Wimbledon again, for the twenty-third time, and was defeated in the third round by Sweden's Carina Karlsson.

FRENCH SINGLES CHAMPIONSHIPS

Year	Champion	Defeated
1925	Suzanne Lenglen	Kathleen McKane
1926	Suzanne Lenglen	Mary Browne
1927	Ked Bouman	G. Peacock
1928	Helen Wills	Helen Jacobs
1929	Helen Wills	René Simone Mathieu
1930	Helen Wills Moody	Helen Jacobs
1931	Cilly Aussem	Betty Nuthall
1932	Helen Wills Moody	René Simone Mathieu
1933	Margaret Scriven	René Simone Mathieu
1934	Margaret Scriven	Helen Jacobs
1935	Hilda Krahwinkel Sperling	René Simone Mathieu
1936	Hilda K. Sperling	René Simone Mathieu
1937	Hilda K. Sperling	René Simone Mathieu
1938	René Simone Mathieu	N. Landry
1939	René Simone Mathieu	Jadwiga Jedrzejowska
1940-45	not played	
1946	Margaret Osborne	Pauline Betz
1947	Patricia Todd	Doris Hart
1948	N. Landry	Shirley Fry
1949	Margaret Osborne du Pont	N. Adamson
1950	Doris Hart	Patricia Todd
1951	Shirley Fry	Doris Hart
1952	Doris Hart	Shirley Fry
1953	Maureen Connolly	Doris Hart
1954	Maureen Connolly	G. Bucaille
1955	Angela Mortimer	Dorothy Knode
1956	Althea Gibson	Angela Mortimer
1957	Shirley Bloomer	Dorothy Knode
1958	Z. Kormoczy	Shirley Bloomer
1959	Christine Truman	Z. Kormoczy
1960	Darlene Hard	Yola Ramirez
1961	Ann Haydon	Yola Ramirez
1962	Margaret Smith	Lesley Turner
1963	Lesley Turner	Ann Haydon Jones
1964	Margaret Smith	Maria Bueno
1965	Lesley Turner	Margaret Smith
1966	Ann Haydon Jones	Nancy Richey
1967	Francoise Durr	Lesley Turner
1968	Nancy Richey	Ann Haydon Jones
1969	Margaret Smith Court	Chris Evert
1970	Margaret Smith Court	H. Niessen
1971	Evonne Goolagong	Helen Gourley
1972	Billie Jean King	Evonne Goolagong
1973	Margaret Smith Court	Chris Evert
1974	Chris Evert	Olga Morozova
1975	Chris Evert	Martina Navratilova
1976	Sue Barker	Renata Tomanova
1977	Mima Jausovec	Florenza Mihai
1978	Virginia Ruzici	Mima Jausovec
1979	Chris Evert Lloyd	Wendy Turnbull
1980	Chris Evert Lloyd	Virginia Ruzici

Year	Champion	Defeated
1981	Hana Mandlikova	Sylvia Hanika
1982	Martina Navratilova	Andrea Jaeger
1983	Chris Evert Lloyd	Mima Jausovec
1984	Martina Navratilova	Chris Evert Lloyd

FRENCH DOUBLES CHAMPIONSHIPS

Year	Champions
1925	Suzanne Lenglen/Didi Vlasto
1926	Suzanne Lenglen/Didi Vlasto
1927	G. Peacock/E. L. Heine
1928	Phoebe Watson/Eileen Bennett
1929	Lili de Alvarez/Ked Bouman
1930	Helen Wills Moody/Elizabeth Ryan
1931	Betty Nuthall/Eileen Fearnly Whittingstall
1932	Helen Wills Moody/Elizabeth Ryan
1933	René Simone Mathieu/Elizabeth Ryan
1934	René Simone Mathieu/Elizabeth Ryan
1935	Margaret Scriven/Kay Stammers
1936	René Simone Mathieu/Billie Yorke
1937	René Simone Mathieu/Billie Yorke
1938	René Simone Mathieu/Billie Yorke
1939	René Simone Mathieu/Jadwiga Jedrzejowska
1940-45	not played
1946	Louise Brough/Margaret Osborne
1947	Louise Brough/Margaret Osborne
1948	Doris Hart/Patricia Todd
1949	Margaret Osborne du Pont/Louise Brough
1950	Shirley Fry/Doris Hart
1951	Shirley Fry/Doris Hart
1952	Shirley Fry/Doris Hart
1953	Shirley Fry/Doris Hart
1954	Maureen Connolly/Nell Hopman
1955	Beverly Fleitz/Darlene Hard
1956	Angela Buxton/Althea Gibson
1957	Shirley Bloomer/Darlene Hard
1958	Rosie Reyes/Yola Ramirez
1959	Sandra Reynolds/Renée Schuurman
1960	Maria Bueno/Darlene Hard
1961	Sandra Reynolds/Renée Schuurman
1962	Sandra Reynolds/Renée Schuurman
1963	Ann Haydon Jones/Renée Schuurman
1964	Margaret Smith/Lesley Turner
1965	Margaret Smith/Lesley Turner
1966	Margaret Smith/Judy Tegart
1967	Françoise Durr/Gail Sherriff
1968	Françoise Durr/Ann Haydon Jones
1969	Françoise Durr/Ann Haydon Jones
1970	Françoise Durr/Gail Chanfreau
1971	Françoise Durr/Gail Chanfreau
1972	Billie Jean King/Betty Stove
1973	Margaret Smith Court/Virginia Wade
1974	Chris Evert/Olga Morozova

Year	Champion
1975	Chris Evert/Martina Navratilova
1976	Fiorella Bonicelli/Gail Chanfreau Lovera
1977	Regina Marsikova/Pam Teeguarden
1978	Mima Jausovec/Virginia Rucizi
1979	Betty Stove/Wendy Turnbull
1980	Anne Smith/Kathy Jordan
1981	Rosalyn Fairbank/Tanya Harford
1982	Martina Navratilova/Anne Smith
1983	Rosalyn Fairbank/Candy Reynolds
1984	Martina Navratilova/Pam Shriver

WIMBLEDON SINGLES CHAMPIONSHIPS

Year	Champion	Defeated
1884	Maud Watson	L. Watson
1885	Maud Watson	Blanche Bingley
1886	Blanche Bingley	Maud Watson
1887	Lottie Dod	Blanche Bingley
1888	Lottie Dod	Blanche Bingley Hillyard
1889	Blanche Bingley Hillyard	L. Rice
1890	L. Rice	M. Jacks
1891	Lottie Dod	Blanche Bingley Hillyard
1892	Lottie Dod	Blanche Bingley Hillyard
1893	Lottie Dod	Blanche Bingley Hillyard
1894	Blanche Bingley Hillyard	L. Austin
1895	Charlotte Cooper Sterry	H. Jackson
1896	Charlotte Cooper Sterry	W. H. Pickering
1897	Blanche Bingley Hillyard	Charlotte Cooper Sterry
1898	Charlotte Cooper Sterry	L. Martin
1899	Blanche Bingley Hillyard	Charlotte Cooper Sterry
1900	Blanche Bingley Hillyard	Charlotte Cooper Sterry
1901	Charlotte Cooper Sterry	Blanche Bingley Hillyard
1902	Muriel Robb	Charlotte Cooper Sterry
1903	Dorothea Douglass	Ethel Thomson
1904	Dorothea Douglass	Charlotte Cooper Sterry
1905	May Sutton	Dorothea Douglass
1906	Dorothea Douglass	May Sutton
1907	May Sutton	Dorothea Douglass Chambers
1908	Charlotte Cooper Sterry	A. Morton
1909	Dora Boothby	A. Morton
1910	Dorothea Douglass Chambers	Dora Boothby
1911	Dorothea Douglass Chambers	Dora Boothby
1912	Ethel Thomson Larcombe	Charlotte Cooper Sterry
1913	Dorothea Douglass Chambers	R. McNair
1914	Dorothea Douglass Chambers	Ethel T. Larcombe
1915-18	not played	
1919	Suzanne Lenglen	Dorothea D. Chambers
1920	Suzanne Lenglen	Dorothea D. Chambers
1921	Suzanne Lenglen	Elizabeth Ryan
1922	Suzanne Lenglen	F. Mallory
1923	Suzanne Lenglen	Kathleen McKane
1924	Kathleen McKane	Helen Wills
1925	Suzanne Lenglen	J. Fry

Year	Champion	Defeated
1926	Kathleen McKane Godfree	Lili de Alvarez
1927	Helen Wills	Lili de Alvarez
1928	Helen Wills	Lili de Alvarez
1929	Helen Wills	Helen Jacobs
1930	Helen Wills Moody	Elizabeth Ryan
1931	Cilly Aussem	Hilda Krahwinkel
1932	Helen Wills Moody	Helen Jacobs
1933	Helen Wills Moody	Dorothy Round
1934	Dorothy Round	Helen Jacobs
1935	Helen Wills Moody	Helen Jacobs
1936	Helen Jacobs	Hilda Krahwinkel Sperling
1937	Dorothy Round	Jadwiga Jedrzejowska
1938	Helen Wills Moody	Helen Jacobs
1939	Alice Marble	Kay Stammers
1940-45	not played	
1946	Pauline Betz	Louise Brough
1947	Margaret Osborne	Doris Hart
1948	Louise Brough	Doris Hart
1949	Louise Brough	Margaret Osborne du Pont
1950	Louise Brough	Margaret Osborne du Pont
1951	Doris Hart	Shirley Fry
1952	Maureen Connolly	Louise Brough
1953	Maureen Connolly	Doris Hart
1954	Maureen Connolly	Louise Brough
1955	Louise Brough	Beverly Fleitz
1956	Shirley Fry	Angela Buxton
1957	Althea Gibson	Darlene Hard
1958	Althea Gibson	Angela Mortimer
1959	Maria Bueno	Darlene Hard
1960	Maria Bueno	Sandra Reynolds
1961	Angela Mortimer	Christine Truman
1962	Karen Hantze Susman	Vera Sukova
1963	Margaret Smith	Billie Jean Moffitt
1964	Maria Bueno	Margaret Smith
1965	Margaret Smith	Maria Bueno
1966	Billie Jean King	Maria Bueno
1967	Billie Jean King	Ann Haydon Jones
1968	Billie Jean King	Judy Tegart
1969	Ann Haydon Jones	Billie Jean King
1970	Margaret Smith Court	Billie Jean King
1971	Evonne Goolagong	Margaret Smith Court
1972	Billie Jean King	Evonne Goolagong
1973	Billie Jean King	Chris Evert
1974	Chris Evert	Olga Morozova
1975	Billie Jean King	Evonne Goolagong Cawley
1976	Chris Evert	Evonne Goolagong Cawley
1977	Virginia Wade	Betty Stove
1978	Martina Navratilova	Chris Evert
1979	Martina Navratilova	Chris Evert Lloyd
1980	Evonne Goolagong Cawley	Chris Evert Lloyd
1981	Chris Evert Lloyd	Hana Mandlikova
1982	Martina Navratilova	Chris Evert Lloyd
1983	Martina Navratilova	Andrea Jaeger
1984	Martina Navratilova	Hana Mandlikova

WIMBLEDON DOUBLES CHAMPIONS

Year	Champions
1913	R. McNair/Dora Boothby
1914	A. Morton/Elizabeth Ryan
1915-18	not played
1919	Suzanne Lenglen/Elizabeth Ryan
1920	Suzanne Lenglen/Elizabeth Ryan
1921	Suzanne Lenglen/Elizabeth Ryan
1922	Suzanne Lenglen/Elizabeth Ryan
1923	Suzanne Lenglen/Elizabeth Ryan
1924	Hazel Wightman/Helen Wills
1925	Suzanne Lenglen/Elizabeth Ryan
1926	Mary Browne/Elizabeth Ryan
1927	Helen Wills/Elizabeth Ryan
1928	Peggy Saunders/Phoebe Watson
1929	Peggy Saunders Mitchell/Phoebe Watson
1930	Helen Wills Moody/Elizabeth Ryan
1931	Phillis Mudford/Dorothy Shepherd Barron
1932	Doris Metaxa/Josane Sigart
1933	René Simone Mathieu/Elizabeth Ryan
1934	René Simone Mathieu/Elizabeth Ryan
1935	Freda James/Kay Stammers
1936	Freda James/Kay Stammers
1937	René Simone Mathieu/Billie Yorke
1938	Sarah Palfrey Fabyan/Alice Marble
1939	Sarah Palfrey Fabyan/Alice Marble
1940-45	not played
1946	Louise Brough/Margaret Osborne
1947	Pat Todd/Doris Hart
1948	Louise Brough/Margaret Osborne DuPont
1949	Louise Brough/Margaret Osborne DuPont
1950	Louise Brough/Margaret Osborne DuPont
1951	Doris Hart/Shirley Fry
1952	Doris Hart/Shirley Fry
1953	Doris Hart/Shirley Fry
1954	Louise Brough/Margaret Osborne DuPont
1955	Angela Mortimer/Anne Shilcock
1956	Angela Buxton/Althea Gibson
1957	Althea Gibson/Darlene Hard
1958	Althea Gibson/Maria Bueno
1959	Jeanne Arth/Darlene Hard
1960	Maria Bueno/Darlene Hard
1961	Karen Hantze/Billie Jean Moffitt
1962	Billie Jean Moffitt/Karen Hantze Susman
1963	Maria Bueno/Darlene Hard
1964	Margaret Smith/Lesley Turner
1965	Maria Bueno/Billie Jean Moffitt
1966	Maria Bueno/Nancy Richey
1967	Rosemary Casals/Billie Jean King
1968	Rosemary Casals/Billie Jean King
1969	Margaret Smith Court/Judy Tegart
1970	Rosemary Casals/Billie Jean King
1971	Rosemary Casals/Billie Jean King

Year	Champions
1972	Billie Jean King/Betty Stove
1973	Rosemary Casals/Billie Jean King
1974	Evonne Goolagong/Margaret Michel
1975	Ann Kiyomura/Kazuko Sawamatsu
1976	Chris Evert/Martina Navratilova
1977	Helen Gourley/JoAnne Russell
1978	Kerry Reid/Wendy Turnbull
1979	Billie Jean King/Martina Navratilova
1980	Kathy Jordan/Anne Smith
1981	Martina Navratilova/Pam Shriver
1982	Martina Navratilova/Pam Shriver
1983	Martina Navratilova/Pam Shriver
1984	Martina Navratilova/Pam Shriver

U.S. SINGLES CHAMPIONS

Year	Champion	Defeated
1887	Ellen Hansell	L. Knith
1888	Bertha Townsend	Ellen Hansell
1889	Bertha Townsend	L. Voorhes
1890	Ellen Roosevelt	Bertha Townsend
1891	Mabel Cahill	Ellen Roosevelt
1892	Mabel Cahill	Bessie Moore
1893	Aline Terry	A. Schultze
1894	Helen Hellwig	Aline Terry
1895	Juliette Atkinson	Helen Hellwig
1896	Bessie Moore	Juliette Atkinson
1897	Juliette Atkinson	Bessie Moore
1898	Juliette Atkinson	Marion Jones
1899	Marion Jones	M. Banks
1900	Myrtle McAteer	Edith Parker
1901	Bessie Moore	Myrtle McAteer
1902	Marion Jones	Bessie Moore
1903	Bessie Moore	Marion Jones
1904	May Sutton	Bessie Moore
1905	Bessie Moore	Helen Homans
1906	Helen Homans	Maud Barger Wallach
1907	Evelyn Sears	Carrie Neely
1908	Maud Barger Wallach	Evelyn Sears
1909	Hazel Hotchkiss	Maud Barger Wallach
1910	Hazel Hotchkiss	L. Hammond
1911	Hazel Hotchkiss	F. Sutton
1912	Mary Browne	Eleonora Sears
1913	Mary Browne	Dorothy Green
1914	Mary Browne	M. Wagner
1915	Molla Bjurstedt	Hazel Hotchkiss Wightman
1915	Molla Bjurstedt	L. Raymond
1916	Molla Bjurstedt	L. Raymond
1917	not played	
1918	Molla Bjurstedt	Marion Zinderstein
1919	Hazel H. Wightman	Marion Zinderstein
1920	Molla Bjurstedt Mallory	Marion Zinderstein
1921	Molla Bjurstedt Mallory	Mary Browne

Year	Champion	Defeated
1922	Molla Bjurstedt Mallory	Helen Wills
1923	Helen Wills	Molla B. Mallory
1924	Helen Wills	Molla B. Mallory
1925	Helen Wills	Kathleen McKane
1926	Molla Bjurstedt Mallory	Elizabeth Ryan
1927	Helen Wills	Betty Nuthall
1928	Helen Wills	Helen Jacobs
1929	Helen Wills	Phoebe Watson
1930	Betty Nuthall	L. Harper
1931	Helen Wills Moody	Eileen Fearnly Whittingstall
1932	Helen Jacobs	Carolin Babcock
1933	Helen Jacobs	Helen Wills Moody
1934	Helen Jacobs	Sarah Palfrey
1935	Helen Jacobs	Sarah Palfrey Fabyan
1936	Alice Marble	Helen Jacobs
1937	Anita Lizana	Jadwiga Jedrzejowska
1938	Alice Marble	N. Wynne
1939	Alice Marble	Helen Jacobs
1940	Alice Marble	Helen Jacobs
1941	Sarah Palfrey Cooke	Pauline Betz
1942	Pauline Betz	Louise Brough
1943	Pauline Betz	Louise Brough
1944	Pauline Betz	Margaret Osborne
1945	Sarah Palfrey Cooke	Pauline Betz
1946	Pauline Betz	Patricia Todd
1947	Louise Brough	Margaret Osborne
1948	Margaret Osborne du Pont	Louise Brough
1949	Margaret Osborne du Pont	Doris Hart
1950	Margaret Osborne du Pont	Doris Hart
1951	Maureen Connolly	Shirley Fry
1952	Maureen Connolly	Doris Hart
1953	Maureen Connolly	Doris Hart
1954	Doris Hart	Louise Brough
1955	Doris Hart	P. Ward
1956	Shirley Fry	Althea Gibson
1957	Althea Gibson	Louise Brough
1958	Althea Gibson	Darlene Hard
1959	Maria Bueno	Christine Truman
1960	Darlene Hard	Maria Bueno
1961	Darlene Hard	Ann Haydon
1962	Margaret Smith	Darlene Hard
1963	Maria Bueno	Margaret Smith
1964	Maria Bueno	Carole Caldwell Graebner
1965	Margaret Smith	Billie Jean Moffitt
1966	Maria Bueno	Nancy Richey
1967	Billie Jean King	Ann Haydon Jones
1968	Virginia Wade	Billie Jean King
1969	Margaret Smith Court	Nancy Richey
1970	Margaret Smith Court	Rosemary Casals
1971	Billie Jean King	Rosemary Casals
1972	Billie Jean King	Kerry Reid
1973	Margaret Smith Court	Evonne Goolagong
1974	Billie Jean King	Evonne Goolagong
1975	Chris Evert	Evonne Goolagong

Year	Champion	Defeated
1976	Chris Evert	Evonne Goolagong
1977	Chris Evert	Wendy Turnbull
1978	Chris Evert	Pam Shriver
1979	Tracy Austin	Chris Evert Lloyd
1980	Chris Evert Lloyd	Hana Mandlikova
1981	Tracy Austin	Martina Navratilova
1982	Chris Evert Lloyd	Hana Mandlikova
1983	Martina Navratilova	Chris Evert Lloyd
1984	Martina Navratilova	Chris Evert Lloyd

U.S. DOUBLES CHAMPIONS

Year	Champions
1890	Ellen Roosevelt/Grace Roosevelt
1891	Mabel Cahill/W. Fellowes Morgan
1892	Mabel Cahill/A. M. McKinlay
1893	Aline Terry/Hattie Butler
1894	Helen Hellwig/Juliette Atkinson
1895	Helen Hellwig/Juliette Atkinson
1896	Elizabeth Moore/Juliette Atkinson
1897	Juliette Atkinson/Kathleen Atkinson
1898	Juliette Atkinson/Kathleen Atkinson
1899	Jane W. Craven/Myrtle McAteer
1900	Edith Parker/Hallie Champlin
1901	Juliette Atkinson/Myrtle McAteer
1902	Juliette Atkinson/Marion Jones
1903	Elizabeth Moore/Carrie Neely
1904	May Sutton/Miriam Hall
1905	Helen Homans/Carrie Neely
1906	L. S. Coe/D. S. Platt
1907	Marie Weimer/Carrie Neely
1908	Evelyn Sears/Margaret Curtis
1909	Hazel Hotchkiss/Edith Rotch
1910	Hazel Hotchkiss/Edith Rotch
1911	Hazel Hotchkiss/Eleonora Sears
1912	Dorothy Green/Mary Browne
1913	Mary Browne/R.H. Williams
1914	Mary Browne/R. H. Williams
1915	Hazel Hotchkiss Wightman/Eleonora Sears
1916	Eleonora Sears/Molla Bjurstedt
1917	not played
1918	Marion Zinderstein/Eleanor Goss
1919	Marion Zinderstein/Eleanor Goss
1920	Marion Zinderstein/Eleanor Goss
1921	Mary Browne/R. H. Williams
1922	Marion Zinderstein Jessup/Helen Wills
1923	Kathleen McKane/Phyllis Covell
1924	Hazel Hotchkiss Wightman/Helen Wills
1925	Mary Browne/Helen Wills
1926	Elizabeth Ryan/Eleanor Goss
1927	Kathleen McKane Godfree/Ermyntrude Harvey
1928	Hazel Hotchkiss Wightman/Helen Wills
1929	Phoebe Watson/Peggy Saunders Michell
1930	Betty Nuthall/Sarah Palfrey

Year	Champions
1931	Betty Nuthall/Eileen Fearnly Whittingstall
1932	Helen Jacobs/Sarah Palfrey
1933	Betty Nuthall/Freda James
1934	Helen Jacobs/Sarah Palfrey
1935	Helen Jacobs/Sarah Palfrey
1936	Marjorie Gladman Van Ryn/Carolin Babcock
1937	Sarah Palfrey Fabyan/Alice Marble
1938	Sarah Palfrey Fabyan/Alice Marble
1939	Sarah Palfrey Fabyan/Alice Marble
1940	Sarah Palfrey Fabyan/Alice Marble
1941	Sarah Palfrey Fabyan/Margaret Osborne
1942	Louise Brough/Margaret Osborne
1943	Louise Brough/Margaret Osborne
1944	Louise Brough/Margaret Osborne
1945	Louise Brough/Margaret Osborne
1946	Louise Brough/Margaret Osborne
1947	Louise Brough/Margaret Osborne
1948	Louise Brough/Margaret Osborne
1949	Louise Brough/Margaret Osborne
1950	Louise Brough/Margaret Osborne
1951	Shirley Fry/Doris Hart
1952	Shirley Fry/Doris Hart
1953	Shirley Fry/Doris Hart
1954	Shirley Fry/Doris Hart
1955	Louise Brough/Margaret Osborne du Pont
1956	Louise Brough/Margaret Osborne du Pont
1957	Louise Brough/Margaret Osborne du Pont
1958	Jeanne Arth/Margaret Osborne du Pont
1959	Jeanne Arth/Darlene Hard
1960	Maria Bueno/Darlene Hard
1961	Lesley Turner/Darlene Hard
1962	Maria Bueno/Darlene Hard
1963	Margaret Smith/Robyn Ebbern
1964	Billie Jean Moffitt/Karen Hantze Susman
1965	Carole Caldwell Graebner/Nancy Richey
1966	Maria Bueno/Nancy Richey
1967	Billie Jean King/Rosemary Casals
1968	Maria Bueno/Margaret Smith Court
1969	Margaret Smith Court/Virginia Wade
1970	Margaret Smith Court/Judy Tegart Dalton
1971	Rosemary Casals/Judy Tegart Dalton
1972	Françoise Durr/Betty Stove
1973	Margaret Smith Court/Virginia Wade
1974	Billie Jean King/Rosemary Casals
1975	Margaret Smith Court/Virginia Wade
1976	Delina Boshoff/Ilana Kloss
1977	Martina Navratilova/Betty Stove
1978	Martina Navratilova/Billie Jean King
1979	Wendy Turnbull/Betty Stove
1980	Martina Navratilova/Billie Jean King
1981	Kathy Jordan/Anne Smith
1982	Wendy Turnbull/Rosemary Casals
1983	Martina Navratilova/Pam Shriver
1984	Martina Navratilova/Pam Shriver

AUSTRALIAN SINGLES CHAMPIONSHIPS

Year	Champion	Defeated
1922	M. Molesworth	Esna Boyd
1923	M. Molesworth	Esna Boyd
1924	Sylvia Lance	Esna Boyd
1925	Daphne Akhurst	Esna Boyd
1926	Daphne Akhurst	Esna Boyd
1927	Esna Boyd	Sylvia Lance Harper
1928	Daphne Akhurst	Esna Boyd
1929	Daphne Akhurst	Louie Bickerton
1930	Daphne Akhurst	Sylvia L. Harper
1931	Coral Buttsworth	J. Crawford
1932	Coral Buttsworth	K. Le Messurier
1933	Joan Hartigan	Coral Buttsworth
1934	Joan Hartigan	M. Molesworth
1935	Dorothy Round	Nancy Lyle
1936	Joan Hartigan	Nancye L. Wynne
1937	Nancye L. Wynne	Emily Westacott
1938	Dorothy Bundy	D. Stevenson
1939	Emily Westacott	H. C. Hopman
1940	Nancye Wynne	——
1941-45	not played	
1946	Nancye Wynne Bolton	Joyce Fitch
1947	Nancye Wynne Bolton	H. C. Hopman
1948	Nancye Wynne Bolton	M. Toomey
1949	Doris Hart	Nancye Wynne Bolton
1950	Louise Brough	Doris Hart
1951	Nancye Wynne Bolton	Thelma Long
1952	Thelma Long	H. Angwin
1953	Maureen Connolly	Julia Sampson
1954	Thelma Long	J. Staley
1955	Beryl Penrose	Thelma Long
1956	Mary Carter	Thelma Long
1957	Shirley Fry	Althea Gibson
1958	Angela Mortimer	L. Coghlan
1959	Mary Carter Reitano	Renee Schuurman
1960	Margaret Smith	J. Lehane
1961	Margaret Smith	J. Lehane
1962	Margaret Smith	Maria Bueno
1963	Margaret Smith	J. Lehane
1964	Margaret Smith	Lesley Turner
1965	Margaret Smith	Maria Bueno
1966	Margaret Smith	Nancy Richey
1966	Margaret Smith	Nancy Richey
1967	Nancy Richey	Lesley Turner
1968	Billie Jean King	Margaret Smith Court
1969	Margaret Smith Court	Billie Jean King
1970	Margaret Smith Court	Kerry Melville
1971	Margaret Smith Court	Evonne Goolagong
1972	Virginia Wade	Evonne Goolagong
1973	Margaret Smith Court	Evonne Goolagong
1974	Evonne Goolagong	Chris Evert
1975	Evonne Goolagong	Martina Navratilova
1976	Evonne Goolagong Cawley	Renata Tomanova

Year	Champion	Defeated
1977(Jan.)	Kerry Reid	Dianne Fromholtz
1977(Dec.)	Evonne Goolagong Cawley	Helen Cawley
1978	Chris O'Neil	Betsy Nagelsen
1979	Barbara Jordan	Sharon Walsh
1980	Hana Mandlikova	Wendy Turnbull
1981	Martina Navratilova	Chris Evert Lloyd
1982	Chris Evert Lloyd	Martina Navratilova
1983	Martina Navratilova	Kathy Jordan
1984	Chris Evert Lloyd	Helena Sukova

AUSTRALIAN DOUBLES CHAMPIONS

Year	Champions
1922	Esna Boyd/M. Mountain
1923	Esna Boyd/Sylvia Lance
1924	Daphne Akhurst/Sylvia Lance
1925	Daphne Akhurst/Sylvia Lance Harper
1926	Esna Boyd/P. O'Hara Wood
1927	P. O'Hara Wood/Louie Bickerton
1928	Daphne Akhurst/Esna Boyd
1929	Daphne Akhurst/Louie Bickerton
1930	M. Molesworth/E. Hood
1931	Daphne Akhurst Cozens/Louie Bickerton
1932	Coral Buttsworth/Marjorie Crawford
1933	M. Molesworth/Emily Westacott
1934	M. Molesworth/Emily Westacott
1935	Evelyn Dearman/Nancye Wynne
1936	Thelma Coyne/Nancye Wynne
1937	Thelma Coyne/Nancye Wynne
1938	Thelma Coyne/Nancye Wynne
1939	Thelma Coyne/Nancye Wynne
1940	Thelma Coyne/Nancye Wynne
1941-45	not played
1946	Joyce Fitch/Mary Bevis
1947	Nancye Wynne Bolton/Thelma Long
1948	Nancye Wynne Bolton/Thelma Long
1949	Nancye Wynne Bolton/Thelma Long
1950	Louise Brough/Doris Hart
1951	Nancye Wynne Bolton/Thelma Long
1952	Nancye Wynne Bolton/Thelma Long
1953	Maureen Connolly/Julia Sampson
1954	Mary Hawton/Beryl Penrose
1955	Mary Hawton/Beryl Penrose
1956	Mary Hawton/Thelma Long
1957	Althea Gibson/Shirley Fry
1958	Mary Hawton/Thelma Long
1959	Renee Schuurman/Sandra Reynolds
1960	Maria Bueno/Christine Truman
1961	Margaret Smith/Mary Carter Reitano
1962	Margaret Smith/Robyn Ebbern
1963	Margaret Smith/Robyn Ebbern
1964	Judy Tegart/Lesley Turner
1965	Margaret Smith/Lesley Turner
1966	Carole Caldwell Graebner/Nancy Richey
1967	Judy Tegart/Lesley Turner

Year	Champions
1968	Karen Krantzcke/Kerry Melville
1969	Margaret Smith Court/Judy Tegart
1970	Margaret Smith Court/Judy Tegart Dalton
1971	Margaret Smith Court/Evonne Goolagong
1972	Kerry Harris/Helen Gourlay
1973	Margaret Smith Court/Virginia Wade
1974	Evonne Goolagong/Peggy Michel
1975	Evonne Goolagong/Peggy Michel
1976	Evonne Goolagong Cawley/Helen Gourlay
1977(Jan.)	Dianne Fromholtz/Helen Gourlay
1977(Dec.)	no final held
1978	Betsy Nagelsen/Renata Tomanova
1979	Judy Chaloner/Dianne Evers
1980	Martina Navratilova/Betsy Nagelsen
1981	Kathy Jordan/Anne Smith
1982	Martina Navratilova/Pam Shriver
1983	Martina Navratilova/Pam Shriver
1984	Martina Navratilova/Pam Shriver

GRAND SLAM WINNERS

Year	Winner
1953	Maureen Connolly
1970	Margaret Smith Court
1983-84	Martina Navratilova (under new regulations)

TOP 25 CAREER MONEY WINNERS
(As of December 31, 1983)

Ranking	Player	Amount
1	Martina Navratilova	$6,384,089
2	Chris Evert Lloyd	4,796,246
3	Billie Jean King	1,938,112
4	Tracy Austin	1,905,365
5	Wendy Turnbull	1,772,407
6	Virginia Wade	1,469,645
7	Evonne Goolagong Cawley	1,397,706
8	Andrea Jaeger	1,297,807
9	Rosemary Casals	1,280,356
10	Pam Shriver	1,232,818
11	Hana Mandlikova	1,175,609
12	Betty Stove	1,043,917
13	Virginia Ruzici	1,001,653
14	Sue Barker	861,891
15	Mima Jausovec	825,754
16	Kerry Reid	769,681
17	Kathy Jordan	764,958
18	Dianne Fromholtz	725,012
19	Anne Smith	719,993
20	Margaret Smith Court	704,594
21	Sylvia Hanika	699,761
22	Barbara Potter	645,068
23	Bettina Bunge	599,887
24	Ann Kiyomura	535,929
25	Regina Marsikova	440,336

TRACK AND FIELD/DISTANCE RUNNING

A few definitions: field events in which women participate today are the high jump, long jump, shot put, discus, and javelin, which are usually performed in the infield of an arena. Track events are sprinting, running, and hurdles. Distance races, including the marathon, are usually road races; cross country is self-explanatory. Although women ran in the ancient Greek Games of Hera, they were roundly discouraged from participation in the modern events well into the twentieth century. Avery Brundage of the International Olympic Committee declared, "I am fed up to the ears with women as track and field competitors." The women Brundage so opposed had organized the Fédération Sportive Féminine Internationale in 1921, which sponsored the first women's world championships in various events in 1922. Unsuccessful in 1924, the FSFI persuaded officials to include five events for women at the 1928 Olympics: the 100-meter, the 800-meter, the 4 × 100-meter relay, the high jump, and the discus. The victory was hollow. In the 800-meter, most of the women, undertrained and overenthusiastic, sprinted the distance and promptly collapsed. Although six women finished well, their achievement was forgotten in the rush to bar women from distances greater than 200 meters, an Olympic prohibition that stood for 32 years. The other events, over the protests of some officials, remained in Olympic competition; by a very slim margin, the committee voted to include hurdles and javelin at Los Angeles in 1932. The 800-meter was reinstated at the 1960 Olympics, the 1500 introduced at Munich in 1972. Although 234 women ran in the Avon International Marathon in 1980, the I.O.C. had refused to include a 3000-meter for women at the 1980 Moscow Games, since the distance was a "little too strenuous for women." Women knew better: through the 70's, more and more women were running at all distances, and running faster; in 1975 the women's world-best marathon time had been broken three times. In the 80's, it is no longer newsworthy that women enter—and finish—ultramarathons and six-day races. For the first time, in 1984 the Olympics included a women's 3000-meter and a women's marathon; it is hoped by many that intermediate distances will be included in 1988. For "official" marathon records, the International Amateur Athletic Federation recognizes only loop courses— thus, strictly speaking the 1984 Olympic event and some of the best-known marathons do not set records.

Jodi Anderson
born Chicago, Illinois, November 10, 1957

In her first year of competition, Anderson set a junior high school record for the long jump of 16′ 7″; in high school in Los Angeles she competed in four track and field events (the maximum permitted), setting state records; and in college she won the collegiate national long-jump title in 1977 and 1979. She was national long-jump champion 1978-81. Every year from 1977 through 1982, Anderson's long jump was the longest performed in the U.S. She won the collegiate title in the pentathlon (100-meter hurdles, shot put, high jump, long jump, 200-meter dash) in her first year of competition, 1979. In the 1980 Olympic trials Anderson won the pentathlon and long jump, setting an American long-jump record of 22′11¾″ which still stood in the summer of 1984. At the 1984 Olympics at Los Angeles, the pentathlon was replaced by the heptathlon, which adds the javelin throw and the 800-meter run. Sidelined by a serious knee injury for most of 1983, Anderson placed second at the Olympic trials, but injured her leg on the first day of the Los Angeles Games and withdrew after the shot put. Her competition style is serious and impassive, her concentration formidable; the millions who saw her as Pooch in the movie *Personal Best* also remember her warmth.

Evelyn Ashford
born Shreveport, Louisiana, April 15, 1957

Ashford's earliest track experience came in high school, where she was the only girl invited to join the boy's team. Awarded a track scholarship to UCLA, in her freshman year she made the 1976 Olympic team and came in fifth in the 100 meters; within two years she was the number-one sprinter in the U.S. She left UCLA to train full time; in 1979 she set the U.S. record of 21.83 in the 200 meters, won the World Cup 100 meters and 200 meters, and repeated that double victory in 1981. She was national champion in the 60-yard dash 1979-83. But Ashford's career has not been without setbacks, including the U.S. boycott of the 1980 Olympics (where as world champion she was likely to win two gold medals) and a hamstring injury suffered later that year. In 1983 at the U.S.-East Germany meet she lost the 100 meters to Marlies Göhr; in July she broke Göhr's 10.81 world record in the 100 meters set at sea level, with a time of 10.79 at the National Sports Festival in Colorado. Then came the 1983 world championships in Helsinki; after winning her heats in the quarterfinals and semifinals, Ashford reinjured her hamstring and fell in the finals. She sat out the indoor season, returning to competition in April 1984 with a 100-meter victory in a wind-aided time of 10.88, and finished second in the 400 meters, which she ran for training. Going into the 1984 Olympics, she said, "I'm gonna be fit, I'm gonna be mentally prepared, and I'm gonna be curious." Injury at the trials limited her to one individual Olympic event, the 100 meters—and at the Los Angeles Games she won the gold medal in 10.97. (She also was a member of the gold-winning 4 × 400-meter relay team.) After the Games, she faced Göhr—who had not competed in Los Angeles because of the East German boycott—in a meet in Zurich. When the race was over the two top women sprinters of the world had six victories apiece, and Ashford had won this one in 10.76, setting a new—and sea-level—world record.

Joan Benoit
born Cape Elizabeth, Maine, May 16, 1957

A skier since childhood, Benoit began running to get back in shape after a skiing accident in which she broke her leg. She liked running and was good at it. In her senior year in high school, she qualified for the Junior Olympics; in 1979, in her second try at the distance, she won the Boston Marathon in 2:35:15, setting an American record. Her tenth marathon was Boston again, in 1983; again she won, and again she set a record—a remarkable world-best time of 2:22:43. She has set American records at 10K, the half marathon, 10 miles, and 25K. Her 10K of 31:36, run in October 1983, was faster than Grete Waitz's recent times at that distance. (Going into the 1984 Olympics, the Norwegian Waitz, the most consistent of the top runners, had won ten of the eleven races in which both women had competed.) Very simply, Benoit loves to run, and her training reflects that: May-November 1983 she was doing over 100 miles a week, including at least one 20-mile run. Noticing signs of staleness and overtraining, she eased off in early 1984, choosing not to compete in the world cross-country championships in March. Even so, she required surgery on her right knee in April, and it was doubtful she would run in the Olympic marathon trials 17 days later. Not only did she run, she won, in 2:31:04. When the day came, Benoit took the lead before the 3-mile mark and never relinquished it, to win the gold medal in the first Olympic women's marathon in 2:24:52; Waitz was second in 2:26:18. Six weeks later Benoit set a world record of 1:08:34 for the half marathon in the Philadelphia Distance Run. She

Diane Dixon, U.S. indoor champion at 440 yards, 1983 and 1984.

shared the 1984 Women's Sports Foundation's designation of Sportswoman of the Year with a fellow Olympian, the gymnast Mary Lou Retton.

Francina "Fanny" Blankers-Koen
born Amsterdam, The Netherlands, April 26, 1918

When Blankers-Koen was training for the 1948 Olympics, every day she wheeled a baby carriage to the Amsterdam stadium and parked it next to the track while she worked out. Although she had qualified for the Olympics in 1936 (and tied for sixth in the high jump), she had to wait 12 years, until the first post-World War II Games, for her next Olympic chance. She was thirty years old and the mother of two children, born in 1941 and 1945. Like Babe Didrikson Zaharias before her, Blankers-Koen was proficient in more events than the Olympic rules permitted a single athlete to compete in. Blankers-Koen held the world record in the 100-yard dash, the 80-meter hurdles, the long jump, high jump, and two relay events. Limited to three individual events at the London Games in 1948, Blankers-Koen chose the 100-meters, the 200-meters, the 80-meter hurdles and the 4 × 100-meter relay—and won gold medals in each. Had she been permitted to compete in the high jump and the long jump, she probably could have had two more golds, since the winners fell consistently short of her records. She was a national hero on her return to Amsterdam, and she looked forward to the 1952 Olympics in Helsinki. But when the time came, illness, blood poisoning, and a boil on her leg forced her to withdraw from three events; she started the 80-meter hurdles but could not finish. Modest and gallant, she retired with the love of a nation. She was named to the Women's Sports Hall of Fame in 1982.

Valerie Brisco-Hooks
born July 6, 1960

After her son was born in 1982, Brisco-Hooks was 40 pounds overweight and not inclined to run. With her husband's encouragement, she returned to training and competition. In June 1984, trim and elegant, she ran her best time to date in the 200 meters, coming in first in 22.16. She was 1984 national indoor champion in the 220-yard dash, and at the outdoor nationals she won the gold medal in the 400 meters in 49.83, thus becoming the first American woman to break 50 seconds in the event. She lowered that time at the Olympic trials, running 49.79, but came in second to Chandra Cheeseborough, who took first in 49.28. Both women improved even those excellent performances at the Los Angeles Games. Brisco-Hooks took the gold medal in 48.83, breaking the Olympic record of 48.88 set by Marita Koch of East Germany in 1980 and establishing a new American record, and Cheeseborough won the silver in 49.05. That medal was not Brisco-Hooks's only gold: she won the 200 meters in 21.81 (another Olympic record) and shared in the U.S. victory in the 4 × 100-meter relay.

Zola Budd
born Bloemfontein, Orange Free State, South Africa, May 26, 1966

"She looks like a twelve-year-old, runs like a twenty-five-year-old, and is only seventeen. She's unbelievable." This appraisal of Budd was made by Ingrid Kristiansen in May 1984, after a 10K race in Oslo in which Budd placed third, behind Norwegian stars Grete Waitz and Kristiansen. In January 1984 Budd had run 5000 meters in 15:01.83, seven seconds faster than previous records established by Mary Decker of the U.S. and by Waitz. (Decker's time of 15:08.26 was not officially lowered until Kristiansen ran 14:58.89 in June 1984.) South Africa has been suspended by the International Amateur Athletic Federation because of its policy of apartheid, and until Budd became a British citizen in April 1984 her records were "unofficial" and she was ineligible for international competition. Since then, she won the 1500 meter event in the British track and field championships with a time of 4:4.39, and she qualified for the British Olympic team in a 3000-meter race that she won in 8:40.2, a time that set a new European junior record. In July 1984 she ran 2000 meters in a record 5:33.15. On the track Budd runs barefoot, as schoolchildren do in South Africa. Her long thin legs move in a unique stride for distance runners, with little knee lift but a tremendous kick in back. Her training is mostly distance, with little speedwork. She looks forward to running longer distances as she matures, the half marathon and the marathon— she has already done ten miles in 55:28. At the Los Angeles Games, she tangled with Mary Decker in the 3000 meter final; Decker fell to the track, could not continue, and later blamed Budd for interfering, although other runners stated that Budd was not at fault. Because of the incident, Budd finished a disappointing seventh in the race.

Chandra Cheeseborough
born Jacksonville, Florida, January 10, 1959

When Cheeseborough runs, she doesn't hear the crowds or the music— she is totally concentrated on her own performance. As soon as the event is over, she is affable and easygoing with public and press. She went to the Montreal Olympics in 1976, finishing sixth in the 100-meter dash (.06 of a second behind teammate Evelyn Ashford). In 1980 she again made the Olympic track team, but the U.S. boycotted the Moscow Games. She was indoor national champion in the 220-yard dash in 1979 and 1981-83. Like her idol, Wilma Rudolph, Cheeseborough comes from Tennessee State University; in 1981 she was a member of the national championship Tennessee State team that set world indoor records in both the 880-yard sprint medley relay (1:42.17) and the 640-yard relay (1:08.9). Cheese-borough excels at distances ranging from the 60-yard dash (she placed second in the national championship in 1983, first in the 1984 Millrose Games event, and first in the 55 meters at the 1984 Vitalis/U.S. Olympic Invitational) to the 400 meters (she set an American record of 49.28 seconds when she won that event at the 1984 Olympic trials). At the Los Angeles Games, Cheeseborough's 49.28 record was broken by teammate Valerie Brisco-Hooks, who won the event in 48.83; Cheeseborough won the silver medal in her own best time of 49.05. Later that week she was a member of the gold-medal-winning U.S. team in the 4 × 400-meter relay, which set an Olympic record of 3:18.29 (breaking the previous Olympic record, established by the East German team at Montreal in 1976, of 3:19.23), and the victorious 4 × 100-meter relay team.

Chandra Cheeseborough

Mary Decker

Mary Decker
born Flemington, New Jersey, August 4, 1958

According to Frank Shorter, 1972 Olympic gold medalist in the marathon, "Mary is that remarkable combination of form and strength." Decker has tremendous stamina and is a joy to watch. But her amazing career has been studded with injuries and enforced layoffs—in ten years of running, 1983 was the first year she ran injury-free. At fifteen she set three world records (the outdoor 800 meters, indoor 880 yards, and indoor 1000 yards). But, perhaps from too much too soon, she developed severe shin splints that were finally successfully treated by surgery in 1977 and 1978. In the first nine months of 1980, apparently stronger than ever, she set a world outdoor record in the mile (4:21.7) and world indoor records in 1500 meters (4:00.8), 880 yards (1:59.7) and a world best indoor mile of 4:17.55 set on an oversized track (greater than 220 yards) and thus not considered an official record. Then, more injuries and little running in 1981. After recovery, more records, including the world records at 5000 and 10,000 meters, fell to her in 1982, and that year she was the first woman to receive the Jesse Owens Award, which is presented annually to the best U.S. track and field athlete; in 1983 she was the sixth woman to receive the Sullivan Award and was Women's Sports Foundation Sportswoman of the Year for the third time (she had been named previously in 1980 and 1982). At the 1983 world championships in Helsinki she won gold medals in the 1500 and 3000 meters. As for the Olympics: in 1972 she was barely fourteen and not ready, shin splints kept her out in 1976, the U.S. boycott kept her out in 1980. In 1984, she qualified for both the 1500 and 3000 meters in the Olympic trials, but at the Los Angeles Games she chose to run in only the 3000 to maximize her chance of a gold medal. With three laps to go in the final, she tripped and fell in an entanglement with Zola Budd of Great Britain, and injured her hip; she could not finish.

Marlies Göhr
born East Germany

At the time of the 1976 Montreal Olympics, Göhr was still Marlies Oelsner, and her performance also seems to belong to someone else: she finished eighth in the 100-meter dash (her time: 11.34), behind both Evelyn Ashford (fifth) and Chandra Cheeseborough (sixth) of the U.S. Beginning in 1977, Göhr held the world record in the 100 meters most of the time over the next six years. By June 1983 she had lowered the world-best time to 10.81; a month later, in the thinner air of Colorado, Ashford took it down to 10.79. Göhr won the gold medal at the world championships in Helsinki in August 1983 (Ashford was injured in the race and did not finish), and was a member of the first-place East German 4 × 100-meter relay team. Göhr did win a gold medal at Montreal in 1976, sharing in the victory of the East German 4 × 100-meter relay team; in 1980, at the Moscow Olympics (where the U.S. did not compete), she won the silver medal in the 100 meters, losing to Ludmila Kondratyeva of the Soviet Union by .01 of a second. East Germany did not compete in the 1984 Los Angeles Olympics; in a Soviet-bloc meet in July, Göhr ran 100 meters in 10.91, her sixth race under 11 seconds in 1984, and at the Soviet-sponsored Friendship-84 games in August, she won the 100 meters in 10.95.

Stephanie Hightower set U.S. records in 100-meter hurdles (1982) and 60-yard and 60-meter hurdles (1983).

Marita Koch
born Wismar, East Germany

An all-around sprinter, Koch feels that work at the various distances improves her overall performance: the starts in the shorter events help her speed in the 400's, the 400's give her strength and endurance to go all out in the shorter distances. She was on the East German Olympic team at Montreal in 1976 and was a favorite to win the 400 meters, but she was injured in the semifinal and had to withdraw. She began medical studies in 1977 on a long schedule that would allow her time for training and competing, and in 1979 she broke the 400-meter world record three times and 200-meter once. (She was the first woman to run the 400 meters in under 49 seconds, the first to break 22 seconds in the 200.) In the 1980 Olympic Games at Moscow, Koch won the 400 meters handily, setting an Olympic record of 48.88 (.28 of a second slower than her own world best). She planned to retire after 1984 to pursue her studies; she was a favorite to repeat her victory in the 200 at the 1984 Olympics in Los Angeles, but East Germany did not compete. In a Soviet-bloc meet in July 1984, she duplicated her 1979 world record and ran the 200 meters in 21.71.

Jarmila Kratochvilova
born Golcuv Jenikov, Czechoslovakia, January 26, 1951
Unlike many world-class athletes, Kratochvilova did not come from a sports-conscious family, nor was she particularly talented athletically as a child. But she was gifted with prodigious strength and determination and, as she has put it, "In the morning I always came out for the training. I knew that if I kept up the hard training, the successes would slowly come." They did, despite illness and injury. Her progress in the 70's was slow going, but at the Moscow Olympics in 1980 she won the silver medal (to East German Marita Koch's gold) in the 400 meters with a time of 49.46. She defeated Koch in the World Cup 400 in 1981. Her great year was 1983; she had an undefeated season, crowned by her performance at the world championships in Helsinki. The scheduling of events was horrendous: Kratochvilova had to run her 800-meter final only half an hour after her 400 semifinal. She won the 800 in 1:54.68, and the next day won the 400 final, setting a world record of 47.99. She was then thirty-two years old. Two weeks earlier, in Munich, she had set a world record in the 800 meters of 1:53.28. Kratochvilova had hoped to cap her 17-year career with an Olympic gold medal in 1984 and retire. That dream was gone with Czechoslovakia's withdrawal from the Los Angeles Games. But she did defeat an Olympic gold-medal winner (indeed, a triple gold-medal winner), when she outran Valerie Brisco-Hooks of the U.S. in the 400 meters at the International Cologne Sports Festival later that August with a time of 49.56 to Brisco-Hooks's 49.83.

Carol Lewis
born Willingboro, New Jersey, August 8, 1963
Six days a week, Lewis trains by running and weightlifting. Jumping? Only once a week. "Once you've learned the technique," she has pointed out, "you don't lose it—you perfect it." Lewis has perfected her indoor long jump to the American record of 22' 2¼", set in February 1984. Her best outdoor jump, unaided by wind, is 22' 10½". In outdoor competition, she was national long jump champion in 1982 and 1983, and won the bronze medal at the 1983 world championships in Helsinki. Since early 1984 she wears eyeglasses in competition; her astigmatism cannot be fully corrected by her contact lenses, and she was pulling to the side

as she approached her jump. Like her brother Carl, she is accomplished
in more than one event; she has performed well in hurdles, high jump,
and shot put. She made the 1980 Olympic team, which did not compete
at Moscow; in 1984 at Los Angeles, she placed ninth, with a jump of
21′ 1¼″

Carol Lewis

Canadian Britt McRoberts, 1984
winner of the Mobil Mile, the U.S.
indoor championship

Ulrike Meyfarth
born Köln-Rodenkirchen, West Germany, May 4, 1956

In 1972 high jumper Meyfarth was a sixteen-year-old schoolgirl. She
was also the youngest athlete, man or woman, to win an individual Olympic
track and field gold medal. She had finished third in the West German
Olympic trials for the Munich Games, and not much was expected of her.
But at the Games she jumped 2¾″ higher than she ever had before, to
equal the then world record of 6′ 3½″. At the Montreal Games in 1976,
Meyfarth was eliminated in an early round, and in 1980 West Germany
boycotted the Moscow Games. Meyfarth continued to jump higher and
higher; in 1983 she won the silver medal at the world championships in
Helsinki (Tamara Bykova of the Soviet Union won the gold), and she
achieved 6′ 8″ at the European Cup competition, which was bettered by
¼″ when Bykova set a new world record a week later. (In June 1984
Bykova went to 6′ 8¾″, and in July Ludmila Andonova of Bulgaria set a
new world record with a jump of 6′ 9½″; neither Bykova nor Androva
competed at the 1984 Los Angeles Olympics because of the Soviet-led
boycott.) Twelve years after her first Olympics, Meyfarth came to the Los
Angeles Games and won the gold medal in the high jump with an Olympic
record jump of 6′ 7½″.

Irina Press
born Leningrad, Soviet Union, March 10, 1939

Tamara Press
born Leningrad, Soviet Union, May 10, 1937

The greatest of Soviet women athletes in the 60's in field events, the Press sisters between them won one silver and five gold Olympic medals, and set 26 world records. Tamara was unexcelled at the shot put—she broke the women's world record six times outdoors, three times indoors, and was the first woman to exceed 60'. At the 1960 Rome Olympics she won the gold medal in shot put, setting an Olympic record of 56' 10", and the silver medal in the discus throw; Irina won the gold medal in 80-meter hurdles, ahead of the field from start to finish (she had set an Olympic record of 10.6 in the semifinals). In 1964, at the Tokyo Games, Tamara won the gold medal in shot put for the second time (with an Olympic record of 59' 6¼") and was first in discus as well, setting an Olympic record of 187' 10", which was considerably short of her own then world record of 194' 5¾". For the first time the pentathlon appeared on the Olympic schedule: Irina won it, beating her own world record in total points with 5,246. The following year Tamara competed in the shot put event at the U.S. national indoor championships, winning with 57' 2½", a meet record that stood for 13 years. Officials on that occasion remember not only her performance but also her manner and sportsmanship: after the shot put competition was finished, she walked back to the ring to shake hands and thank them—a gesture no other athlete, American or foreign, ever made. A few months later, in September, she set another of her world records at the European championships, putting the shot 61' on her first try.

Louise Ritter
born Red Oak, Texas

One of a large family active in sports, Ritter was a good high school athlete in a number of events, the high jump emerging as her favorite. As a freshman at Texas Woman's University in 1977, she changed her technique from straddle to flop, and a few months later won the first of her three national collegiate championships. She continued with track in college, and her sprint work has given her an exceptionally fast approach to her jump. In 1978 she won the national outdoor title, and in 1979 she took the gold medal at the Pan American Games. She won the high jump event at the 1980 Olympic trials, but had to stay home from Moscow because of the U.S. boycott. She had down years in 1981 and 1982 because of injury, but returned to a full schedule in 1983 and had a splendid year, jumping an average of 6' 6" in ten meets. At the Millrose Games in January she won the gold medal with a jump of 6' 5"; she won the bronze medal at the world championships in Helsinki with 6' 4¾"; and in September she jumped a 6' 7", setting an American record. But 1984 was less consistent, because of injury and possibly overtraining, and at the Los Angeles Olympics she placed eighth with a jump of 6' 3¼".

Allison Roe
born Auckland, New Zealand, May 30, 1957

Proficient in swimming and ballet, Roe was Auckland under-sixteen tennis champion and a member of the national under-twenty-three tennis team. She started running at seventeen; at eighteen she was New Zealand cross-country champion. After an injury in early 1980, she began doing longer-distance work. She finished fourth in the 1980 Tokyo Women's Marathon in 2:42:24, and ran the Auckland Marathon in 2:36. Her winning performance in April 1981 in the Boston Marathon (2:26:46) set a course record and cut more than seven minutes off the previous women's best time. Six months later, Roe was the first woman to finish in the 1981 New York City Marathon, and her 2:25:29 set a world record. For most of 1982 Roe suffered from achilles tendon injury and other lower leg problems; in March she ran the Seoul Marathon in 2:43:12, but severe leg cramps caused her to drop out of the Boston Marathon in the seventeenth mile the following month, and because of continuing achilles difficulties she did not run the New York event. Injuries were troubling also in 1983; in 1984 she finished seventh in the Osaka Women's Marathon, and in the Boston Marathon she was fourth woman at the 25-mile-mark when again leg cramps forced her withdrawal. After her tremendous 1981 win in the New York City Marathon, Roe predicted that a woman would break the 2:25 mark. Less than two years later, Joan Benoit took only 2:22:43 to run the Boston Marathon, and women are now looking straight at 2:20.

Wilma Rudolph
born St. Bethlehem, Tennessee, June 23, 1940

Born prematurely to a large and caring family in rural Tennessee, Rudolph's childhood was a nightmare of polio, scarlet fever, double pneumonia; she could not walk without a brace until she was eleven. After she was stricken her family took turns massaging the affected leg four times a day for two years, and her mother took her weekly to Nashville, 45 miles away, for heat treatments and hydrotherapy. When she was eight she could walk with a brace; by the time she was eleven she had graduated to corrective shoes. The shoes didn't stop her from playing basketball with her brothers; and when in time they proved a hindrance rather than a help she played barefoot. In high school she made the basketball team and was all-state at fifteen; by sixteen she was a fine runner, winning state high school titles at 50, 75, and 100 yards. She qualified for the 1956 Olympics team (after only a year of high school competition) and shared in the bronze medal for the 4 × 100-meter relay. Two months before the next Olympiad, at Rome in 1960, Rudolph had set a world record of 22.9 seconds in the 200 meters. Running into a strong wind, she couldn't beat that time in Rome, but the gold medal was hers. She also won the gold medal in the 100 meters, but this time the wind was at the runners' backs, so her 11 seconds flat did not establish a record. Her third gold medal came to her as a member of the first-place U.S. team in the 4 × 100-meter relay. After the 1960 Olympics Rudolph set new world records in the 100 and 200 meters which survived the next Olympiad. She was a cheerful and popular competitor, and after the Rome Games, her coach, Ed Temple, said, "She's done more for her country than the United States could pay her for." She was AP Athlete of the Year in 1960 and 1961, and won the Sullivan Award in 1961; she was named to the Women's Sports Hall of Fame in 1980.

Wilma Rudolph

Willye White, five-time U.S. Olympian

Ria Stalman
born The Netherlands

Discus thrower Stalman has a "special relationship" with the U.S., training in America and competing with the Los Angeles Track Club; she was even a U.S. collegiate champion. Internationally, she competes for The Netherlands. She was national collegiate champion in her days at the University of Texas/El Paso (1978) and Arizona State (1979, 1981). In spring 1983 she had a world-best throw of 220′ 6″, bettered later in the year when Galina Savinkova of the Soviet Union hurled 240′ 4″ (since then, in August 1984, Irina Mesynski of East Germany threw a world-record 240′ 8″, surpassed ten days later when Czechoslovakian Zdena Silhava threw 244′ 11″). At the world championships at Helsinki in August, Stalman finished seventh, behind six Soviet and East European athletes (but ahead of Savinkova, who placed eleventh). Competing in the U.S. in 1984, Stalman set an American record in June when she threw 221′ 9″ to win the gold medal at the national outdoor track and field championships; at that competition she took the shot put as well, with 59′ 1½″. Less than a month before the Los Angeles Olympic Games, Stalman made a throw of 233′ 8″. When reporters asked her what she thought the reaction would be in The Netherlands, she said, "I think they'll go bonkers when they read of this one!" The Dutch had more to celebrate in August, when at the Los Angeles Games (where the Soviets and most East Europeans did not compete) Stalman won the gold medal with a throw of 214′ 5″.

Helen Stephens
born Fulton, Missouri, February 13, 1918

In high school, informally timed by her coach, Stephens did 50 yards in 5.8 seconds—that matched the existing world record. The next year, 1935, was her first appearance at the national track and field championships: she won the 50-meter dash, the standing long jump, and the shot put, and repeated that performance in 1936. At the time of the Olympics in 1936, she held the world record in the 100 meters with a time of 11.6; at the Berlin Games she won the event in a wind-aided 11.5. She won a second gold medal as a member of the winning U.S. 4 × 100-meter relay team. Hitler asked to meet her, and she returned his Nazi salute with "a good old Missouri handshake." No doubt as forthrightly, she declined his suggestion of a weekend together. Back in the U.S., she won national titles in 1937 in the 50-meter dash, the shot put, and the 200-meter dash, and then retired, undefeated on the track. Almost 50 years later she was competing again, in the Senior Olympics—and, through 1983, is still undefeated.

Irina Kirszenstein Szewinska
born Leningrad, Soviet Union, May 24, 1946

Despite her birthplace, Kirszenstein Szewinska is Polish, and she competed for Poland at the Olympic Games—five of them. In her first, the Tokyo Games in 1964, she won silver medals in the 200 meters and the long jump, and was a member of the gold-medal-winning 4 × 100-meter relay team. At Mexico City in 1968 she won the gold medal in the 200 meters with a world-record time of 22.5 and came in third in the 100 meters. Before the Munich Games in 1972 she had given birth to a son; nonetheless, she won the bronze medal in the 200 meters. In 1972 Kirszenstein Szewinska began training for the 400 meters, and in her second 400-meter race, in 1974, she was the first woman to break 50 seconds for the distance. Between 1974 and 1978—when she was age twenty-eight to thirty-two—she won 34 consecutive 400-meter races; she was finally defeated by Marita Koch of East Germany at the 1978 European championships. Returning to Olympic competition at the Montreal Games, she won the gold medal in her new distance, setting a world record of 49.29. She competed again at the Moscow Games in 1980, but pulled a muscle in the 400-meter semifinal and had to withdraw. Twice she competed in the U.S. track and field championships—1969 and 1973—and won the gold medal in the long jump both times.

Wyomia Tyus
born Griffin, Georgia, August 29, 1945

Tennessee State University has been home to great American women athletes for 30 years. One of its daughters was Wilma Rudolph, and another was Tyus, who was the first to equal Rudolph's world record of 11.2 seconds in the 100 meters. Tyus achieved that time in a preliminary heat at the 1964 Tokyo Olympics; in the final her time was slower (11.4) but good enough for the gold. At Tokyo, Tyus also won a silver medal in the 4 × 100-meter relay. After the Olympics her family wanted her to retire from competition; athletics, they felt, was unfeminine. Instead Tyus proceeded to win three consecutive 60-yard-dash national championships (1965-67), setting world records twice (6.8 in 1965, 6.5 in 1966). She was preparing for the 1968 Olympics, and again met with discouragement: the competition would be formidable, and no one had ever won the Olympic 100-meter twice in a row. At Mexico City Tyus did just that. Facing a field that included the four other holders of the then world record of 11.1, she brought the record down to 11.0 and had her gold medal. She shared in another gold medal at Mexico City when the U.S. team won the 4 × 100-meter relay in a world-record 42.8. She was inducted into the Women's Sports Hall of Fame in 1981, and in 1983, when track and field sportswriters and statisticians picked an All-Time Team, the woman sprinter named was Tyus.

Grete Andersen Waitz
born Oslo, Norway, October 1, 1953
   "I'm just a very, very normal person and I just happen to run fast." Waitz has certainly run into the hearts of New Yorkers: her manner is serene and confident, yet modest and unpretentious, and she has won the New York City Marathon six times (1978-80, 1982-84). Her background is on the track: she was Norwegian junior champion in the 400 meters and 800 meters. She qualified for the Olympics in the 1500 meters in 1972 and 1976, but did not make the finals either time. She won the World Cup 3000 meters in 1977 and in 1978 achieved times of 4:00.55 in the 1500 and 8:31.75 in the 800, but she felt she had reached her limit. Then she found her distance in the marathon. She has said, "I think the main reason I've run well in the marathon is my strength. My running technique is not very good for track. The reason I have run fast times on the track is because I'm strong." Her time in her first marathon, 2:32:30 at New York in 1978, took 2 minutes off the existing world record. Since then she has lowered the world record by 9 minutes, and until the 1984 Olympics she had won every marathon she has completed (she could not finish the 1981 New York City Marathon because of shin splints, and in 1982 she had to drop out of the Boston Marathon at mile 23 with cramps in her quadriceps muscles). In 1983 she won the London Marathon in 2:25:29 and the world championship in 2:28:09. With her 1984 victory in the L'Eggs Mini Marathon (10K) in New York, she has won the event five times; she is also a five-time winner of the world cross-country championships. Runners talk of "running within yourself"; that is what Waitz does, running a controlled, beautiful race from start to finish. In the first Olympic women's marathon, held at the 1984 Los Angeles Games, she won the silver medal with a time of 2:26:18. Twelve weeks later, overcoming heat, humidity, stomach cramps, and diarrhea, Waitz bravely won her sixth New York City Marathon on October 28, 1984, in 2:29:30.

Mildred "Babe" Didrikson Zaharias
born Port Arthur, Texas, June 26, 1914; died September 27, 1956
   A teammate at the 1932 Olympics, Jean Shiley, later said, "Muhammad Ali wasn't the first to say, 'I am the greatest.' Babe was." And perhaps

she was. From a large, active, and sports-minded family, Didrikson Zaharias was a star high school basketball player and twice named All-American, her nickname reflected her baseball prowess, and before her eighteenth birthday she held three national track and field records. The 1932 national track and field championships served also as the Olympic trials. Didrikson Zaharias entered eight of the ten events, won five (shot put, baseball throw, long jump, 80-meter hurdles, and javelin throw), and tied Shiley for first in the high jump. That day her hurdles, javelin throw, and high jump set world records. At the Olympics she was limited to three individual events; she chose her world-record three. She won gold medals in the javelin throw, setting an Olympic record of 143' 4", and the 80-meter hurdles, setting a world record of 11.7 seconds. In the high jump she competed again against Shiley. The two tied on their first jump, a world record 5' 5¼"; both failed the next jump, 5' 6". A jump-off at 5' 5¾" was held; both women cleared, but the judges decided Didrikson Zaharias's style—a version of the later, and legal, Fosbury flop—was illegal, since her head cleared the bar before her body. That year she won the first of her five AP Athlete of the Year Awards. Suspended from amateur competition because she had permitted her name and likeness to be used in a car ad, she began a varied sports/entertainment career, playing exhibitions in baseball, tennis, and basketball. She began playing golf seriously in 1934, and had a stunning career. She won her third U.S. Open—by a comfortable 12 strokes—two years before her death from cancer. **See also Golf.**

OLYMPIC RECORDS
Track Events

Event	Record-holder	Country	Time	Year
100M	Evelyn Ashford	USA	10.97	1984/Los Angeles
200M	Valerie Brisco-Hooks	USA	21.81	1984/Los Angeles
400M	Valerie Brisco-Hooks	USA	48.83	1984/Los Angeles
800M	Nadezhda Olizarenko	USSR	1:53.42	1980/Moscow
1500M	Tatyana Kazankina	USSR	3:56.6	1980/Moscow
3000M	Maricica Puica	Romania	8:35.96	1984/Los Angeles
Marathon	Joan Benoit	USA	2:24.52	1984/Los Angeles
100M Hurdles	Vera Komisova	USSR	12:56	1980/Moscow
400M Hurdles	Nawal El Moutawakil	Morocco	54.61	1984/Los Angeles
4 × 100M relay	East Germany		41.60	1980/Moscow
4 × 400M relay	USA		3:18.29	1984/Los Angeles

Field Events

Event	Record-holder	Country	Distance	Year
High Jump	Ulrike Meyfarth	West Germany	6' 7.5"	1984/Los Angeles
Long Jump	Tatiana Kilpakova	USSR	23' 2"	1980/Moscow

Event	Record-holder	Country	Distance	Year
Shot Put	Ivanka Hristova	Bulgaria	69' 5.25"	1976/Montreal
Discus Throw	Evelin Schlaak	East Germany	229' 6"	1980/Moscow
Javelin Throw	Tessa Sanderson	Great Britain	228' 2"	1984/Los Angeles
Heptathlon	Glynis Nunn	Australia	6390 pts.	1984/Los Angeles

WORLD RECORD-HOLDERS
Track Events Indoor

Event	Record-holder	Country	Time	Year
50 yards	Evelyn Ashford	USA	5.73	1983
50 meters	Marita Koch	East Germany	6.11	1980
60 yards	Evelyn Ashford	USA	6.54	1982
60 meters	Marita Koch	East Germany	7.08	1983
100 yards	Marlies Göhr	East Germany	10.29	1980
100 meters	Marita Koch	East Germany	11.15	1980
200 meters	Marita Koch	East Germany	22.39	1983
300 yards	Merlene Ottey	Jamaica	32.63	1982
300 meters	Merlene Ottey	Jamaica	35.83	1981
400 meters	Jarmila Kratochvilova	Czechoslovakia	49.59	1982
500 yards	Rosalyn Bryant	USA	1:03.3	1977
500 yards	Janine MacGregor	Great Britain	1:03.3	1982
500 meters	Lorna Forde	Barbados	1:10.5	1978
600 yards	Delisa Walton	USA	1:17.38	1982
600 meters	Anita Weiss	East Germany	1:26.2	1980
800 meters	Olga Vakrusheva	USSR	1:58.4	1980
1000 yards	Mary Decker	USA	2:23.8	1978
1000 meters	Brigitte Kraus	West Germany	2:34.8	1978
1500 meters	Mary Decker	USA	4:00.8	1980
1 mile	Mary Decker	USA	4:20.5	1982
3000 meters	Mary Decker	USA	8:47.3	1982
2 miles	Jan Merrill	USA	9:31.7	1979
2 miles	Mary Decker	USA	9:31.7	1983
50Y Hurdles	Johana Klier	East Germany	6.2	1978
50M Hurdles	Annelie Ehrhardt	East Germany	6.74	1973
50M Hurdles	Zofia Bielczyk	Poland	6.74	1981
60Y Hurdles	Stephanie Hightower	USA	7.36	1983
60M Hhurdles	Bettine Jahn	East Germany	7.75	1983

Field Events Indoor

Event	Record-holder	Country	Distance	Year
High Jump	Tamara Bykova	USSR	6' 7.5"	1983
Long Jump	Anisoara Cusmir	Romania	22' 9.25"	1983
Shot Put	Helena Fibingerova	Czechoslovakia	73' 10"	1977

Track Events Outdoor

Event	Record-holder	Country	Time	Year
100 meters	Evelyn Ashford	USA	10.76	1984
200 meters	Marita Koch	East Germany	21.71	1979
400 meters	Jarmila Kratochvilova	Czechoslovakia	47.99	1983
800 meters	Jarmila Kratochvilova	Czechoslovakia	1:53.28	1983
1000 meters	Tatyana Providokhina	USSR	2:30.6	1978
1500 meters	Tatyana Providokhina	USSR	3:52.47	1980
1 mile	Maricica Puica	Romania	4:17.44	1982
2000 meters	Maricica Puica	Romania	5:35.5	1979
3000 meters	Tatyana Kazankina	USSR	8:22.62	1984
5000 meters	Ingrid Kristensen	Norway	14:58.89	1984
10,000 meters	Olga Bondarenko	USSR	31:13.78	1984
15,000 meters	Silvana Cruciata	Italy	49.44.0	1981
100M Hurdles	Grazyna Rabsztyn	Poland	12.36	1980
400M Hurdles	Margarita Ponomaryova	USSR	53.58	1984
4 × 100M relay	East Germany		41.53	1983
4 × 400M relay	East Germany		3:15.92	1984

Field Events Outdoor

Event	Record-holder	Country	Distance	Year
High Jump	Ludmila Andonova	Bulgaria	6' 9.5"	1984
Long Jump	Anisoara Cusmir	Romania	24' 4.5"	1981
Shot Put	Natalia Lysovskaya	USSR	73' 11"	1984
Discus Throw	Zdena Silhava	Czechoslovakia	244' 11"	1984
Javelin Throw	Tilina Lillak	Finland	245' 3"	1983
Heptathlon	Sabine Paetz	East Germany	6867 pts.	1984

U.S. RECORD-HOLDERS
Track Events Indoor

Event	Record-holder	Time	Year
50 yards	Evelyn Ashford	5.73	1983
50 meters	Jeanette Bolden	6.13	1981
60 yards	Evelyn Ashford	6.54	1982
60 meters	Jeanette Bolden	7.21	1981
220 yards	Chandra Cheeseborough	23.25	1982
300 yards	Diane Dixon	33.83	1983
300 meters	Diane Dixon	37.50	1983
400 meters	Diane Dixon	53.17	1983
440 yards	Lori McCauley	53.29	1983
500 yards	Rosalyn Bryant	1:03.3	1977
500 meters	Edna Brown	1:11.1	1984
600 yards	Delisa Walton	1:17.38	1982
600 meters	Delisa Walton	1:26.56	1981
800 meters	Mary Decker	1:58.9	1980
880 yards	Mary Decker	1:59.7	1980
1000 yards	Mary Decker	2:23.8	1978

Event	Record-holder	Time	Year
1000 meters	Diana Richburg	2:40.1	1982
1 mile	Mary Decker	4:20.5	1982
2000 meters	Mary Decker	5:51.1	1982
3000 meters	Mary Decker	8:47.3	1982
2 miles	Mary Decker	9:31.7	1983
5000 meters	Margaret Groos	15:34.5	1981
50Y Hurdles	Deby LaPlante	6.37	1978
50M Hurdles	Candy Young	6.85	1983
60Y Hurdles	Stephanie Hightower	7.36	1983
60M Hurdles	Stephanie Hightower	8.02	1983
4 × 200M relay	Morgan State	1:36.8	1981
4 × 400M relay	University of Texas	3:37.88	1981

Field Events Indoor

Event	Record-holder	Distance	Year
High Jump	Colleen Sommer	6'6.75"	1982
Long Jump	Carol Lewis	22'2.25"	1984
Shot Put	Maren Seidler	61'2.25"	1978

Track Events Outdoor

Event	Record-holder	Time	Year
100 meters	Evelyn Ashford	10.76	1984
200 meters	Evelyn Ashford	21.83	1979
400 meters	Chandra Cheeseborough	49.28	1984
800 meters	Mary Decker	1:57.60	1983
1000 meters	Madeline Manning	2:37.30	1976
1500 meters	Mary Decker	3:57.12	1983
1 mile	Mary Decker	4:18.08	1982
2000 meters	Mary Decker	5:38.90	1982
3000 meters	Mary Decker	8:29.71	1982
5000 meters	Mary Decker	15:08.26	1982
10,000 meters	Mary Decker	31.35.3	1982
15,000 meters	Nancy Conz	53:06	1981
100M Hurdles	Stephanie Hightower	12.79	1982
400M Hurdles	Lori McCauley	55.69	1983
4 × 100M relay	U.S. team	41.61	1983
4 × 400M relay	U.S. Olympic team	3:18.29	1984

Field Events Outdoor

Event	Record-holder	Record	Year
High Jump	Louise Ritter	6' 7"	1983
Long Jump	Jodi Anderson	22' 11.75"	1980
Shot Put	Maren Seidler	62'7.75"	1979
Discus Throw	Leslie Deniz	213' 11"	1984
Javelin Throw	Kate Schmidt	227' 5"	1977
Heptathlon	Jane Frederick	6714	1984

BOSTON MARATHON CHAMPIONS

Year	Champion	Country	Time
1972	Nina Kuscsik	USA	3:10:26
1973	Jacqueline Hansen	USA	3:05:59
1974	Miki Gorman	USA	2:47:11
1975	Liane Winter	West Germany	2:42:24
1976	Kim Merritt	USA	2:47:10
1977	Miki Gorman	USA	2:48:33
1978	Gayle Barron	USA	2:44:52
1979	Joan Benoit	USA	2:35:15
1980	Jacqueline Gareau	Canada	2:34:28
1981	Allison Roe	New Zealand	2:26:46
1982	Charlotte Teske	West Germany	2:29:33
1983	Joan Benoit	USA	2:22:43
1984	Lorraine Moller	New Zealand	2:29:28

NEW YORK CITY MARATHON CHAMPIONS

Year	Champion	Country	Time
1971	Beth Bonner	USA	2:55:22
1972	Nina Kuscsik	USA	3:18:42
1973	Nina Kuscsik	USA	2:57:08
1974	Kathrine Switzer	USA	3:07:29
1975	Kim Merritt	USA	2:46:15
1976	Miki Gorman	USA	2:39:11
1977	Miki Gorman	USA	2:43:10
1978	Grete Waitz	Norway	2:32:30
1979	Grete Waitz	Norway	2:27:33
1980	Grete Waitz	Norway	2:25:42
1981	Allison Roe	New Zealand	2:25:29
1982	Grete Waitz	Norway	2:27:14
1983	Grete Waitz	Norway	2:27:00
1984	Grete Waitz	Norway	2:29:30

TRIATHLON

Some may call it lotus-land, but think again: California is the birthplace of the triathlon, a combination of three demanding endurance sports, biking, running, and swimming. In the 70's bike clubs in that state began combining their races with other sports, often with running and swimming, sometimes with kayaking. (Strictly speaking, of course, a triathlon can be a combination of any three physical contests.) The event that put the triathlon on the map was the first Hawaii Ironman Triathlon in 1978, combining the distances of three important Hawaii races: the Waikiki Rough-Water Swim (2.4 miles), the Around-the-Island Oahu Bicycle Race (112 miles), and the Honolulu Marathon (26.2 miles). There were 15 participants, all men, 12 of whom finished; in 1984 hundreds of contenders took part, many of them women. This race, now known as the Budweiser Light Ironman Triathlon World Championship, is the toughest. An "iron" athlete originally meant one who participates in all three segments, as opposed to a member of a relay team; lately, the term has been used to refer to events of ultra distances, while shorter races have been called "tinmans." Like the distances, the sequence of the three segments is not fixed, although for safety reasons the usual order is swim-bike-run. Self-reliance is an important part of the triathlon philosophy; in many triathlons there are no pit stops and in the cycle segment drafting is illegal. The first New York Triathlon was held in August 1984 (a 1.9-mile swim from the Statue of Liberty to the Battery, a 21.3-mile bike ride, and a 7.4-mile run in Central Park—the first woman finisher was **Jann Girard** of Austin, Texas, in 2:19:54). There is talk of an Olympic triathlon by 1992; in the meantime, California provided another leap forward, the first all-women triathlon, sponsored by Bonne Bell, held in 1983, which attracted 630 women competing as individuals and 117 relay teams. **Lyn Lemaire** of the U.S. was the first woman to finish the Hawaii Ironman, completing the 1979 event in 12:55:38 (five years later, Lemaire founded *Ultrasport* magazine, of which she is publisher). For consistency and performance, veteran **Sally Edwards** is the top American endurance athlete, competing in marathons, ultramarathons, and triathlons since 1978. Her record in the Hawaii Ironman includes a second-place finish, two third places, and a fifth place in October 1983—at the age of thirty-seven. The increasing quality and depth of the women's field is demonstrated by the record achieved by fellow American **Lyn Brooks**: when she finished her first Hawaii Ironman (February 1981) she came in third, with a time of 12:42; in February 1982 she took 52 minutes off her time (finishing faster than the previous year's first-place woman) and tied for third. In October 1982 she knocked another 32 minutes off—and finished fifth. In July 1983 Brooks placed second in the three-day Ultimate Endurance Triathlon, from Sacramento to San Francisco, with a total time of 14:44:52 for a 6K swim, 153-mile cycle, and a 50K run. **Sylviane** and **Patricia Puntous** of Montreal train eight hours a day, with remarkable results. The twins are known for their hand-in-hand finishes, and in 1982 and 1983 they had nine ties for first, two ties for second, and two finishes with Sylviane in first, Patricia second. One of these one-two performances was in the October 1983 Hawaii Ironman: Sylviane's time was 10:43:37, and Patricia, who had taken about six minutes to change a punctured bicycle tire, did 10:49:18; the previous month they had taken the U.S. national championship with a first-place tie in 2:48:18 for a 2K swim, 40K cycle, 15K run. In 1984, at the all-women Bonne Bell Triathlon, Sylviane finished first (1:38:06), Patricia second (1:38:21); when in September they won the Mighty Hamptons Triathlon (1½-mile swim, 25-mile cycle, 10-mile run) in a dead heat in 2:40:33, it was the tenth time in 14 triathlons they had tied for first place. Their year was capped by their finish in the Hawaii Ironman in October: Sylviane was the women's winner in 10:25:13, and Patricia was in second with 10:27:28.

VOLLEYBALL

High-speed cameras and biomechanical analysis by computer are today vital aids in training women volleyball players—who hit harder, jump higher, move faster than the men the game was designed for could have imagined. Invented in 1895 by William G. Morgan, a physical education director at the Holyoke, Massachusetts, YMCA, volleyball was intended for middle-aged men who were not up to basketball. Through the international Y organization, the sport spread, and was one of the events at the 1913 Far East Games in Manila; the game went to Europe with the doughboys of World War I. In the U.S., the first national championship (for men only) was won in 1922 by the Brooklyn, New York, YMCA. The U.S. Volleyball Association was founded in 1928, and since then has sponsored the national championships, establishing the women's open title in 1949. At the college level, women's volleyball is especially popular in the West; today, more than 700 teams across the country field teams. International in volleyball was sparked by American soldiers in World War II, who played it enthusiastically and taught it to others. Their aptest pupils were the Japanese. Volleyball became an Olympic sport for men and women at the 1964 Tokyo Games, and the aggressive performance of the gold-winning Japanese women's team stunned the world. Over the past 20 years of international competition, the strongest teams have been Japan, the Soviet Union, China, and Cuba. In 1974 the USVBA established a year-round training center for the U.S. team—the first such for any U.S. Olympic team sport, and a bold and successful move. Although the team did not even qualify for the 1976 Olympics, in less than five years it was ranked fifth in the world and in 1979 second. The U.S. boycott of the 1980 Games, for which the team had qualified, was a tremendous setback, but the team reorganized and recovered; in 1983 the Women's Sports Foundation named it the Team of the Year. In the 1982 world championships, held in Lima, China was first, Peru second, and the U.S. was third. The U.S. went on to defeat world-champion China both at the Varna Cup tournament in Bulgaria in August 1983 and at the Bremen International tournament in January 1984. At the Los Angeles Olympics in August 1984, China won the gold medal, the U.S. the silver, and Japan the bronze. After the Olympics the present U.S. team, several of whose members had played together for a decade, disbanded. The Chinese team they had faced in Los Angeles was younger, quicker, stronger; particularly outstanding were **Lang Ping,** the best spiker on the team (and possibly in the world), and **Zhang Rong-fang**, an excellent blocker. The silver-winning Japanese team benefited by the fine performances of eighteen-year-old **Kumo Nakada,** who had led her club to the national championship for three years in a row, and **Yuko Mitsuye**, a veteran hitter and a bold and aggressive player. But overall, in the history of Olympic women's volleyball one name leads the rest: **Inna Ryskal** of the Soviet Union played on her country's team in four Games, 1964-76: thus Ryskal holds four Olympic volleyball medals, two silvers, won at Tokyo in 1964 and Montreal in 1976, and two golds, won at Mexico City in 1968 and Munich in 1972.

Patricia Ann "Patti" Bright
born Chicago, Illinois

A veteran of two Olympics as setter/hitter on the U.S. team—Tokyo in 1964, Mexico City in 1968—Bright is volleyball coach at Santa Monica High School; one of her players is her daughter. For Bright, volleyball is a family affair—she learned the game from her mother. In her college days at Michigan State University, Bright practiced with the men's team, then transferred to the University of Southern California to be able to play with top-level clubs. She was a member of the silver-winning U.S. team at the Pan American Games in 1963 (her first international tournament). Just before the 1964 Tokyo Olympics she married Mike Bright, a fellow Olympian—he was on the men's volleyball team. In the Games the women's team did better than the men's, finishing fifth, with a win-loss match record of 1-5. (These were the Games at which the tremendous performance of the Japanese women astounded the world.) Bright played four years later in the Mexico City Games, and although the team's record was worse than in 1964 (eighth place, 0-7), Bright had her moment: as server, she aced the Soviet team—which ultimately won the gold medal—as she recalls, "four or five points in a row." That was the only game the U.S. won in the entire tournament.

Rita Crockett
born San Antonio, Texas, November 2, 1957

Crockett can jump so high that she's observed, "You think you're down, but you're not down yet." She can also hit—like teammate Flo Hyman, she is a powerful spiker (and, like Hyman, she is one of six women in the world named to the All-World Cup team). She is believed by some to be the best U.S. woman athlete playing today in any sport. Her early athletic experience was in track and basketball as well as volleyball; she decided to concentrate on volleyball when her junior college team won the national title and she herself was named All-American. In 1978 she joined the U.S. team as hitter/blocker; she was Rookie of the Year. A member of the 1980 Olympic team that never went to Moscow, she played on the 1982 bronze-medal world championship U.S. team and the silver-winning U.S. team at the 1984 Olympics at Los Angeles.

Debbie Green
born South Korea, June 25, 1958

A world-class player who's 5' 4"? Unlikely—unless you happen to be just about the best setter in the game. Green wasn't always that good—she had a weak serve—but persistence paid off. She played for the junior national team as starting setter 1974-78, and led her school (the University of Southern California) to collegiate championships. At seventeen (in 1975) she was the youngest U.S. Volleyball Association All-American. She moved up to the U.S. national team in 1978, and played in the 1979 Pan American Games tournament (the U.S. took fourth place). She was on the non-playing U.S. Olympic team in 1980, and on the bronze-winning U.S. team in the world championships in 1982. At the 1984 Olympic Games at Los Angeles, the U.S. played well but was defeated by China in the finals, to win the silver medal in the tournament. Seeing the closeness and pride of the U.S. team even in defeat, one understood Green's remark, "I've got eleven sisters."

Flo Hyman
born Inglewood, California, July 29, 1954

Senior member of the U.S. team, Hyman began playing relatively late, when she was already tall (she is 6' 5"). This, she feels, has made it a little harder for her to push herself to hit the floor, to follow the ball wherever it goes. But she has learned that, as she puts it, "Pushing yourself over the barrier is a habit." There is little question she has acquired the habit. Named Most Valuable player at the 1979 North/Central and Caribbean American (NORCECA) championship (at which the U.S. team was runner-up), she was Best Hitter at the 1981 World Cup Games in Tokyo and chosen for the All-World Cup team, of which only six women in the world are members. One of the world's most powerful volleyball hitters, Hyman also worked hard to develop a solid defense game. Coach Arie Selinger has described Hyman as "a leader on the court. If Flo plays well, the team follows." At the Los Angeles Olympics in 1984 she played well—but not well enough for gold against the strong Chinese team. When it was over, Hyman said, "We accomplished a lot. We're proud of our silver medal."

Sue Woodstra
born Colton, California, May 21, 1957

Captain of the U.S. team since 1980, Woodstra is generally agreed to be the best all-round player on the squad. There's not much she can't do: she sets those balls teammate Debbie Green can't reach, she's a fine hitter, and she has made a specialty of the receive of serve. She is 5' 9"; if she were taller, says coach Arie Selinger, "she would be the most awesome talent we have." An active child, Woodstra played a number of sports; though she did not have much volleyball experience she was invited to join the junior team in 1973 because she was so obviously a naturally gifted athlete. A member of the senior team since 1978, she played on the 1981 World Cup team (fourth place) and the gold-medal North/Central and Caribbean American (NORCECA) championship team; in 1982 she was a member of the bronze-winning U.S. team in the world champion-ships. She was hampered by injuries in 1984, but nevertheless played on the silver-winning U.S. Olympic team at Los Angeles.

OLYMPIC CHAMPIONSHIPS

Year	Gold	Silver	Bronze
1964 Tokyo	Japan	USSR	Poland
1968 Mexico City	USSR	Japan	Poland
1972 Munich	USSR	Japan	North Korea
1976 Montreal	Japan	USSR	South Korea
1980 Moscow	USSR	East Germany	Bulgaria
1984 Los Angeles	China	USA	Japan

WORLD CHAMPIONSHIPS

Year	Gold	Silver	Bronze
1952	USSR	Poland	Czechoslovakia
1956	USSR	Romania	Poland
1960	USSR	Japan	Czechoslovakia
1962	Japan	USSR	Czechoslovakia
1967	Japan	USA	South Korea
1970	USSR	Japan	North Korea
1974	Japan	USSR	South Korea
1978	Cuba	Japan	USSR
1982	China	Peru	USA

U.S. COLLEGIATE CHAMPIONS

Year	School
1981	Southern California
1982	University of Hawaii
1983	University of Hawaii

WOMEN'S SPORTS FOUNDATION
AWARD WINNERS

HALL OF FAME PIONEERS	HALL OF FAME CONTEMPORARY
1980	**1980**
Patty Berg	Janet Guthrie
Amelia Earhart	Billie Jean Moffitt King
Gertrude Ederle	Wilma Rudolph
Althea Gibson	
Eleanor Holm	
Mildred "Babe" Didrikson Zaharias	
1981	**1981**
Glenna Collett Vare	Peggy Fleming Jenkins
	Chris Evert Lloyd
	Sheila Young Ochowicz
	Wyomia Tyus
	Mickey Wright
1982	**1982**
Francina "Fanny" Blankers-Koen	Olga Korbut
Sonja Henie	Carol Mann
	Annemarie Moser-Pröll
1983	**1983**
Tenley Albright	Donna de Varona
Andrea Mead Lawrence	Maxine "Micki" King Hogue
Helen Stephens	
1984	**1984**
Marion Ladewig	Martina Navratilova
Suzanne Lenglen	Kathy Whitworth
Patricia Keller McCormick	
Eleonora Sears	

INDEX

A

Aarons, Ruth Hughes, 133
Adamek, Donna, 10
Addie, Pauline Betz, 137
Agache, Lavinia, 57
Ahm, Tonni Olsen, 1
Albright, Tenley, 70
Alcott, Amy, 39, 40
Anders, Beth, 36
Andersen, Greta, 129
Anderson, Jodi, 165
Andersson, Agneta, 17
Angelakis, Jana, 28
Arendsen, Kathy, 101
Armstrong, Deborah, 90
Ashford, Evelyn, 165
Austin, Tracy, 135

B

Badminton, 1–2
Basketball, 3–9
Bassett, Carling, 136
Beloglazova, Galina, 56
Benoit, Joan, 166
Berg, Patty, 40
Berglund, Marianne, 19
Berube, Michelle, 56
Bhushan, Insook, 134
Blalock, Jane, 41
Blanchard, Theresa Weld, 71
Blankers-Koen, Francina "Fanny," 167
Blazejowski, Carol, 4
Bleibtrey, Ethelda, 108
Boekhorst, Fieke, 35

Bowling, 10–16
Boxberger, Loa, 11
Bradford, Vincent, 28
Bright, Patricia Ann "Patti," 186
Brinker, Maureen Connolly, 138
Brisco-Hooks, Valerie, 167
Brooks, Lyn, 184
Brown, Carol, 89
Budd, Zola, 167
Bueno, Maria, 138
Burke, Donna, 86
Burr, Leslie, 25
Burton, Beryl, 20

C

Canins, Maria, 20
Canoeing, 17–18
Caponi, Donna, 42
Carner, JoAnne Gunderson, 41, 42
Carpenter-Phinney, Connie, 20
Carton, Cheryl, 2
Casals, Rosemary, 138
Čáslavská, Vera, 57
Caulkins, Tracy, 109
Cawley, Evonne Goolagong, 140
Chadwick, Florence, 130
Cheeseborough, Chandra, 168, 169
Cheeseman, Gwen, 36
Cheng Min-chih, 134
Chin, Tiffany, 72
Choi, Aei Young, 3
Clapp, A. Louise Brough, 137
Cochran, Barbara Ann, 91
Cohen, Tiffany, 109
Colledge, Cecilia, 72
Comaneci, Nadia, 57, 58

191

ACKNOWLEDGMENTS

The authors wish gratefully to acknowledge the assistance of the following: Mimi Fahnestock, librarian, the International Running Center Library, New York; Diane Holum, speed-skating coach, U.S. Olympic team; Bill Plummer, Amateur Softball Association of America; the staff of Westchester Book Composition, Inc., especially Patricia Murphy, Eileen Misiunas, and Joan Lee; and the sports organizations and their press offices that were so helpful in providing information.